Musical Meaning and Interpretation
Robert S. Hatten, editor

NAOMI ANDRÉ

Voicing Gender

Castrati, Travesti, and the Second Woman in Early-Nineteenth-Century Italian Opera

INDIANA UNIVERSITY PRESS
Bloomington and Indianapolis

Publication of this book is made possible in part with the assistance of a Challenge Grant from the National Endowment for the Humanities, a federal agency that supports research, education, and public programming in the humanities.

This book is a publication of

Indiana University Press
601 North Morton Street
Bloomington, IN 47404-3797 USA

http://iupress.indiana.edu

Telephone orders   800-842-6796
Fax orders   812-855-7931
Orders by e-mail   iuporder@indiana.edu

© 2006 by Naomi André

The paper used in this publication meets the minimum requirements of American National Standard for Information Sciences—Permanence of Paper for Printed Library Materials, ANSI Z39.48-1984.

Manufactured in the United States of America

Library of Congress Cataloging-in-Publication Data

André, Naomi Adele.
  Voicing gender : castrati, travesti, and the second woman in early-nineteenth-century Italian opera /
Naomi André.
    p. cm. — (Musical meaning and interpretation)
  Includes bibliographical references and index.
  ISBN 0-253-34644-4 (cloth : alk. paper) — ISBN 0-253-21789-X (pbk. : alk. paper)
  1. Opera—Italy—19th century—History and criticism. 2. Feminism and music. 3. Heroines in opera. I. Title.
II. Series.
  ML1733.4.A53 2006
  782.1′0945′09034—dc22

                                                                          2005016783

1 2 3 4 5   11 10 09 08 07 06

Contents

Illustrations

Acknowledgments

This project has benefited from the generous support and guidance of a few institutions and a lot of people. At an early stage of this project, the American Association of University Women awarded me a generous grant, and my special thanks also go to the local Ann Arbor, Michigan, chapter, the members of which were especially enthusiastic about my work in its early stages.

My deep appreciation goes to my two wonderful editors at Indiana University Press who shepherded this book through the publication process. Gayle Sherwood, whose elegant style guided this project through the early stages, wisely chose excellent readers and made extremely insightful comments herself. Suzanne Ryan came in at the production stage and gracefully worked with me to get the manuscript off my computer and into book form—on the shelves in print. Many thanks go to Donna Wilson, who seamlessly kept things knit together during this transition. I am also very appreciative of Andrea Reinkemeyer, who provided invaluable help with setting the music examples.

I would like to thank the University of Michigan for a subvention to help cover publication costs and for salary support throughout this project. Further thanks to the Institute for Research on Women and Gender, the Office of the Provost on Multicultural Academic Affairs, and Rackham for additional research funding. My special gratitude goes to Paul Boylan (former Dean of the School of Music) and Lester Monts (Associate Vice Provost), who hired me when I was at the end of my Ph.D. studies and who believed in me from the very beginning of my professional career. Their insightful leadership provided an encouraging and enriching environment for new directions in research. Several colleagues at the School of Music have read early sections of the manuscript and have given me thoughtful feedback: Richard Crawford, Judith Becker, Kevin Korsyn, Martha Sheil, and Shirley Verrett. Several have helped me shape this project through probing, yet supportive, conversations: John Wiley, Andrew Mead, Evan Chambers, Carolyn Helton, and Wayne Petty. Special thanks are also extended to my opera classes on whom I tried out several of the ideas that led to themes further explored in this book. The opportunity to share my work with performers who are creating and interpreting music daily, especially those working with opera (singers, conductors, composers, accompanist/coaches, orchestra players), has been very important in shaping my overall approach to this material.

I have been extremely fortunate to have a diverse and rich intellectual community throughout the University of Michigan. This has included two formal writing groups, an informal review committee, and individuals who have listened and constructively challenged me to clarify my ideas. All of these people have felt like intellectual "life savers" as I navigated the difficulties in shaping and articulating this project; my deepest gratitude goes to them for their support while letting me take a chance with these ideas (even when things were still at a very formative stage). I was delighted to be included in a writing group of savvy recently tenured scholars whose projects, in various disciplines, all incorporate feminist directions; my deepest gratitude goes to the FFB, who truly helped me find my voice: Liz Wingrove, Yopie Prins, Catherine Brown, and Kali Israel. At a later, yet still critical, stage of this project I had the pleasure and great fortune to receive feedback from two music scholars whose innovative and groundbreaking work I admire: many thanks to Marion Guck and Amy Stillman. The Women's Studies review team, led by Abby Stewart and Sid Smith, came to my project at a turning point, and I am very grateful for their guidance in helping me narrow down this project and work with pages and pages of text that needed much revision. Individuals who have made a strong impact on my thinking include Kelly Askew, Rachel Andrews, Kathy Battles, Suzanne Camino, and Arlene Keizer. I also have a terrific cadre of current and former doctoral students, several now in the midst of their own academic careers, who were especially generous in their support and willingness to actually listen to my ideas after asking the seemingly innocent question "How is your work going?" These colleagues are Amanda Eubanks-Winkler, Kyra Gaunt, Candida Jaquez, Mark Katz, Inna Naroditskaya, Jill Pearon, Eric Saylor, Rebecca Schwartz-Bishir, Adele Smaill, and Shinobu Yoshida.

Many people outside of the University of Michigan have been crucial to my academic survival and well-being. I would like to thank Reinhold Brinkmann and Kay Kaufman Shelemay for continuing to watch over me as I navigated the transitional and complicated years post-Ph.D. and pre-tenure; I am very grateful for their bedrock of support. I also wish to thank Tara Browner, Ellie Hisama and Anton Vishio, Linda Hutcheon, Ingrid Monson, and Guthrie P. Ramsey, Jr., for their encouragement and help over the past several years. My heart and thanks go to my many caring friends based in Ann Arbor, Cambridge, California, Paris, New York, and beyond: Caroline Gaither; Edie Lewis; the wonderful women of WOCAP; Fatimah Bolhassan; Mary Lee Ingbar; Margot Gill; Paula Szocik; Siew Ho Schleyer; JoAnne Moody; Paul Franklin; Eric, Tina, and Tom Mitchko; Wendy Giman; Leone Rendon Litt and Ken Litt; Céline Beaulieu; and the late Mary Leake and Jacqueline Beaulieu.

I wish to thank those in my closest immediate family for their continuing support, especially my aunt Helen and uncle Denis Sullivan and their "Red Room" where I spent many productive hours reading, thinking, and writing. Zeke and Elliott have given me their unfailing support in too many ways to list. Finally, I want to express my deepest esteem to my mother, Diane Adele Pomeroy, whose love and faith have always been there for me.

Prelude: Hearing Voices

This is a book that asks what happens when we *listen* to women in opera. By listen, I mean listening to—hearing—the sounding of their voices as well as attending to their plight within the narrative of the story. This might be a fairly easy task if I were writing about opera performers today; I would have the luxury of going to their performances and experiencing the sound of their voices myself. I would also have the options of writing to individual singers, having their published interviews at my fingertips, and, perhaps, gaining an interview myself. However, my project is different; I am writing about operas that were written and the singers who premiered them in the nineteenth century.

"Hearing" the voices of these operatic women is the central idea that holds the narrative of my story, this book, together. I am interested in how the voices of female singers, through the characters they portrayed, produced meaning on nineteenth-century opera stages in Italy, Paris, and London.[1] My interest in this question and time period did not spring from a purely abstract notion of "I wonder what the voices of opera singers sounded like before the technology of recorded sound; say, for example, what did Bellini's first Norma sound like?" Instead, this project started out as a way to examine how women were characterized in opera. My original question was "Why do women in opera always die at the end?" As an avid opera-goer, the death of the heroine seemed to say less about her strength of character and more about the fulfillment of an odd convention. At the beginning of this project and now, as I am finishing it, I have been unwilling to believe that the heroine's untimely death is the primary criterion, or requirement, for hers to be the central role. After having experienced the power of the live performance of these roles in the theater myself, I am convinced that the presence of these characters is not overcome or ultimately defeated by the device of their demise at the opera's conclusion.

One way to address this question was to draw on my memory of the leading female roles of opera characters who do not die at the final curtain. In fact, an earlier title of this project was *Surviving Opera*. This inquiry centered on the operas of Giuseppe Verdi. I realized that, while most of the female characters in his operas do, indeed, die, a few of them get to live. As a graduate student in the late 1980s through the mid-1990s, I found that these questions regarding characterization and gender in opera were fairly new for musicologists to ask. However, I found this area to be provocative and made it the topic of my dissertation.[2] To choose a manageable study, I focused on three leading female roles in Verdi's middle and late operas who do not die: Azucena from *Il trovatore* (1853), the Princess Eboli from *Don Carlos* (1867), and Amneris from *Aida* (1871). What stood out as a result of that study were three shared features among all three female characters: (1) each survives the end of the opera, and (2) at least in modern productions, all three are performed by singers who are generally thought of as mezzo-sopranos and contraltos. Third, each opera has two leading principal female characters.[3] I came to think of the project as one looking at Verdi's operatic writing for women's lower voices. This seemed to be the best way to differentiate between the women in opera who died (the high sopranos) and those who get to survive ("my" mezzos and contraltos). The central difference proved to be the pairing of voice type and character type.

The more I began to think about Italian opera in the nineteenth century, the more a couple of questions kept resurfacing. What was the context for these Verdian heroines? While the three female characters I had featured in my dissertation were uncommon in the second half of the nineteenth century for surviving, precedents can be found in opera from the beginning of the nineteenth century for the leading woman (or, when there was more than a singular prima donna role, women) not to die. In fact, it turned out that women who died at the end of operas were rather rare before 1830.

I have developed two terms that I have found useful in conceptualizing this project: the *second woman* and the *period ear*. My aim is not to flatten things out so as to contrive a teleological progression, but rather to acknowledge a more detailed picture in its complexity. Though more in-depth discussions follow in the first chapter, I offer here two succinct, albeit unconventional, ways of thinking of the second woman and period ear. Throughout this project I have thought of the second woman as the interesting character whom no one knows how to categorize. Surprising us as sometimes a man (meaning: a female singer performing a male character) or sometimes a woman, sometimes heroic or sometimes spiteful, she is invariably the less predictable, though certainly the more animated, of the principal roles for women. As I came to understand her function and character, I decided that she was definitely the one I would rather sit next to at a dinner party.

In quite a different vein, an early epiphany that later led to the concept of the period ear came unexpectedly while I was taking a break. I had been struggling mightily as I tried to frame and organize what I wanted to do with women on the early-nineteenth-century Italian opera stage and the phenomenon of their sounding voices producing both male and female characters. It was the end of a fall semester, and the holidays were approaching. I decided that I wanted to do some "extracurricular pleasure reading" (meaning: not related to my research), when a good friend gave me a copy of Natalie Angier's *Woman: An Intimate Geography,* which had just come out. Not being a staunch follower of the latest medical or women's psychology books, I was very pleasantly surprised when I found Angier's book to be not just accessible (after all, she had won a Pulitzer Prize for her writing on biology in *The New York Times*) but also engaging, entertaining, and fun. It was then, in the first chapter about fertility, ovaries, and eggs, that I had a sudden revelation. In a description about harvesting eggs for fertility treatments, Angier writes that the doctor "does the entire extracting procedure by watching the ultrasound screen, where the image of the ovary looms in black and white, made visible by bouncing high-frequency sound waves."[4] I suddenly had an image that worked: the ultrasound sonogram. A sonogram produces images from sound waves—a picture drawn by sound.

Though sound and image usually are placed on opposite spectrums denoting a dichotomous relationship, I wanted to break down this binary opposition. Instead of thinking about how sound and image differ, I found that I was linking the two so that they each informed the other. This was borne out in my mind's eye—and my mind's ear—when I saw pictures of early-nineteenth-century female opera singers dressed as the heroine in one opera and then cross-dressed as the hero in a different opera. In some cases the same singer would be known for singing as a male character one night and then in a female role a few nights later. As I listened to modern recordings of these roles and attended opera performances, I found that I was hearing the male and female characters differently. This was true even when I heard the same singer's voice sing a female character in one opera and then a male character in another. The relationship between the sound and the visual image did not seem to match up; I realized that the voice I heard was influencing me to see the singer differently, and seeing the singer was distorting what I heard. The sonogram, where sound generates the image, became my first metaphor for linking women's operatic voices to their visual presence onstage (in both male and female characters). The framework the ultrasound provides became a critical touchstone for this book.

In a project that came from a curious opera lover sitting in the audience and refusing to write off the dying heroine as only, or exclusively, weak and helpless, I am recapturing the strength I hear in so many opera characters from nineteenth-century Italian opera. Though the first women who premiered these roles were not recorded on modern technology, I would like to assert that the sounding of their voices has not been entirely lost. By constructing our period ears for female singers in nineteenth-century Italian opera we can hear an aural genealogy received by the female characters in the second half of the nineteenth century as a legacy from their ancestors.

Voicing Gender

1   Sounding Voices:
Modeling Voice and the *Period Ear*

As opera-goers, we enjoy and indulge the suspension of disbelief that enables us to accept a woman dressed as a male character and hear her voice as "his" voice. Today, as sophisticated listeners at the beginning of the twenty-first century, we join audiences from the late twentieth century who readily responded when, for example, Marilyn Horne sang (male) title roles in Handel's *Rinaldo* and Rossini's *Tancredi* as well as Arsace from Rossini's *Semiramide,* and then portrayed Rosina in *Il barbiere di Siviglia,* the title role in Bizet's *Carmen,* and Delila in Saint-Saëns's *Samson and Delila.* In the 1980s the late Tatiana Troyanos's repertory included the diverse roles of Strauss's Octavian (*Der Rosenkavalier*) and the Composer (*Ariadne auf Naxos*) as well as Wagner's Kundry (*Parsifal*) and Berg's Countess Geschwitz (*Lulu*). Since the mid-1990s, houses everywhere have been sold out when Cecilia Bartoli sings: whether it be a concert of Rossini *travesti* roles (male characters written to be performed by female singers), the title role in Rossini's *La Cenerentola,* or Mozart's Susanna and Despina, in *Le nozze di Figaro* and *Così fan tutte,* respectively.[1] And Frederica von Stade has been long beloved on the stage as, alternatively, Mozart's Cherubino (*Figaro*) and Charlotte in Massenet's *Werther.* Since the 1990s, a new generation of divas, among them Vesselina Kasarova, Jennifer Larmore, and Susan Graham, also sing both in trousers and in skirts. Hence, this agile tradition in which women move back and forth across gender boundaries in the characters they portray is not in danger of disappearing. Additionally, a new generation of countertenors, such as Brian Asawa, David Daniels, and Bejun Mehta, have begun to engage in similar vocal timbre crossings. Their ambiguously gendered, flexible treble voices render a similar critical space where the performance of sound traverses gender.

Despite the ease of linking the current popularity of female singers whose repertories include trouser roles from Rossini through Strauss to contemporary discourses of changing gender roles, these performers must be understood within a complex and varied history of representing and performing women's voices.[2] The contemporary sounds of women's voices cross-dressed as male characters are infused by an older, and at times nearly forgotten, aesthetic: one that privileges flexible treble timbres to cross gender boundaries. In the pages that follow I explore this earlier aesthetic and the changing meaning in the sound of women's voices during the nineteenth century, and examine how these changes affect characterizations within opera plots.

Catherine Clément's groundbreaking book *Opera, or the Undoing of Women,* along with Susan McClary's noteworthy "Foreword," provided a critical step for a long overdue analysis of what happens to many women in opera. The translation of Clément's book into English in 1988 gave feminist opera criticism in musicology the much-needed stimulus to grapple with the complicated position of women in opera and, more specifically, the configuration of women in nineteenth-century opera. Though there are exceptions, in most Romantic operas after 1830 the heroine, and sometimes also the hero, dies at the opera's conclusion. The comic tradition in nineteenth-century opera outside of Rossini (e.g., *Il barbiere di Siviglia*, 1816; and *L'italiana in Algeri*, 1813) and Donizetti (e.g., *La fille du regiment*, 1840; and *Don Pasquale*, 1843) has not had extensive exploration. Nonetheless, and despite these exceptions, the situation still presents a seeming contradiction. On the one hand, the conceit of the dying Romantic heroine who always meets her untimely end reinforces her status as a victim. On the other hand, this same heroine has a seemingly contradictory strength in her central position within the dramaturgy and, despite her ultimate death at the opera's conclusion, the sound of triumph heard in her soaring voice.[3]

The issue of "voice" in musicology has received attention through different constructions of how voices in music produce meaning. From Edward Cone's multiple "voices" in music (e.g., the composer's, the poet's, the performer's), Carolyn Abbate's "envoicing" of "unsung" musical and narrative structures, and Mary Ann Smart's analyses of the voices of specific nineteenth-century opera divas (French grand opera singer Rosine Stolz and early Verdi interpreter Erminina Frezzolini), music scholarship has addressed the implied and hidden voices embedded within musical discourse.[4] Likewise, recent collections in opera studies have explored varied theoretical constructs of the voice, from how voice resonates in culture and art to how gender and sexuality are represented in opera.[5]

In the past twenty-five years, the female operatic voice specifically has generated much interest. From the voices of African American opera and concert singers (when opera stages were slow to become integrated) to the erotic desire heard in individual divas' voices, the sonic spaces of women's voices in opera have been recovered, deconstructed, and theorized as contested sites that welcome interpretation.[6] Building on the work of Michel Poizat, and focusing on the arenas of nineteenth-century literature and opera, Felicia Miller Frank developed the idea of the constructed female operatic voice that simultaneously looks back to the Italian castrato tradition and forward to technological advances of modernity at the end of the century. Women's voices echo as "otherworldly" and "inhuman," not only through an aestheticized virtuosity encompassing the object of musical pleasure and the sublime, but also through the development of the mechanical doll (e.g., Offenbach's Olympia in *Les contes d'Hoffmann*) and the technological reproductions of the voice through the early phonograph.[7]

My inquiry is not rooted in reading the female voice through the bifocal lens of literature and mechanical reproductions of sound, like Miller Frank's. Rather, it is concerned with the development of the female operatic voice from the time of the castrato through the aesthetics that guided women's voices in opera in the second half of the nineteenth century. A significant part of this book examines the castrato and cross-dressed female heroic roles that coexisted with, and eventually replaced, the castrati in the *primo ottocento* (the early part of the nineteenth century in Italy). Heather Hadlock is another opera scholar whose work has covered women singing male characters in a similar time period and beyond. She has written on Cherubino in Mozart's *Le nozze di Figaro* (1786) through the nineteenth century with Nick- lausse in Offenbach's *Les contes d'Hoffmann* (1881) up to the fin-de-siècle world of Massenet's *Chérubin* (1905) and Richard Strauss's *Der Rosenkavalier* (1911). In an essay on Mozart's Cherubino and Massenet's Chérubin, she explored the open- ing up of an erotic aural soundscape that a woman's voice singing as a male char- acter can engender. Hadlock's examination of the primo ottocento also includes three singers central to the cross-dressing travesti tradition: Rosamunda Pisaroni, Giuditta Pasta, and Marietta Brambilla.[8]

My concern in the following chapters is not on a history of women singing male characters, but to trace the continuum of roles that women in Italian opera sang in the first half of the nineteenth century. This is made possible by placing cross- dressed roles within the context of the larger spectrum of roles that women sang. Seen together with the female characters, I contend that the travesti heroes and pageboy roles opened up further opportunities in the characterization of the fe- male heroines that prima donnas performed in the 1830s through the second half of the century.

Men's Voices and Women's Voices

Opera scholarship has noted that the primo ottocento was a time of tran- sition. At stake was the voice of the hero. The eighteenth-century heroic voice, par excellence, was that of the ever-flexible and awe-inspiring castrati (singers whose voices were altered as the result of surgery before a boy entered puberty). By the end of the eighteenth century, the presence of the castrati on the opera stage waned. Even the last of the best, Giambattista Velluti, retired in 1830, but by the early years of the nineteenth century the castrati had already become anachronistic and appeared with decreasing frequency in opera. But, as has been noted by opera scholars Rodolfo Celletti, John Rosselli, and others, the tenor did not achieve his full status in opera as the leading male character until the 1830s.[9]

The otherworldly and ethereal voices of the castrati had been well suited to en- tertain the eighteenth-century monarchs whose political, social, and cultural po- sition endowed them with supreme rights: they represented an embodiment of divine power. No longer considered a court entertainment whose primary respon- sibility was to reflect the grandeur of its aristocratic and royal patrons, operas in the primo ottocento (especially in the 1830s–40s) began to reflect the difficulties, and sometimes hopelessness, of more "real" (albeit exaggerated) human emotions and situations. Though there were still Italian opera theaters that maintained their royal and patrician connections, the business of what happened onstage regard- ing the structure of the plot and the fleshing out of the characters underwent a palpable shift.

The tenor embodied the Romantic epoch's reconstruction of what was consid- ered to be the ideal heroic sound. The Romantic tenor exhibited groundbreaking vocal achievements and a different articulation of verisimilitude than the uncanny voices of the castrati. The Italian heroic Romantic tenor sound resulted from developments in vocal technique, specifically the *do di petto* (the "chest voice" high C), and a heavier post-Rossinian style of writing for the voice with a larger orchestral accompaniment.

The tenor's voice came to more appropriately represent what was heard as sounding more natural. In early-nineteenth-century Italian opera, this helped shape the new conception of the heroic male leading character. The Romantic tenor exemplified the new and increasing power attained by aristocrats and the rising bourgeoisie. His voice was more "human" as he produced a "natural" (unaltered surgically), yet still operatically stylized, sound. This was the voice of the nineteenth-century hero whose character, despite weaknesses and shortcomings, aspired to a noble struggle against oppression, corruption, and immorality.

The interest in having a closer connection between the voices of the male heroic characters onstage and real-life men offstage had far-reaching consequences. As the number of male singers who were schooled in the art of singing grew, the tenor came into his own—vocally—as the *primo uomo* (leading man).[10] With predecessors in the late eighteenth century (such as Anton Raaf, Mozart's first Idomeneo in his opera of that title), by 1830 the tenor became the leading male protagonist and the new ideal hero for the soprano prima donna.

The development of the tenor as a full-fledged virtuosic voice and his ultimately replacing the female heroic travesti tradition were two innovations of Romantic opera. In light of the increasing prominence the tenor achieved in opera throughout the nineteenth and up through the twentieth century, scholarship has explored the development and path of the Romantic tenor hero.[11] However, what has not received as much attention is the impact that the subsequent decline of the heroic travesti tradition had on roles for women in the nineteenth century.

In these first decades of the nineteenth century, between the reign of the castrati and the rise of the tenor, women's lower voices (the mezzo-sopranos and contraltos) came to occupy a critical space; they replaced the castrato and embodied the sound of the hero. Although the substitution of women for castrati singers when the latter were not available had been common in the eighteenth century, in the primo ottocento women's lower voices took on a new meaning: they became the voice of the hero.

The distinction between the types of roles women sang in terms of vocal category (soprano, mezzo-soprano, contralto) and the gender of the character was most pronounced in the primo ottocento travesti tradition. High sopranos sang the female heroine, and women with lower voices sang the leading heroic male character. However, this vocal coding became less stable as, at the same time, other operas with two female *characters* (and a tenor hero) opened up further opportunities for female singers. In the operas with two female characters, vocally the roles tend to be rather similar in range in comparison with the more disparate ranges of the two female singers in the travesti operas. In the travesti operas, vocal type, character, and gender are linked together; the gender of the role is primarily articulated through the *tessitura* (general range where the role has the most notes) of the vocal line. As mentioned above, the higher soprano part is the female heroine, and the lower part is the male hero. In the operas with two female characters, by contrast, the differences in vocal types are less striking and become increasingly subtle; it is then that the character type, the portrayal of each woman in the plot, becomes the critical factor.

To illustrate these differences in singing ranges between the heroic travesti–female character and the two female character roles more concretely, let me cite a few examples drawn from this study: Rossini's *Tancredi* (1813), Donizetti's *Anna Bolena* (1830), and Bellini's *Norma* (1831). In *Tancredi* the range for the heroic travesti title character is two octaves: G below middle C to G two octaves above. The range for the principal female role, Amenaide, is audibly higher: middle C to C♯ two octaves and a half step above. Hence, Tancredi's range descends down a perfect fourth below Amenaide's lowest note, and her music extends up a tritone above Tancredi's highest note. Yet for the two operas, each with two female leading characters, the ranges are almost identical. The range for Anna Bolena is B♭ below middle C to high C two octaves and a whole step above. The range for Giovanna Seymour is the same B♭ below middle C up two octaves and a half step to B♮. Bellini's *Norma* has the same range as Anna Bolena. Adalgisa's range is middle C to high C two octaves above. In both cases the difference in range for each pair of women is minimal: a half step for Anna and Giovanna (both have same lowest note, Anna sings a half step above Giovanna) and a whole step for Norma and Adalgisa (both have the same highest note, Norma sings a whole step lower than Adalgisa).

What differentiate the music of the two female characters are their individual tessituras, the style of singing in that tessitura (e.g., lots of leaps versus smooth legato stepwise lines), and the orchestration accompanying them. Therefore, through the music each character is given a distinctive sound. It is these sophisticated associations between the sounding voice and the character portrayed that I seek to "listen to" and understand.

Plot and Characterization:
The *First Woman* and the *Second Woman*

As I examine the configuration of women in primo ottocento opera, their role in the drama is critical for understanding what kind of meaning their presence had in opera. George Bernard Shaw's overview of opera plots, a story where a tenor and soprano want to get together but the baritone and mezzo-soprano get in their way, might seem to work for many operas; however, it oversimplifies the motivations for this pattern and the history for how it became a norm. In each of their essays in *Siren Songs*, both Catherine Clément and Heather Hadlock address the larger scheme of patterns relating voice and character type.

Approaching opera from a philosophical and psychoanalytical perspective, Clément's discussion of voice types, character, and drama encompasses a wide range of operas spanning the Enlightenment through the twentieth century, with an emphasis on Italian, French, and German opera from the nineteenth century.

Beginning with a disclaimer, Clément begins her section subtitled *Individual voices and social roles:* "No scheme that correlates voice types—soprano, tenor, baritone—and types of characters will apply to every opera in the repertory, but some generalizations are possible."[12] Reinforcing her earlier study, *Opera, or the Undoing of Women,* Clément now places women's voices in four different categories. For nineteenth-century heroines, under the subheading "Soprano: Persecuted Victim," she demonstrates that practically all sopranos are victims who are "humiliated, hunted, driven mad, burnt alive, buried alive, stabbed, committing suicide." Her one notable exclusion is a "symbolic exception of the early twentieth century: Turandot."[13] As for the mezzo-soprano, under the subheading "Mezzo-Soprano: Resistance, Witchcraft, and Treason," Clément compares her to the baritone as an older, and more calculating, type of character: "I insist on this similarity—'like the baritone'—for perceptions of the mezzo often focus on her 'masculine' way of life."[14] Though she signals an association, neither in this section nor in other parts of her essay does Clément follow up on this connection between the mezzo-soprano and some articulation of masculinity. Nor does she ever refer to the mezzo-soprano in her role as a heroic travesti character. The one time Clément includes cross-dressed characters is when she mentions "a certain feminine weakness in the voices of mezzo-sopranos disguised as young boys: Cherubino in *Le nozze di Figaro* and Octavian in *Der Rosenkavalier.*"[15]

For Clément the contralto and the voice of the bass are "voices of spirit and power." Regarding characterization, she asserts "they do not really impersonate, but rather act in a sacred field, shamanistic or religious."[16] As a contrast to the mezzo-soprano singing the pageboy and resonating with weakness, Clément hears the deep contralto voice as bordering on the divine and infused with power.

Hadlock supports Clément's position of the "weak" cross-dressed pageboy roles regarding their resistance to a clear-cut category. Hadlock augments the picture by noting that the pageboy can be best understood as a "'liminal' presence within opera's increasingly gendered spheres of action." She also notes that, unlike the hapless soprano heroine, the cross-dressed female singer generally survives the end of the opera.[17]

My analysis of how women's voices sounded within the context of the plot provides a different analysis from the "weak" and "powerful" categories of Clément's taxonomy. I am less concerned with the organization of all vocal and character types in all of nineteenth-century opera than in an understanding of how women's voices conveyed different meanings in Italian opera from the first half of the nineteenth century. I find Hadlock's construction of the pageboy's "'liminal' presence" and "gendered spheres of action" to be quite helpful in my discussion of the pageboy. My interest is in contextualizing the shifting gendered spaces for a wider range of women's voices within the primo ottocento; I present a continuum of the different types of roles that women's voices assumed at different points in the first decades of the century. Rather than a fixed association between voice and role, I find that the aesthetics surrounding what was heroic, masculine, and feminine shifted around 1830, and that the preferred sounds for heroism changed. Along with the timbral differences between voice and role, the trajectory of the plot shifted so that the endings provided different outcomes.

In my analysis of how voice, gender, and character interact, I explore the different types of roles for women's voices that emerge in the first half of the nineteenth century. I refer to the two female characters in primo ottocento opera as the *first woman* and *second woman;* however, in my usage these two terms do not imply a hierarchical relationship either in their relative importance in the plot or in the range of each of their voices. In the second half of the nineteenth century, the norm in Italian opera is for one prima donna soprano. If there is another female role that extends beyond the chorus, she is generally labeled a *comprimaria* or *seconda donna* and is relegated to the role of an attendant, friend, or minor rival to the primary heroine.

In my terminology the first woman is the soprano who loves the tenor and is loved in return; the second woman is the soprano who frequently loves the tenor, but is not loved (or is loved less) in return. The first woman is usually the higher soprano; in ensembles she almost always gets the top line. The second woman might also have very high notes, yet she generally has a wider range (with more low notes), lower tessitura, and heavier sound to her voice with more weight and heft.

The beginning decades of the nineteenth century provide several types of romantic pairings for women's voices. In the heroic travesti tradition, a high soprano female character is paired with a lower soprano (mezzo-soprano or contralto) singing the part of a male character—a woman dressed as the hero (singing *en travesti*). If you take this same pair of women and then add a Romantic tenor, a new configuration arises. The singer who had sung the heroic travesti role becomes a female character; I refer to her in this new role, now as a woman in the opera plot, as the second woman. I want to make clear that there is an overlapping sonic phenomenon between the character types and the sound of the voice of the travesti hero and the second woman: the same voice, and frequently the same singer, who was heard as a male character travesti hero in one opera on one night was also heard as a second woman in a different opera on another night. The other female singer, the first woman, always remains the heroine; she is the female character paired with the travesti hero, and when she is the love interest to the tenor hero, she is frequently the rival to the second woman.

While the opera plot has been important for other scholars who have focused on where the leading heroine ends up (after 1830 she usually dies), what is critical to my analysis are the recurring patterns associated with both the first woman and the other role for the leading female singer, whether she sings the male hero en travesti or another female character (the second woman). The patterns in the twists of the plot are, basically, formulaic. My analysis examines these formulas as they are connected to specific types of voices, revealing the codes that emerge between what was heard onstage vocally and what the character does in the plot. These "codes" serve as a lens into the basic understandings audience members witnessed and experienced as the performance practices of the time.

There are three further twists in the conventions as opera plots evolve and employ (1) the inevitable tragic ending, (2) the tenor replacement of the heroic travesti role, and (3) the smaller number of leading women in the plot, which changes from two to one. Both in literature and on the dramatic stage, the aesthetics of Romanticism replaced the eighteenth-century norm for a sanguine resolution of the conflict in the plot. Rather than the happy ending (frequently accomplished through a deus ex machina) that worked out the problems of the drama, the "serious" operas of the 1830s and 1840s (that stemmed from the eighteenth-century *opera seria* tradition) moved in a few different directions.

The nineteenth-century comic opera tradition, born out of eighteenth-century *opera buffa,* became decreasingly common in Italy toward the middle and second half of the nineteenth century.[18] The more popular genres were the "serious" operas that included the continued *opera seria* tradition and the *semiseria* genre, a "mixed" genre that blended together comic and dramatic elements.[19] None of the principals dies in the comic opera tradition, and, though the threat of imminent danger lurks in the background, an eleventh-hour reprieve in semiseria operas untangles the confusion concluding the drama with a *lieto fine* (happy ending). In the serious operas with tragic plots (the operas that become the most common in the second half of the nineteenth century), one or more of the principal characters dies; almost invariably, this includes the Romantic heroine.

As the aestheticized beauty of the bel canto flexible treble voice of the castrato tradition was transferred to the female heroic travesti roles in the primo ottocento, the plot structure followed the older eighteenth-century tradition of the happy ending where the leading characters survive the end of the opera.[20] When the female travesti singer sang the second woman and the tenor became the new hero, the triangulation of the plot usually featured the two principal female characters (the first and second women) vying for the affection of the tenor. Within this trio the first woman would most likely be paired with the tenor, and the second woman would end the opera either coupled with the baritone, or alone.[21] Sometimes the two principal women were paired with two different male characters (the tenor and the baritone), and then the conflict in the plot involved either the love of the same man (the tenor) and/or the desire of a higher social position (e.g., becoming the new Queen).[22]

As the middle of the nineteenth century approached, the structure of Italian opera plots continued to undergo transformation; the number of roles for principal female singers moved from two (the first woman and the travesti or second woman) to one (the new Romantic heroine). In these operas with one leading female role, the primary focus of the drama was on the plight keeping the leading tenor and the Romantic heroine apart and the unfortunate situation that led to one—or both—of their deaths.

Given the success the first woman had gaining the tenor's affection in operas with two female characters, it would make sense to assume that the new singular Romantic heroine was an outgrowth of the first woman character type. Yet the Romantic heroine, the normative leading role for a woman in opera in the second half of the nineteenth century, was actually a *hybrid* role that included a combination of elements from both the first and the second women of the primo ottocento.

Moreover, what this means is that behind the suffering undone heroine of Italian Romantic opera is the history of the heroic travesti role. Hence, the dying heroine in opera from the second half of the nineteenth century is a more complicated character than one who only suffers and expires.

The Conceit of Sounding Voices and the *Period Ear*

What does all of this say about the sound of women's voices in primo ottocento opera? It becomes clear that there is something about the voice of the women who sang both the travesti roles and the second women that primo ottocento audiences could easily hear (and accept) as both a male and female voice. Thus, part of the primo ottocento aural codes for opera allowed a female voice to perform a male character one night, and a few nights later the same singer could portray a woman. Therefore, the sound of such a woman's voice was contextualized within the world of the opera for the type of character she was given. The conventions regarding sound were not dependent upon the gender of the character: the same voice could, and did, sound as a man some nights and a woman on others. In subsequent chapters I trace this aural genealogy from the eighteenth-century castrati to the nineteenth-century articulation of their bel canto tradition in the female heroic travesti singers, the rise of the tenor as the heroic ideal, and the emergence of the Romantic heroine. However, I also position this aural soundscape within a set of sophisticated coexisting practices; the operatic conventions, understood by the audience, dictate the gendering of a woman's voice.

As I "listen" to the voices of the women in these early-nineteenth-century Italian operas, I draw on a conceptualization that I have adapted from art historian Michael Baxandall's *Painting and Experience in Fifteenth-Century Italy*. Baxandall developed the *period eye* as a way to think about the beginning of perspective painting in fifteenth-century Renaissance Italy, and how it reflects the time's culture and beliefs. Baxandall defines the period eye as a "Quattrocento cognitive style as it relates to Quattrocento pictorial style." He further elaborates:

> Some of the mental equipment a man orders his visual experience with is variable, and much of this variable equipment is culturally relative, in the sense of being determined by the society which has influenced his experience. Among these variables are categories with which he classifies his visual stimuli, the knowledge he will use to supplement what his immediate vision gives him, and the attitude he will adopt to the kind of artificial object seen. The beholder must use on the painting such visual skills as he has, very few of which are normally special to painting, and he is likely to use those skills his society esteems highly.[23]

Far from saying that a period eye is necessary for enjoying fifteenth-century Italian painting, Baxandall's argument reveals that the intended audience for this art shared some of the same "mental equipment"—methods for interpretation—that was culturally specific to that community. While accounting for the variable of individual opinions, Baxandall highlights the interaction between the fifteenth-century Italian observer and the understood codes that were embedded within the paintings of that time. In his conclusion he observes that

> An old picture is the record of visual activity. One has to learn to read it, just as one has to learn to read a text from a different culture, even when one knows, in a limited sense, the language: both language and pictorial representation are conventional activities.[24]

Baxandall argues that the picture—though it might seem self-evident as recognizable colors, angles, and images on a surface for viewers today—is also a coded space for interpretation.

Baxandall's study highlights several examples that explore the connections between aspects of daily life and the images in paintings from fifteenth-century Italy. Frequently the arrangement of individuals on a canvas corresponds to the placement of people in various dances from the time (e.g., the *bassa danza*) and reflects a social ordering of the community. Another example comes from understanding that spiritual lessons were portrayed in religious paintings, and hence, those works had both a decorative and instructive purpose to their original viewers. A third example reveals that by realizing that fifteenth-century developments (or rediscoveries) in geometry and mathematical ratios (illustrated in the calculated placement of buildings and archways) imposed a vanishing point and created the innovative illusion of three-dimensional space, we can better appreciate the experience of the first observers.[25] Baxandall posits that these visual works, rather than being archaic museum pieces, come alive when we begin to appreciate how they originally fit into the everyday experiences of their first intended audience.

I am suggesting that there is a connection between the ways in which the fifteenth-century paintings Baxandall refers to were seen and the music of primo ottocento opera was heard. The first viewers of perspective painting in fifteenth-century Italian art performed a suspension of disbelief when they allowed the geometric depiction of three dimensions to be graphically represented on a two-dimensional surface. In a similar way, early-nineteenth-century Italian audiences suspended their disbelief when a woman's voice performed as a male heroic character on the opera stage. In both situations, the culture of the period dismantled a binary truth of what was, and was not, the "real" thing. Visual art and music are both media that open up critical spaces that were, and still are, experienced in different cultural contexts.

Cultural anthropologist Clifford Geertz has also made use of Baxandall's conceit of the period eye as a means for understanding how art can be interpreted by its intended audience and function as a communal artistic expression. In his essay "Art as a Cultural System," Geertz states,

> The capacity, variable among peoples as it is among individuals, to perceive meaning in pictures (or poems, melodies, buildings, pots, dramas, statues) is, like all other fully human capacities, a product of collective experience which far transcends it, as is the far rarer capacity to put it there in the first place. It is out of participation in the general system of symbolic forms we call culture that participation in the particular we

call art, which is in fact but a sector of it, is possible. A theory of art is thus at the same time a theory of culture, not an autonomous enterprise.[26]

Geertz's "collective experience" that involves a "participation in the general system of symbolic forms" provides another way of saying that interpretation is not based on a single, so-called objective mode of understanding. Making meaning out of the past involves not only our collection of data, so that we can piece together a version of the historical truth, but also our interaction with our reconstruction of the broader cultural context the original audience experienced.

Baxandall's period eye, reinforced by Geertz's emphasis on how art works within culture, inspired my own formulation of the *period ear* as a similar process for reconstructing a larger musical context that nineteenth-century opera-goers could have experienced. The specific context I propose takes into account the changing functions of sound—the specific vocal timbres of women's voices—and a way of thinking about the sonic world of nineteenth-century Italian opera. While Baxandall focuses on the use of examples from everyday life that may be read into and cited within the painting, my analysis is less reliant on connecting daily experiences to what happens on the opera stage. This is because opera, unlike visual art (such as paintings in fifteenth-century Italy), unfolds over time as a kinetic phenomenon and creates its own world within the theater. I am concerned with the sounding of the voices in opera houses as a temporal event and the experience that the performance creates.

Before moving away from this discussion of the period ear, I will draw on one more interdisciplinary model, once again from art history, that emphasizes seeing and the process of experiencing art. In an essay that appears in her collection *The Politics of Vision: Essays on Nineteenth-Century Art and Society,* Linda Nochlin presents the image of the "unassuming eye," which she also refers to as the "neutral eye," in her discussion of Camille Pissarro and his position in the Impressionist art movement as compared to those of Paul Cézanne and Paul Gauguin. Resisting the move to minimize Pissarro's innovation and his connectedness to Impressionist ideology, Nochlin writes,

> The whole notion that it is possible to divorce seeing from its cognitive, emotional, and social context is as idealistic, in its way, as any classical norm. The idea that there can be such a thing as a neutral eye, a passive recorder of the discrete color sensations conveyed by brilliant outdoor light is simply an element of Impressionist ideology, like their choice of "ordinary" subjects and "casual" views, not an explanation of the style itself.[27]

Though Nochlin writes from the standpoint of the artist as the one who sees, she expresses the same imminent interaction between the viewing of the work and the idea of the work as an image. this is not a neutral, passive, or unassuming relationship. The viewer—both the artist looking at his or her own work and the audience seeking admission to a production—performs a translation while experiencing the artwork. Nochlin writes of this process as providing the work with a "cognitive, emotional and social context"—the parameters she outlines as giving the work meaning. A few lines later she continues, "what an artist sees, as revealed by the evidence of the painted image, would seem to depend to an extraordinary degree on *when* he is looking and *what* he has chosen to look at."[28]

With her emphases on *when* and *what,* Nochlin situates the image and the artist's interpretation as a fluid exchange between the content of the image and the time and place in which the artist is working. By substituting the experience of the visual artist with the experience of nineteenth-century listeners of Italian opera, and the visual object produced by the artist with the aural images created by each member of the audience, Nochlin's paradigm presents a compelling case for how Baxandall's period eye and my period ear operate. As the nineteenth-century audiences of Italian opera across Europe—whether they were in the Teatro San Carlo in Naples, La Fenice in Venice, the Théâtre Italien in Paris, or Covent Garden in London—made sense of what they experienced in the theater, they produced an aural image that brought together what they saw and heard on the opera stage.

I propose that the sound of operatic singing had encoded meanings and associations for who a character was. In this vein the nineteenth-century Italian audience was able to ascertain a character's position in an opera plot by the timbral sound of the voice. Different connotations for characterization in opera were elicited by the sound of a high soprano voice as opposed to a lower contralto. These following chapters trace the development and evolution of the period ear and present a "listening" to the aural associations evoked by women's voices in the first decades of the nineteenth centuries and how they changed in meaning.

In assessing the implications of these operatic conventions and practices, I argue that attending to women's voices unsettles our assumptions about gender. As the aural legacy of the castrati haunts the beginning of the nineteenth century in the travesti heroes, so the travesti roles then cast their shadow throughout the rest of the century and inform the female characters that emerge over the course of the nineteenth century. Since the voice of the second woman used to be heard as that of a man, how can her voice not present a different articulation of femininity in opera than that of the first woman? This study explores the meaning of this aural genealogy: how a woman's voice represents both male and female characters and the relationship between voice and gender signification. I propose a model for listening to these provocative voices, the treble timbres produced by female bodies, allowing them to survive multiple meanings. This project is a critical intervention in theorizing voice more historically and historicizing voice more theoretically.

Overview

The voice of the castrato was the hidden aesthetic resonating in the female travesti roles of the early-nineteenth-century stage. In chapter 2 I "listen" to the castrati's cross-dressed voices (the voices of the women who replaced the castrati) and explore the instability between the changing configurations of "masculine" and "feminine" sounds as they are projected from the eighteenth century onto the primo ottocento stage. To understand the castrati's influence in the beginning of the nineteenth century, I highlight four aspects of their legacy as they relate to female singers: the continued preference for treble vocal timbre, the use of heroic travesti roles, their virtuoso singing styles, and the transmission of their technique through pedagogy and treatises.

In his 1830 novella *Sarrasine,* Balzac provides a reflection of the tension between erotic desire, gender, voice, singer, and character in the first decades of the nineteenth century. Balzac's evocation of the castrati in the early-nineteenth-century imagination reveals a continuing fascination with how their voices articulated the aesthetics of previous generations and how they continued to linger into the present of the 1830s. As in Balzac's *Sarrasine,* and in the nonfictional world of the primo ottocento, the heroic function of the castrato's voice is transferred to female singers. Working through the framework of the destabilization and reconfiguration of the categories of sex and gender from the seventeenth through nineteenth centuries, I employ Thomas Laqueur's models of premodern and modern gender constructions and Marjorie Garber's work on cross-dressing to provide a framework for contextualizing the changing meanings behind ideological and visual codes.[29] My work adds the third dimension of sound (the voice) as it interacts with visual images (a woman's body playing a male role) and the aesthetic ideology that accepted this combination as "heroic."

In chapter 3 Giacomo Meyerbeer's last—and best-known—opera for Italy, *Il crociato in Egitto* (*The Crusader in Egypt,* 1824) is analyzed as a case study in the principal treble voices, here further complicated through the device of masquerade. *Il crociato* was the culmination of Meyerbeer's Italian operatic repertoire and provided his entrée into Parisian operatic circles.[30] Frequently cited as the last opera by a major composer with a role for a castrato, *Il crociato* exploits the opportunities Meyerbeer had at his disposal. The castrato, a Knight of Rhodes, assumes the identity of an Egyptian Saracen, and the second woman, a low-voiced female singer, is a female character dressed as a Knight of Rhodes. In addition to the castrato and cross-dressed female character, a heroic tenor takes the role of the Grand Master of the Knight of Rhodes. Rounding out the story is the first woman, a higher soprano, who depicts a Saracen who has abandoned her Muslim religion for Christianity (so that she can marry the castrato).

As a German who traveled to Italy to learn the principles of writing opera in Rossini's heyday, Meyerbeer's fame today is primarily based on his success as an important developer of French grand opera. However, the "internationalism" of Meyerbeer's Parisian style owes much to the conventions he learned in Italy. Meyerbeer's last Italian opera provides a melting pot of the norms of northern Italian primo ottocento opera and illustrates an alternative, yet complementing, view of opera to the one seen in Rossini's career after he accepted his position at the southern Teatro San Carlo in Naples.

The Interlude acts as a hinge to connect the dual streams of influence that energized the primo ottocento. While the first chapters look backwards to the older traditions that shaped early-nineteenth-century Italian opera, the next two chapters (4 and 5) look ahead to practices and new constructions that continue into the secondo ottocento. The central questions are, first, how do we get to the Romantic heroine who dies at the end of the opera, and, second, what is the meaning behind the sounding of her voice given its earlier history on the stage? In sum, what are plausible interpretations of women's voices on the primo ottocento stage by a period ear?

A chronological approach to these questions does not work. The castrati did not stop singing on the opera stage before the female heroic travesti came to be the most common voice for the hero. Nor did the tenor suddenly emerge as the voice to replace the female heroic travesti singers in a specific given year. In fact, all three of these practices occurred concurrently; occasionally, as in the case of Meyerbeer's *Il crociato*, all three could collide in the same opera. In the background of the primo ottocento the castrato aesthetics for heroism give way to the new voice of the Romantic tenor, and opera plots change so that the lieto finale is ultimately supplanted by the tragic ending. The Interlude also allows the opportunity to set up the four operas that will be used as the major case studies in the last two chapters (a subgroup I call the "Queen" operas) and the concept of hybridity as a means for hearing the transformation of how women's voices moved from the heroic travesti to the pageboy and how the two leading female singers (the first and second women) were brought together to become the Romantic heroine.

In the libretto excerpts quoted in chapters 4 and 5, I have italicized the lines that I specifically refer to in my discussion. None of these internal italicized emphases are in the original libretto; I added them to aid the reader by quickly drawing attention to the sections I have cited and treated in some depth. As in chapter 3, the formal designations in some of the arias and duets in chapters 4 and 5 are also noted in italics (*cantabile, cabaletta*, etc.—these terms are defined in the Glossary) and are my own additions to aid the reader in following the libretto; they are not in the original.

Chapters 4 and 5 focus on operas written by composers who made their reputation in Italy and spent the majority of their opera careers there (unlike Meyerbeer, in chapter 3, who went on to settle in Paris).[31] Chapter 4 examines the evolving norm to render women's cross-dressed voices less central by taking away their heroic capabilities and making them a court page. With comparisons to Mozart's Cherubino, I demonstrate how the pageboy is rearticulated in the nineteenth century. I discuss Smeton (from Donizetti's *Anna Bolena*, 1830) and Arturo (from Donizetti's *Rosmonda d'Inghilterra*, 1834) as pageboys who maintain their connection to the heroic travesti tradition. In what I call hybrid roles, Smeton and Arturo combine their dramatic function as the young adolescent page to the court with moments when their voices are center staged and echo their heroic legacy. As they sing in situations with the high soprano first woman, their voices evoke aural memories of the heroic travesti. Caught between the evolving nature of their dramatic and vocal positions, their voices resonate with an echo of the past and relevance for the present.

Chapter 5 examines the configuration of two leading female characters who both spend an entire opera as women. Neither playing female travesti characters (heroic or pageboy) nor in disguise (as in Meyerbeer's Italian operas), these two female singers present the juxtaposed characterizations and voices of the first and second women. I focus on the ways in which the two women are distinguished in the plot—who is loved by the hero, who has the most power, who dies—and how their two roles are interconnected. The subtle pairing between vocal type and character enriches our view of the range of roles available to women during this time.

In chapter 5 I also expand my purview of the primo ottocento to include the transition between the voices and characters that led into the *secondo ottocento* (the second half of the nineteenth century in Italy). As the first half of the nineteenth century gave way to the second half when the operas of Verdi dominated Italy through the end of the century, the emergence of the singular prima donna heroine becomes the norm. Rather than an exclusive adaptation of either the first or the second woman, the Romantic heroine—this new singular prima donna—turns out to be an amalgamation of both character types and voices.

The transitions between the changing conventions of how the hero and heroine were gendered and voiced in opera during the primo ottocento produced singers who were able to excel in both types of roles. Generally female singers tended to specialize in one type of role; this would be either the first woman heroine or a heroic travesti singer; the latter might also add second woman roles as the tenor came into prominence and eliminated the travesti heroes. Sometimes women specialized in the heroic travesti roles. Other women would not sing travesti roles and would focus only on female characters.

In my narrative of women in primo ottocento opera, the leading soprano Giuditta Pasta (1797–1865) plays an important role in the history of the Italian prima donna. She was central in the development of the repertory, vocal sound, and different representations of women on the nineteenth-century opera stage. Having performed as the hero en travesti, the first woman, the second woman, and the prototypical Romantic heroine, Pasta's was a "gendered voice" that resonated as an aural site of multiple possibilities. In the roles she premiered and the signature roles with which she was associated, Pasta's voice and dramatic presence were critical in bridging the distance between the castrato bel canto aesthetics and the conventions of the secondo ottocento. In addition to the words about her operatic performances by her contemporaries, the patterns in the plots of several of "Pasta's operas" and the interactions between the leading roles for female characters provide a more fleshed-out picture of how the Romantic heroine in opera came to be.

The Coda of this study makes a few speculations about situating the Romantic heroine in opera within the context of her time in the Italian *Risorgimento* (the nineteenth-century Italian unification movement). I suggest links between the trajectory undertaken by women's voices, and the roles they brought to life, with the historical and political context of Italy in the first half of the nineteenth century and the struggle for a united national identity. As heroism is rearticulated in the European arena in the aftermath of the French Revolution and the Napoleonic regime, the changing sound of operatic heroism presents a compelling counterpoint that helps illustrate how opera and drama voiced gender in their own time.

2   Haunting Legacies: The Castrato in the Nineteenth Century

The figure of the castrato in opera has caused much speculation: both during the lifetime of the castrati as well as during their afterlife in the nineteenth century and up to the present. Scholarship has shown that at the end of the eighteenth century the castrati were becoming less common in opera, and by the beginning of the nineteenth century they were indeed anachronistic in almost all situations.[1] This is borne out in the operas from the beginning of the nineteenth century; roles for the castrati become increasingly rare and disappear almost entirely by the end of the first decade. However, the castrati were still present in significant numbers to occupy Roman church choirs throughout the nineteenth century and into the first decade of the twentieth century. A nice piece of evidence cited (alas, not reproduced) in Patrick Barbier's *The World of the Castrati* is an 1898 photograph of the Sistine Chapel choir that identifies a quarter of the choir to be castrati: seven castrati out of a total of twenty-eight singers.[2]

Yet most people who care about nineteenth-century Italian opera do not put the castrati and early Romantic opera together as having any relationship to each other. At best, those who remember that Rossini wrote one operatic role for a castrato (Arsace in *Aureliano in Palmira*, 1813) or that Meyerbeer is generally considered the last major composer to write a role for a castrato (Armando in *Il crociato in Egitto*, 1824) might think these occurrences as bizarre, archaic, and having little to do with anything current at that time. Besides, *Aureliano* was an early work for Rossini and *Il crociato* was written before Meyerbeer went to Paris and became the chief architect of French grand opera; clearly they represent early efforts before these two composers became famous for their more paradigmatic works.

However, the castrati singers still appeared in operas—albeit infrequently—in the first decades of the nineteenth century. The last two great castrati in opera were Girolamo Crescentini (1762–1846) and Giambattista Velluti (1781–1861), and both had careers into the nineteenth century; Velluti was the last to retire, in 1830.[3]

Many castrati who had retired at the end of the eighteenth century lived for many years into the nineteenth century.[4] With so many accomplished and once-famous castrati living in the primo ottocento (and the others whose names have not been remembered), we can see how the nineteenth-century bel canto tradition is informed by the practitioners of the eighteenth-century bel canto techniques in significant and tantalizing ways.

Giambattista Velluti, one of the last castrati in opera, as a young man, as he appeared in *Il Trajano.* Most likely this was Giuseppe Nicolini's *Traiano in Dacia,* which Velutti premiered in February 1807 at the Teatro Argentina in Rome. *The Harvard Theatre Collection, The Houghton Library.*

In this chapter I will argue that the castrato's influence in the nineteenth century extended beyond their mere presence as retired opera singers and curiosities of Roman church choirs. The sound of their voices haunted and shaped the development of opera singing throughout the primo ottocento and into the second half of the century. Their voices resonated not only in the early-nineteenth-century preference for flexible treble timbres in the heroic roles (the female travesti singers), but also in the development of the nineteenth-century bel canto technique that included an adaptation of the dazzling fioratura and seamless sound from blending the vocal registers. The interaction between sound and image produced new meanings regarding the characterization of the hero. As women's bodies, en travesti, became the accepted site for the male hero, the rising prominence of the tenor presented an alternative sound and image of masculinity. The image of the castrati also haunted the nineteenth-century's vision of itself. Honoré de Balzac's 1830 novella *Sarrasine* examines the tension between erotic desire, gender, voice, singer, and character. I use Balzac's contemporary account to aid my "listening" of the castrati's voices and exploration of the instability between the changing configurations of "masculine" and "feminine" sounds. With their close proximity to the eighteenth century, the "period ears" of the audiences in the first decades of the nineteenth century were attuned to hearing the past while simultaneously creating something new in the present.

Listening to the Castrati

The decade of the 1990s gave us two examples (or "versions") of castrato voices on compact disc: the early-twentieth-century recordings (made in 1902 and 1904) of the last castrato in the Sistine Chapel choir, and the voice created for the 1994 movie *Farinelli*.[5] Gérard Corbiau, the director of *Farinelli*, made a bold decision for representing the voice of Farinelli, the stage name of Carlo Broschi, arguably the most famous of all castrati.

Rather than use a countertenor or a female singer, the two voices most frequently used to perform castrato roles in modern productions today, Corbiau decided to combine the voices of soprano Ewa Mallas-Godlewska and countertenor Derek Lee Ragin as the voice of Farinelli. He digitally remastered recordings of both voices singing the same music and created a new hybrid voice.[6] The decision to manufacture such a voice was a bold one that worked quite effectively. The resulting sound is uncanny, yet impressive and beautiful. In a movie about the otherworldly, awe-inspiring voice of the most legendary castrato, it would have been anticlimactic if Farinelli's voice were recognizable as the voice of a famous singer from the 1990s. Besides, how could any singer today live up to the almost mythical status of the great Farinelli?

The resultant hybrid voice was familiar enough to modern ears to sound believable, and yet it evoked a sound and technical capability that was almost unbelievable and virtually impossible. In their own time, the castrati voices were altered voices and would not occur without a type of surgery called an orchiectomy. Today, the technically manufactured voice of the movie is an apt metaphor for the historical castrati whose voices were altered via their surgery and then greatly manipulated in the six to twelve years of vocal training in conservatories.

The second recording is a rerelease of the voice of Alessandro Moreschi (1858–1922), the last castrato who sang in the Sistine Chapel choir until his retirement in 1913. The sound of this digitally remastered compact disc was transferred from recordings that had been made by Fred and Will Gaisberg, British pioneers of the Gramophone Company, in 1902 and the American engineer W. Sinkler Darby, who worked for the same company, in 1904. Ironically, this "real" voice of Moreschi,

Portrait of "Carlo Broschi, called Farinelli." *The Harvard Theatre Collection, The Houghton Library.*

historically preserved, sounds as though it is veiled through a filter of older performance practice styles and ancient technology.

On the recording Moreschi employs a singing style that involves a pronounced *portamento* (literally "carrying") from one note to the next when the two notes span an interval greater than a third, and usually in intervals of a sixth or larger.[7] Most modern ears are accustomed to a limited use of portamenti in certain contexts for added expressive affect.[8] To many listeners today, Moreschi's portamenti sound like sobbing effects for the smaller intervals and wild swooping gestures for the larger intervals, resulting in a general feeling of imprecise vocal attacks. Despite the admirable efforts of the production staff, the static crackles and hissing sounds from the aging original gramophone records (the transferring process was not able to erase all of these) is also quite distracting. However, the most vexing of all is the "Producer's note" at the end of the booklet that accompanies the compact disc. It states:

> The pitching of Moreschi's records presented us with some problems since no-one [*sic*] had the slightest idea of what his voice ought to sound like. However, we discovered that when we pitched both the 1902 and 1904 recordings of Rossini's *Crucifixus* to the score key of A flat, all of the records made at both sessions fell into score keys or *unreasonable* keys, and sounded vocally correct to several musicians for whom they were played.[9]

With this disclaimer, our understanding of what it means to listen to an "authentic" castrato voice in the late twentieth century must be shaped. Since this voice no longer exists today, even when confronted with it, we do not know what it is supposed to sound like. What does it mean to sound "vocally correct" with such an enigmatic lost voice? Our contemporary ears cannot tell what has been distorted and what is out of tune.

I hear both of these recordings as approximations of the castrati voices I read about from the seventeenth and eighteenth centuries. Ideologically and aurally, the manufactured hybrid voice from *Farinelli* works well for me. The vocal singing is dazzling and displays all of the effects that were praised during the seventeenth and eighteenth centuries. Breath control, evenness of tone, and acrobatic fioratura are all there and evoke a sonic world that is at once almost familiar, and yet borders on being eerie. My late-twentieth-century ears find the sound satisfying, even though I know it was not a "real" voice. In the world of the ever-increasing power of the Internet and technology, I was comfortable with this "virtual" voice.

The voice on the compact disc that represents, or masquerades as, Moreschi's voice is aurally and ideologically disturbing. Vocally it seems out of control and less predictable. It sounds as though his voice encompasses a couple of different voices within the expanse of his range. The high register sounds secure, like it is floating, and the lower register sounds harsh and heavy. In fact, it is precisely the features of evenness of tone and smoothness between registers for which the castrati were particularly well known that seems to be missing from Moreschi's voice.

The act of listening to Moreschi's voice today recalls some of the original audiences' reactions to the castrati in the mid-nineteenth century; for both them and us, the voice of the castrato elicits a guilty sense of pleasure and horror.[10] A letter from Marie d'Agoult, a companion of Liszt's who was active in the Parisian salon culture, to German conductor and composer Ferdinand Hiller from April 6, 1839, reveals her impressions of hearing the castrati in Rome. Besides her disappointment in the castrati themselves, she describes the audience's agitated anticipation to hear these celebrated voices:

> There is no point in telling you that the reputation of the Holy Week ceremonies is greatly exaggerated. You go there with admission tickets as you go to the theatre; you fight, you do battle with old English ladies; nothing could be less religious. The performance of the music is horribly bad. There are too few castrati and they sing out of tune with quavering voices; the cardinals are half asleep or absent-minded; nobody behaves as they should.[11]

With somewhat less clamor than the battling "old English ladies" that d'Agoult refers to, the castrato voice still holds its appeal of uniqueness. For us today, the sound on the recording has become a curiosity element. When we hear Moreschi's voice, we listen for the castration because of its novelty.

For the audiences in the seventeenth and eighteenth centuries, the castrati's virtuosic and flexible treble timbres embodied heroism; this aesthetic was accepted over, or despite, the grisly knowledge of how this sound came to be. From the mid-nineteenth century up through the present, heroism has been represented through the perceived virility of unaltered male voices: the tenor, baritone, and bass. With this new practice, the listening changed because the audience accepted and heard different conventions. The castrato became an outdated spectacle. With our nineteenth-century predecessors, we listen because we want to know what castration sounds like. It is hard not to hear the "sobbing" grace note ornaments in Moreschi's voice as a poignant cry of melancholy that somehow seems to implicate each of us now as we listen, even after all these years. But our listening today only includes a portion of the original total effect. For the mid-nineteenth-century audiences who were still able to hear the castrati in churches, the aural spectacle extended into the visual with the added stimulation of seeing this voice come out of a castrated body.

The Body and Voice in Balzac's *Sarrasine*

As a participant of the nineteenth-century salon culture in Paris, Honoré de Balzac (1799–1850) was thoroughly immersed in the artistic world of his time. Friends with Rossini, Liszt, and Berlioz, Balzac's love of Italian opera (particularly those of Rossini) makes him an astute commentator on the musical cultural life of the city.

Balzac delved into the intersection of the visual and aural that comes together in the body and voice of the castrato. Written in Paris in 1830, his novella *Sarrasine* features a castrato who spans the eighteenth century up to the time of the novel's writing and provides a special historical account of the castrati in the first third of the nineteenth century. Balzac's novella is striking for the view he provides into nineteenth-century conceptions of the castrati; in 1830 the author presents both the body and the voice of the castrato haunting the present and looking back to the past. Though the castrati were not completely unknown in Paris, they never enjoyed the popularity that they had in Italy. Hence, as a Frenchman, Balzac's use of the castrato not only references an older operatic practice no longer popular, but also cites a foreign cultural phenomenon that opens up a transgressive realm of fascination and possibility.

Even the very title—*Sarrasine*—which turns out to be the name of one of the protagonists, connotes an exotic reference to an Orientalized Other. In French "Sarrasine" is the feminine form of the noun "Saracen." In Balzac's time and up through today, a Saracen refers to an Arab and/or Muslim. As a twist on one of the themes embedded within the novella, the French male protagonist named Sarrasine presents the reader with the opportunity to experience the metaphor of a masculine persona embedded within a feminized signifier. Like our title character, at first sight the reader encounters Sarrasine and finds something quite different from what appeared to be obvious based on what was seen.

Balzac's novella, which begins at a ball in Paris hosted by the de Lantry family, is a carefully interwoven narrative that contains a story within a story. The account of Sarrasine is presented as a history to the present time in the novella that the unidentified male narrator tells his young female companion, Béatrix, Countess Arthur de Rochefide.[12] The novella is set around 1830, and the story of Sarrasine, a young male French sculptor, is set in 1758, when he goes abroad to study.[13] While visiting Italy Sarrasine becomes obsessed with "La Zambinella," a singer whom he hears in an opera by Jomelli at the Teatro Argentina in Rome. Balzac vividly describes the first time Sarrasine sees the singer:

> Suddenly a burst of applause which shook the house greeted the prima donna's entrance. She came coquettishly to the front of the stage and greeted the audience with infinite grace. The lights, the general enthusiasm, the theatrical illusion, the glamour of a style of dress which in those days was quite attractive, all conspired in favor of this woman. Sarrasine cried out with pleasure.[14]

Though the singer's appearance enraptures the young sculptor, it is the first encounter with the singing voice that causes him the greatest ecstasy:

> When La Zambinella sang, the effect was delirium. The artist felt cold; then he felt a heat which suddenly began to prickle in the innermost depth of his being, in what we call the heart, for lack of any other word! He did not applaud, he said nothing, he experienced an impulse of madness, a kind of frenzy which overcomes us only when we are at the age when desire has something frightening and infernal about it. . . . The distance between himself and La Zambinella had ceased to exist, he possessed her, his eyes were riveted upon her, he took her for his own. An almost diabolical power enabled him to feel the breath of this voice, to smell the scented powder covering her hair, to see the planes of her face, to count the blue veins shadowing her satin skin. Last, this agile voice, fresh and silvery in timbre, supple as a thread shaped by the slightest breath of air, rolling and unrolling, cascading and scattering, this voice attacked his soul so vividly that several times he gave vent to involuntary cries torn from him by convulsive feelings of pleasure which are all too rarely vouchsafed by human passions. He was presently obliged to leave the theater. His trembling legs almost refused to support him.[15]

This orgasmic description leaves little surprise that for the rest of the novella Sarrasine devotes himself entirely to this singer. He religiously attends every performance of the opera and feverishly devises ways to meet La Zambinella outside the theater. It is not until the very end that he discovers, to his horror, at a concert (not in the opera house) that La Zambinella is a castrato who specializes in female roles on the opera stage.[16] The realization is too much for Sarrasine to bear. Though he is told that La Zambinella is not a woman, Sarrasine does not fully believe it and thinks that there must be a mistake. Sarrasine continues his plan to kidnap the singer for what he had initially hoped would be a romantic tryst; however, he is consequently murdered by La Zambinella's protectors.

Sarrasine, the unsuspecting Frenchman who goes to the Roman opera house, becomes enamored by the physical appearance and voice of La Zambinella. As an outsider to the local customs of performance he is ensnared by both a visual and aural deception: La Zambinella is not a biological woman, and the voice is not a biological woman's voice. Yet neither of these things mattered to Sarrasine's perceptions. Sarrasine heard the voice as the character La Zambinella portrayed. He listened for the heroine in the voice and found her. Packaged in the body of La Zambinella, the voice transcended the "truth" behind the veil of sound mediated by sight.

This account demonstrates the close connection between sound and sight. In primo ottocento opera, these two things are not static, nor are they self-evident. Even during the heyday of the castrati, a person without the cultural knowledge of the aesthetic behind castrato singing could be deceived. Sarrasine shows us that the "period ear" was always a learned way of hearing; even being born in a certain time did not necessarily make you a connoisseur for how sight and sound were interpreted. As the narrator recounts this story to his female companion, he is passing down this knowledge. In a time when the sound of the castrato's voice was almost, but not quite, lost, Balzac writes his novella, telling the young (and reminding the old) among his contemporaries of the castrati from the previous generation. As we read *Sarrasine* today, we are being shown what older members among Balzac's nineteenth-century audience still remembered.

In the present time of Balzac's novella, the elderly gentleman who haunts the de Lantry ball, hovering in the background and raising suspicions among the guests, turns out to be La Zambinella at the age of one hundred. He is described in terms that confirm his antiquity, yet also emphasize conflicting ambiguities that speak of his other-worldliness: the image of death with his penetrating demeanor, his feminine accoutrements with his mawkish grace, and his regal bearing with a foreign exoticism:

> His cadaverous skull was covered by a blond wig whose innumerable curls were evidence of an extraordinary pretension. For the rest, the feminine coquetry of this phantasmagorical personage was rather strongly emphasized by the gold ornaments hanging from his ears, by the rings whose fine stones glittered on his bony fingers, and by a watch chain which shimmered like the brilliants of a choker around a woman's neck. Finally, this sort of Japanese idol had on his bluish lips a fixed and frozen smile, implacable and mocking, like a skull. Silent and motionless as a statue, it exuded the musty odor of old clothes which the heirs of some duchess take out for inventory.[17]

This dual image of La Zambinella as ancient (either near death or from a very old civilization) and attempting to be youthful (with an arrogant vanity) permeates this scene at the ball. Immediately following the description of the elderly gentleman given above, he is juxtaposed with the young Countess the narrator has brought to the ball. Her figure, "in the full bloom of its beauty," and the details of her body (her neck, arms, bosom, and "sweet breath") are described in a fashion remarkably similar to the praise Sarrasine bestows upon La Zambinella when he encounters the singer in Rome.[18] The Countess sets up the first juxtaposition between the beauty of La Zambinella as it is transferred to women in the early nine-teenth century. After the Countess is repulsed by the physical presence of the an-cient man, she flees into a room where a large portrait of Adonis is displayed.[19] She is immediately captivated by the picture, but the irony is later revealed: the canvas she admires is based on Sarrasine's statue of La Zambinella in the crowning glory of his youth when La Zambinella was virtually the same age as the Countess.[20] In the Countess the reader sees how even the younger generation in 1830, Balzac's contemporaries, who might initially be repulsed by the thought of the castrati could still be entranced when presented with them, as the picture of Adonis reveals the hidden Zambinella in her original glory.

One of the most intricately layered juxtapositions in the novella is found in the relationship between Marianina de Lantry and her great-uncle (La Zambinella). Though her role might seem small, it is critical for understanding the legacy she personifies. In his analysis, Barthes theorizes that both Marianina and her brother Filippo "embody a kind of explosion of Zambinellan femininity,"[21] a helpful ap-proach for understanding Marianina's position in the novella. Not only does she represent the propagation of her great-uncle's feminine attributes, she is also given many of the major tropes associated with La Zambinella—an unattainable desir-ability, etherealized beauty, and an aestheticized singing voice. In her first appear-ance the narrator introduces her with the query

> Who wouldn't have married Marianina, a girl of sixteen whose beauty embodied the fabled imaginings of the Eastern poets! Like the sultan's daughter, in the story of the Magic Lamp, she should have been kept veiled. Her singing put into the shade the par-tial talents of Malibran, Sontag and Fodor, in whom one dominant quality has always excluded over-all perfection; whereas Marianina was able to bring to the same level purity of sound, sensibility, rightness of movement and pitch, soul and science, cor-rectness and feeling. This girl was the embodiment of that secret poetry, the common bond among all the arts, which always eludes those who search for it.[22]

Marianina is immediately presented as the object of men's desires—everyone wants to marry her. Despite her family's mysterious source of wealth, the narrator over-hears a philosopher at the ball exclaim: "Even if the Count de Lantry had robbed a bank, I'd marry his daughter any time!"[23] As Sarrasine's infatuation with La Zam-binella began the moment he first saw her, so we, the readers, are presented from the first with the irresistible charms of Marianina. As La Zambinella's old counte-nance was likened to a "Japanese idol," Marianina's beauty is evoked by "Eastern poets"—she is compared to the sultan's daughter, and a noteworthy reference is made to a veil that should keep her beauty's secret well hidden.

Like Sarrasine's first encounter with La Zambinella's voice, the references to Marianina's voice deserve special attention. Her singing is mentioned twice, and both descriptions are steeped in the historical codes of the time. With her first appearance, her voice is compared to a trio of women's voices: Maria Malibran, Henriette Sontag, and Joséphine Fodor-Mainvielle. These three women were among the leading opera singers of their day, with active international careers. Given his love of Italian opera, Balzac had ample opportunities to hear them in Paris, and in the 1820s all three were particularly well-known interpreters of Rossini's operas. The second reference to Marianina's voice is mentioned as a diversion at the ball when she sings "the cavatina from *Tancredi*,"[24] one of Rossini's early Italian serious operas (written in 1813) that was among his most popular in this genre and a signature role of Malibran's.

Rossini's Voice

Balzac's reference to Rossini is telling. At the time when Balzac wrote *Sarrasine*, Rossini was the undisputed leader of opera; Donizetti was just beginning to win serious recognition with *Anna Bolena* (1830); and Bellini was still at an early point in his career with his greatest successes yet ahead of him (both *La sonnambula* and *Norma* are from 1831). Balzac's admiration for Rossini grew out of their friendship and his great love of Italian opera. He considered Rossini "the composer who has conveyed the greatest human passion in the art of music," and his reference to the composer shows an appreciation and knowledge of Italian opera.[25]

Rossini's operas exemplify the hybrid nature of the primo ottocento musical aesthetic that had one ear listening to the past and the other turned to the future. After having taken both Italy and Vienna by storm in the 1810s and 1820s, Rossini made his mark in Paris, then the international operatic center of the world. In 1824 he moved to Paris to assume artistic control of the Théâtre Italien. Throughout the 1820s, several of his Italian operas were revived and adapted for the opera houses in Paris, and he composed new operas for the Opéra.[26] He was a major force in the musical life of Paris in the 1820s through the early 1830s and, to a lesser degree, until his death in 1868.

Rossini revered the voices of the castrati. Though his career coincided with their very last days in opera, he continued to write roles that evoked their bel canto style of singing in florid melodic vocal lines and the practice of keeping the flexible treble timbres in the heroic characters. Most of Rossini's Italian "serious" operas (as opposed to the comic operas) have female travesti roles. By using female voices for the hero, he was preserving the aesthetic of the castrati. In 1813, the same year as *Tancredi*, Rossini wrote his only operatic role for a castrato (Giambattista Velluti): Arsace in *Aureliano in Palmira*. It is quite possible that if the castrati had stayed popular in opera, Rossini might have written more operatic roles for them.

In 1858 Rossini looked back to the age of the castrati with nostalgia and commented on their voices:

> Let's speak first of the voice, the instrument formed. Nature, alas, never creates all parts of a voice perfectly, any more than a pine tree gives birth to a Stradivarius. Just as an instrument maker must construct a Stradivarius so it behaves, so it to fabricate the instrument he counts upon using. And how long and arduous a labor that is!
>
> Among my compatriots, that job formerly was facilitated; in view of nature's refusal to comply, they made castrati. The method, to be sure, was heroic, but the results were wonderful. In my youth it was my good fortune still to be able to hear some of those fellows.

I have never forgotten them. The purity, the miraculous flexibility of those voices and, above all, their profoundly penetrating accent—all that moved and fascinated me more than I can tell you.[27]

Rossini's comments about the castrati and their bel canto tradition of singing are more than solely anecdotal. Having heard the castrati when he was young and then having worked with Velluti in 1813 at a formative early stage in the composer's career, Rossini was able to gain first-hand knowledge of the castrato sound and style of singing. His use of the female travesti singers allowed him to retain a timbre similar to the castrati's and work with the same basic vocal range.

Like many of Rossini's other Italian serious operas, the heroic title role of Tancredi was written as a travesti part for a female singer. Though the cavatina that Balzac mentions is not specified, it is more than likely that Marianina was singing the cabaletta from Tancredi's entrance aria, "Di tanti palpiti" (For so many misgivings [palpitations]); not only was it the most famous tune from *Tancredi*, but it also became one of Rossini's most popular and enduring melodies in the nineteenth century.[28] The last words of the text of "Di tanti palpiti," Sarà felice—il cor mel dice, il mio destino—vicino a te" (I shall be happy—my heart tells me—my destiny is to be near you), echo central themes in *Sarrasine*.[29] At this point in the opera, Tancredi has just arrived at the garden of the palace where he looks forward to seeing his lost beloved. In Balzac's story, Marianina's singing captures the attention of her elderly great-uncle and draws him to her:

> Escaped from his room like a lunatic from his cell, the little old man had obviously slipped behind a hedge of people who were listening to Marianina's voice, finishing the cavatina from *Tancredi*. He seemed to have come out from underground, impelled by some piece of stage machinery. Motionless and somber, he stood for a moment gazing at the party, the noises of which had perhaps reached his ears. His almost sonambulatory preoccupation was so concentrated on things that he was in the world without seeing it.[30]

As Tancredi sings in the garden of a palace, so has La Zambinella been drawn to listen to Marianina from a garden, so to speak, "behind a hedge of people" in the de Lantry mansion. His appearance embodies a simultaneous death and rebirth. As he seemingly emerged from "underground," his frozen countenance keeps him at a distance from the others at the party as he observes, without interacting with, them. The image of the ancient La Zambinella held in rapt attention to Marianina's voice emphasizes his focused concentration; he liminally inhabits two worlds concurrently. He relives the past while he intensely listens to Tancredi's cavatina; as a former singer, his own voice is evoked through the nostalgia for an eighteenth-century bel canto singing style. In this scene in the novella Balzac shows us La Zambinella's ability to listen to two worlds at once—eighteenth-century practices interpreted through nineteenth-century singers. This scene also highlights the interplay of two genders. The memory of singing as La Zambinella is harshly reflected in the decrepit old man. As a relic of a former aesthetic, the ancient castrato as Marianina's great-uncle relives his past as the sought-after La Zambinella who could pass as a woman.

When La Zambinella listens to Marianina he hears a reflection of his own voice. When he watches her sing, he sees an echo of his visage in her presence. While Barthes refers to Marianina and her brother Filippo as embodiments of "Zambinellan femininity," it is only Marianina who sings; she inherits his voice. Marianina's presence and voice are a figurative reincarnation of La Zambinella. As La Zambinella listens to Marianina sing, his attention is firmly rooted in the present as the final words of "Di tanti palpiti" ring with an extra resonance. While Tancredi sings that his destiny is to be near his beloved, La Zambinella hears his legacy in the voice of his great-niece. Marianina, the vocal progeny of La Zambinella, captures the essence of the castrato's voice and theatrical grace in female form.

In Rossini's first version of *Tancredi*, which premiered at the Teatro La Fenice in Venice on February 6, 1813, he set Gaetano Rossi's (the librettist's) altered ending to Voltaire's *Tancrède* (Paris, 1760). Voltaire's play is a tragedy; however, Rossi kept with the current opera trends of the time and used a happy ending, where Tancredi realizes that Amenaide has been faithful to him and they are united to live happily ever after. At the next production several weeks later in Ferrara (March 1813), Rossini decided to preserve Voltaire's original ending and wrote a new tragic finale. Though Tancredi is ultimately convinced in both versions that Amenaide has been true to him all along, in the second version it is too late; he has been mortally wounded in battle. As they are finally united, he bids her farewell and dies.[31]

The two endings provide a telling commentary on the conventions of opera in the first decades of the nineteenth century. The Ferrara version was not well received, and it was Rossini and Rossi's original ending for Venice that gave the opera its great popularity. Besides the tradition for happy endings where things get worked out (this remains the general norm until 1830, when tragic endings become more common), the resolution adds another layer to our view of Balzac's novella. While it is probable that Balzac was familiar with the more popular happy ending of *Tancredi*, the dual ending of the opera reflects the changing codes in sound and gender that this epoch in opera was able to encompass. The fading shadow of La Zambinella looks on with hope and anticipates a basically happy, yet bittersweet, future while listening to the reincarnation of "her" voice in Marianina's. However, the ghostly specter of Marianina's great-uncle foresees his own demise as he hears his voice being replaced by Marianina's.

The Castrato's Physical Presence

In Balzac's novella the substitution of Marianina's voice for La Zambinella's is an echo of what was happening aurally and visually on the early-nineteenth-century opera stage: female singers sang the leading male heroic character. This substitution had far-reaching consequences in terms of how the castrato's image lingered on and his voice echoed throughout the early nineteenth century. Aurally, it was not new for women to sing castrato roles; this had been happening in the eighteenth century when a castrato was not available. What was different was that in the early decades of the nineteenth century what had been the exception became the new norm; the hero was now routinely written for a woman's voice. Visually,

Satire of the castrato's physical appearance (William Hogarth's engraving of Handel's *Flavio*, 1723). The singers are the castrato Farinelli, the soprano Cuzzoni, and the castrato Senesino. The smallest figure is thought to be the bass Berenstadt. *The Harvard Theatre Collection, The Houghton Library.*

the heroic character migrated from a castrato's body to a woman's body. The visual markers of the castrati—their physical characteristics—were remapped onto another type of body.

The orchiectomy left physical consequences beyond the potential for a phenomenal singing voice. After the operation the pituitary gland was not regulated by testosterone. In medical terms the condition caused by the surgery is called primary hypogonadism. The operation severed the blood vessels that carried the hormones from the testes to the rest of the body (it did not actually always remove the testes). As medical doctors Enid and Richard Peschel explain, the effects of the surgery were caused by "the lack of androgen hormone stimulation by the Leydig cells in the testes."[32] Since the operation was performed before puberty, between the ages of six and twelve, the physical development and frequent overactivity of growth hormones led to a set of physical characteristics that marked the castrati visually.

Some of these physical changes were distortions of the visual codes that signified masculinity and femininity. In most portraits of castrati, both on the opera stage and off, they are depicted in men's clothing. This is consistent with the convention that the premier type of operatic role for them to assume was the heroic male lead.[33] Less common are iconographic parodies that picture castrati in women's

28 *Voicing Gender*

clothing. These reference their appearance in women's roles, particularly on the Roman stage where women were banned and castrati (usually young castrati at the beginning of their careers) sang the female parts.[34] Another visual marker of the castrati was that they were frequently taller than their contemporaries, because of their "disproportionately long arm and leg size relative to the torso size."[35] This physical characteristic is consistent with the medical definition of eunuchoid appearance.

Besides their large physical stature and male dress, there were also feminine aspects to the castrato's body and appearance. Castrati did not develop an Adam's apple, and they did not grow beards or mustaches; hence, their faces and throats had a smooth and supple look without the visual markers of adult masculinity. Additionally, again due to the lack of androgen stimulation, unchecked female hormones gave the castrati the tendency to develop extra fatty tissue around their breasts, hips, and thighs. Therefore, their physical appearance generally lacked a hard muscular build and, instead, was more shapely, with the fleshy softness equated with the feminized body.

With both masculine and feminine features encoded in their physical bodies, the castrati were the ideal singing vessels. They could sing both male and female roles convincingly, and they were even able to continue the ability to embody both genders off the stage. Balzac's *Sarrasine* is supported by historical accounts that point out that the castrati could "pass" as either gender, both on and off the stage, should they so desire.[36] An account by Casanova from 1745 while he was in a Roman coffeehouse reveals a real-life Sarrasine-like moment:

> In comes a pretty-faced abate. His hips and thighs make me think him a girl in disguise; I say so to the Abate Gama, who tells me that it is Beppino della Mammana, a famous castrato. The Abate calls him over and laughingly says that I had taken him for a girl. He gives me a bold look and says that if I will spend the night with him he will serve me as a boy or a girl, whichever I choose.[37]

While the castrati were able to pass as women or men offstage (these accounts tend to center in Rome), the more common situation was for the conceit of the cross-dressed disguise itself to be the site of feigned deception and pleasure. Even though most audiences knew that the castrati were not women, it was the believability of the illusion that sustained the thrill. As Johann Wolfgang von Goethe remarked at the end of the eighteenth century:

> I reflected on the reasons why these singers pleased me so greatly, and I think I have found it. In their representations, the concept of imitation and of art was invariably more strongly felt, and through their able performance a sort of conscious illusion was produced. This double pleasure is given, in that these persons are not women, but only represent women. The young men have studied the properties of the female sex in its being and behavior; they know them thoroughly and reproduce them like an artist; they represent not themselves, but a nature absolutely foreign to them.[38]

I am not interested in trying to rigidly define whether the castrati were biologically male or female. Nor am I trying to imply that their contemporary audiences saw them as exclusively one or the other. By bringing together codes for what is considered "masculine" and "feminine," the castrati embodied many ambiguities both in their own time as well as in ours today. As we look back and try to understand how they were configured in opera and by their audiences, we need to take these varying viewpoints into consideration. One thing that is clear is that the castrati resist an explicit definition of being men or women. Instead, they call into question how gender in opera is constructed. To further address this issue, I now shift my emphasis from the visual image of the castrati and complement my discussion of their physical appearance with a focus on the singing voice and their aural presence.

The Castrato's Throat

In an uninterrupted puberty a boy's voice undergoes significant changes that signal his maturation into manhood. This physical process has visual and aural components. As the hormonal changes of puberty take place, the position of the larynx changes, and it moves down. Visually, this is marked by the appearance of an Adam's apple that moves up and down while speaking and singing. Aurally, the sound of the voice is also altered. The pitch drops an octave, and the timbre—the tone color—deepens. These changes are responsible for the lower pitches in these voices as well as the darker, sometimes huskier, sound that characterizes the adult male voice. The changing of boys' voices is not a hidden or instantaneous process. During this time adolescent boys find that they have little control over the placement of their voice. When they try to speak, they find that there are unexpected squeaks and slides in the voice that expose the internal hormonal changes.

The castrato's larynx does not descend, since the voice does not undergo the hormonal effects of puberty; this keeps the pitch as well as the timbre of the voice high. Enid and Richard Peschel approach the relationship between the castrato's voice and his voice as a boy before his surgery through a comparison of the size of boys', girls', women's, and men's vocal chords. Before puberty, the vocal chords of boys and girls are the same size. While (unaltered) men's vocal chords grow dramatically, women's vocal chords stay about the same size or increase only slightly. The castrato's vocal chords remained the same size as they were when the singer was a boy; hence, the correspondence in pitch between castrati's and women's mature voices was quite similar.[39]

A similar description of the castrato's anatomy can be found in a report from the beginning of the twentieth century. Ear, nose, and throat specialist Jean Pierre Sauvage was able to examine three autopsy reports of castrati from the end of the nineteenth and beginning of the twentieth centuries and wrote, "the phonation apparatus of the castrati reveals itself to be extremely original. The size of the larynx was similar to that of a woman of small stature. The size of the thoracic cavity was like that of a large man. The width and consistency of the larynx was like that of a boy."[40]

Although the vocal chords remained the same size, the timbre of the castrato's voice was comprised of a different sound than being an unaltered continuation of his boyhood voice. As the body developed around the larynx, the selection of harmonics and overtones resonating in the voice changed, shaping the ethereal tone color. Another physical development of the castrati was the expansion of the rib cage into a rounder shape. The different position of the larynx and the enlarged rib cage combined with the muscles developed from the rigorous breathing exercises in their training to give the castrati a physical mechanism for singing that blended characteristics from an unaltered male voice with the unique physiological changes they underwent (e.g., their adult lung capacity providing the breath for their boy-sized vocal chords). Hence, they were able to exploit their unusual physical development with their strenuous conservatory training and produce a voice that exceeded the capabilities of unaltered voices.

Patrick Barbier notes that the "castrato embodied the trinity—man, woman and child . . . a voice often judged sublime and sensual by contemporary observers who were certainly more kindly disposed towards artifice than the general public of today."[41] The boy's voice was captured before puberty; the position of the larynx and the smaller-sized vocal chords were aided by plasticity and flexibility. The woman's throat was also invoked through the absence of the Adam's apple and the similarity in the dimensions of the vocal chords and bone structure. Additionally, the pitch of the castrato's voice was the same as a woman's pitch, hence, the easy substitution of female and castrato singers for the same roles without transpositions. Finally, housed in the body of what would have matured into a typical man, the strength and developed musculature gave the castrato's voice a physical power that was forceful and penetrating. The castrato's voice encompassed a stylized sounding of all types of voices. Physically, on the outside the throat looked like a woman's throat with a supple neck, lack of male facial hair, and absent Adam's apple, but on the inside, the castrato's vocal chords were the same size as they had been when he was a boy. Yet their bodies retained many of their male features, namely, their capacity for larger muscle development and a larger body size. The castrati reinterpreted the codes for how gender was articulated by juxtaposing features from men, women, and children in the same throat.

Timbre and the Break

As Wayne Koestenbaum queries the diva's throat in his book *The Queen's Throat*, I would like to examine the throat in the body of the castrato as the origin of sound. Koestenbaum situates the singer's throat as a site of science, pleasure, and erotics. He cites the "break" in the voice, the crossing between registers, as

> The place within one voice where the split between male and female occurs. . . . The singer schooled in *bel canto* will avoid eruptions by disguising the register breaks and passing smoothly over them. The register line, like the color line, the gender line, or the hetero/homo line, can be crossed only if the transgressor pretends that no journey has taken place . . . by revealing the register break, a singer exposes the fault lines inside a body that pretends to be only masculine or only feminine.[42]

Koestenbaum presents the voice trained in the bel canto tradition as a means to negotiate between masculine and feminine aural codes. If the register break (the change from one part of the voice to another, for example, head voice to chest voice) is heard, the illusion is broken.

A break between registers is indicative not only of a faulty technique, but also of a break between aural and visual systems. In singing a vocal line with a wide range, the overtones and resonance between the different physical regions of the body signal different stylized constructions of characterization. The brighter sound of the head voice contrasts with a deeper, somewhat huskier sound of chest voice. A woman singing in her head voice needs to be able to make the smooth transition into her chest voice so that the moment between the two registers is blurred and the two are encompassed into one. If the break is heard, then the image is shattered; the sound is fragmented, and the audible differentiation between registers becomes a disruption between two conflicting voices. In bel canto singing a single body encompasses many voices that are blended into one character though the manipulation of a strong technique.

If the break in the voice can be the audible signal of how gender is heard, the castrati are able to cross back and forth almost imperceptibly. Their physical development and years of intensive musical instruction in the conservatories trained their voices to become the perfect emblems of bel canto aesthetics.

To produce castrati, the orchiectomy was performed before the young boy's voice "broke" at puberty; the goal was to preserve the essence of his voice as a boy. Yet as we have seen the sound of the castrato's voice was not the same as his boyhood voice because the rest of his body grew and, through rigorous training, developed different muscles for sound projection. Given the altered physical mechanism that produced the castrato's voice (as compared to a teenage boy who was not castrated) it is likely that the exact breaks in the castrati's voices differed from those in noncastrated men. Nonetheless, we do know that castration did not prevent voices from developing different registers.

Singing treatises written by castrati repeatedly discuss the importance of producing an even sound between registers. In one of the most influential treatises of the bel canto era, Giambattista Mancini wrote in 1777:

> The great art of the singer consists in acquiring the ability to render imperceptible to the ear, the passing from one register to the other. In other words, to unite the two, so as to have perfect quality of voice throughout the whole range, each tone being on a level with your best and purest tone. This is art and it is not easy to reach the goal. It takes study, work and industry to correct the defects originated from the more or less strong constitution of the vocal organs, and it requires ability and such a careful use of the voice to render it equally sonorous and agreeable, that few students succeed.[43]

This emphasis on a smooth, continuous voice guides the voice student to hide the break in the voice so that it would eventually become "imperceptible to the ear." The castrato aesthetic was a cross-dressing of the voice. Like cross-dressing that retains the mark of both genders, where the pleasure is in the mixing of male and female codes (rather than passing as one or the other), the vocal break symbolizes the mark between male and female. The best of the castrati voices were able to bridge the divide and inhabit the two sonic spheres interchangeably.

Travesti

The metaphor that Balzac constructs of Marianina's singing, as a nineteenth-century projection of La Zambinella's voice, opens up opportunities for hearing gender through sound. Given the ability to portray either men or women both on and off the opera stage, the castrato's voice represented the reenactment of gender codes; the same voice could depict both male and female.

The holdover preference for flexible, high treble voices for the hero brought the sound of the castrati into the nineteenth century. In the first decades of the century women's voices also took on this dual ability, albeit limited to the opera stage, and could represent what was considered "masculine" (when women donned trousers) and what was considered "feminine" (when dressed in skirts). The aural possibilities heard in the castrato's voice were then transferred onto the female travesti singers.

Though the castrati were known to sing the roles of women, their most common function in opera once they had matured was to assume the role of the hero. Given the ban on women performing onstage in the Papal States up through the end of the eighteenth century, it was not uncommon for a young castrato to make his debut on the opera stage in a female role.[44] A few castrati specialized in female roles, as notes Baroque opera scholar Ellen Harris, who cites Girolamo Bartoluzzi (flourished 1719–24) and Andrea Martini (1761–1819). In his well-known book *The Castrati in Opera*, Angus Heriot adds Giuseppe Acquini (flourished 1683) to this group.[45]

Alessandro Scarlatti's opera *Pompeo* (with a libretto by Nicolò Minato) serves as an example of the vocal distribution of roles in two performances that took place at the end of the seventeenth century. First performed in Rome in the private theater of Lorenzo Onofrio Colonna on January 25, 1683, it was revived the next year in Naples. The cast lists reproduced in table 2.1 compare the role, character gender, and type of singer who performed each role.[46]

An unusual feature, for the end of the seventeenth century, in the first performance is that the two leading male characters (Pompey and Mithridates) were sung by tenors (rather than castrati). This premiere also had two male characters that were sung by castrati (Sextus and Pharnaces). The final vocal type of one role (Harpalia) is a little unclear because it is notated in the soprano clef in act 1 and in the tenor clef in act 2; most likely this refers to a change of singer midway through the composition of the opera. In the two performances, women sang the roles of two female characters (Julia and Hypsicratea) and two male characters en travesti (Claudius and Scipio Servilius). In 1684 castrati sang four roles, three of whom are male characters and one, Harpalia, who is a woman.

The only male character that is not performed by a woman or a castrato is Julius Caesar; in both performances he is sung by a bass. Caesar does not have a large role in the main intrigue of the plot, in fact, his role is smaller than Pompey, Mithridates (who is also a father; his son is Pharnaces), Pharnaces, and Sextus. As the father of Julia and Claudius, he is one of the older characters, and his deep voice

Table 2.1. Cast Lists for Two Productions of Alessandro Scarlatti's *Pompeo*
(1683 and 1684)

Role	Character Gender	1683, Rome	1684, Naples
Pompey	Male	Male, Tenor	Castrato
Sextus	Male	Castrato	Male, Tenor
Hypsicrateia	Female	Female	Female
Mithridates	Male	Male, Tenor	Castrato
Pharnaces	Male	Castrato	Male, Tenor
Harpalia	Female	Soprano/Tenor	Castrato
Julius Caesar	Male	Male, Bass	Male, Bass
Claudius	Male	Female	Female
Julia	Female	Female	Female
Scipio Servilius	Male	Female	Castrato

could be heard as a reflection of his age. Combined, his low (unaltered) male voice and secondary position in the drama placed him in his own vocal-dramatic realm, separate from substitutions by treble voices.

The other male characters, with more substantive roles, undergo substitutions between different types of treble voices. The larger, more heroic roles (Pompey, Mithridates, Pharnaces, and Sextus) are sung by either castrati or tenors. Claudius, not a major part, is treated as a travesti role and is sung both times by a woman. Viewed in conjunction with the two leading female roles, Hypsicrateia and Julia, the use of women's voices is more consistent; all three characters are sung by women in both performances. However, the roles of Scipio Servilius (male character sung by a woman and a castrato) and Harpalia (female character probably first sung by a tenor and then a castrato), two subsidiary characters, show the complexity behind the interaction of gender, vocal type, and character. The size of the role and the gender of the character did not determine the gender of the singer.

These two performances of Scarlatti's *Pompeo* also illustrate that character pairings based on romantic or familial relationships within the plot do not simplify the situation. The two female characters, which are sung both times by women, can marry tenors or castrati: Hypsicrateia is married to Mithridates (sung by a tenor and a castrato), and Julia ends up marrying Pompey (sung by a tenor and a castrato). Additionally, women are romantically linked to all types of voices: Hypsicrateia is wooed by Sextus (sung by a castrato and tenor) and Claudius (female singer). Though Julia and Scipio Servilius (sung by a woman and castrato) are in love, she is also pursued by and eventually paired with Pompey (sung by a tenor and castrato). In the midst of such shifting gender ambiguity among singer, voice type, and character, the only relationship that consistently meets the modern sensibilities of verisimilitude is the filial one between Julia (a female character sung by a woman) and her father, Caesar (a male character sung by a low male voice).[47]

This preference for treble voices to assume a variety of male and female roles continued into the eighteenth century. Admired for both their vocal color and agility in technical ability, the interaction of singers and roles complicated the distinctions made between the gender of the performer and the gender of the character being portrayed. As the presence of women in opera became more socially acceptable at the beginning of the eighteenth century, the erotic ambiguity that reconfigured gender on the opera stage continued. Ellen Harris outlines the first performances of Handel's *Rinaldo:* in the original production of 1713 "the castrato Nicolini sang the title role, but the male role of Goffredo was written for a woman. In 1713 the opera was revived with Mrs. [Jane] Barbier singing Rinaldo; in 1717 the part of Goffredo was given to a castrato."[48] When a castrato was not available, reworking a role for a woman singer (when allowed onstage) was frequently done, as the case of *Rinaldo* illustrates.

The fact that women's voices were sometimes substituted for castrato roles, and vice versa, says less about the preference of one type of voice over the other (women singers, though gaining in acceptance and popularity on the opera stage toward the end of the eighteenth century, could not yet approach the prestige given to the best of the castrati), than the Baroque tolerance for sexual ambiguity in the casting of the leading roles. It was the aesthetic for the sounding of high-timbred treble voices produced by castrati and women that pleased sixteenth- and seventeenth-century audiences. The sound of these types of voices in the principal roles were valued above, what would seem to modern audiences today, the cognitive dissonance of men who sound somewhat like women singing male characters, women singing male characters, and, less frequently, men singing female characters.

The example of the two performances of Scarlatti's *Pompeo* in 1683 and 1684 illustrates the different connections between singers and the characters they portrayed on the Baroque stage as compared to the norms that were in place by the mid-nineteenth century and that continue today. That things were different is not new. Celletti cites "the abstract nature of the relationship between sex and role, as symbolized by the castrato and the *travesti*" as one of the defining components of bel canto opera.[49] Regarding the practical side of performing these operas today, Harris supports replacing castrato roles with female voices so as to stay closest to the original timbre and avoid transpositions—even though this can lead to the situation of ending up with almost all-female casts. She continues, "from a historical point of view, range and vocal colour are far more important than sexual identity."[50] Dorothy Keyser strongly characterizes the reception of castrati's and women's voices by their contemporaneous audiences: "choices of vocal timbre, originally made to accommodate the religious scruples of the Catholic church, had effectively erased the association between sung voice register and gender to the baroque ear."[51]

Keyser's point about the "baroque ear" segues nicely into my examination of women's voices in the nineteenth century and searching for a way to conceptualize what the sounding voice could mean. As shown above, flexible treble-timbred voices permeated virtually the entire cast of early operas as women and castrati performed most of the roles. However, rather than "erasing" the associations between vocal register and gender, I think these connections complicate and destabilize the relationship. To the seventeenth- and eighteenth-century ear (for my purposes, I will rework Keyser's phrase), the common substitution between the roles women and castrati performed led their voices to be heard as interchangeable. A woman's voice could be heard singing female as well as male characters. When a female singer sang a male character, either in a role that had been written for a woman's voice en travesti (e.g., Claudius in both productions of *Pompeo* or the role of Goffredo for the original production of Handel's *Rinaldo*) or when replacing a castrato (e.g., the 1713 *Rinaldo* where Mrs. Jane Barbier sang the title role that had originally be written for Nicolini), her voice was heard as a man's voice. The authority and power given to the hero onstage was elicited by and transferred onto a woman's voice. In these productions, when the travesti woman's voice sounded, the audience heard a male character.

The breakdown in the distinctions between a castrato role and a female travesti role in the seventeenth century highlights the shifting identity of the castrato and female voices; both types of voices were heard as sites of multiple possibilities. These voices had the potential to be interpreted in different ways: in some situations they could be identified as male characters, in other circumstances they sang female roles. The sound of their flexible treble timbres was coded to mean more than only one thing to their audience. In the early nineteenth century when the castrato is no longer common on the opera stage, women replaced them in the heroic travesti roles. Women's voices then become the primary site of cross-sexual casting, and the multiple meanings of the flexible treble timbre get transferred on to female singers.

These two features—first, women singing as men and, as a result, second, women's voices being the site of multiple meanings (the potential to portray male and female characters)—were made possible by the continued demand for a castrati vocal aesthetic, even as the castrati disappeared from the opera stage. Audiences in the first decades of the nineteenth century were accustomed to seeing, hearing, and believing in different patterns than we are today. The range of what was considered audibly plausible shifted around 1830 as the stylized sound of the hero moved to the tenor. The legacy the castrati left the early-nineteenth-century Italian stage included a sophisticated constellation of relationships between the sounding voice, the gender of the body producing the voice, and the meanings they generated.

Vocal Instruction

The sounding of the castrato voice was supported by a singing technique that was obtained through a rigorous and intensive period of training.[52] Their formal education generally lasted from the time they underwent the orchiectomy (before puberty, usually any time between the ages of six and twelve years old) through their late teen years and generally lasted a period of six to ten years. Most attended a conservatory that had a specialized program for castrati as well as a more general music education for other, noncastrated, students. The four most famous institutions for training castrati were in Naples (Conservatorio di Santa Maria di Loreto, Pietà dei Turchini, Poveri Gesù Christo, and Saint'Onofrio), but there were also excellent schools in Bologna, Rome, Venice, and other Italian cities.[53]

Given the length and intensity of their training, the castrati studied music quite broadly, far beyond simply having singing lessons. In their extensive music education they studied composition, harmony, and counterpoint, which enabled them to write their own alternative versions of ornaments; Farinelli was known to write three different sets of embellishments so as to continually dazzle his audience with different versions of the same aria. Such knowledge of counterpoint and harmony also led some castrati to become respected composers in their own right. One of the best-known composer-castratos was Nicola Porpora (1686–1766), who was also internationally famous as an opera composer with commissions from houses throughout Italy and in London, Vienna, and Dresden.

The training of castrati was a valued endeavor, and their role as pedagogues became an important way for their techniques to be disseminated. Since the castrati were the leading teachers of opera singing, they were sought out by students for formal training. As Marianina is presented as the vocal progeny of her great-uncle, La Zambinella, a similar genealogy can be traced to the famous castrati; their lineage was remembered and considered prestigious. In addition to his careers as a singer and successful composer, Porpora was also one of the most accomplished teachers of his time, and his students included Carlo Broschi (Farinelli), Gaetano Majorano (Caffarelli), and Antonio Hubert—who took on the name "Porporino" in honor of his esteemed castrato teacher. Such recognition of one's teacher was not uncommon; Gioacchino Conti took on the name "Gizziello" after his teacher Domenico Gizzi, and Angelo Monanni called himself "Manzoletto" after his mentor and instructor, Giovanni Manzuoli.[54] Occasionally a lineage of three generations emerged, such as the case with Francesco Antonio Pistocchi, the founder of the Bolognese school. Pistocchi taught the castrato Antonio Bernacchi, who then trained the castrati Giovanni Tedeschi (known as Amadori) and Tommaso Guarducci.[55]

Pistocchi and Tosi ran one of the most famous schools in Bologna at the beginning of the eighteenth century, and, like many castrati teachers, their legacy was passed on to other castrati and female and noncastrated male singers. Pistocchi's most famous noncastrato singers were the tenors Annibale Pio Fabri and Antonio Passi. Continuing in this Bolognese line, Bernacchi's students included the contralto Vittoria Tesi Tramontini and the tenors Carlo Garlani and Anton Raaff.[56] Hence, even in the height of their popularity in the eighteenth century, the castrato singing style was passed on to other treble voices—tenors and women singers—in formal vocal instruction. Additionally, these students went on to become leading singers in their own right. While it is clear the castrato voice encapsulated the aesthetics of Baroque bel canto singing, my point here is to show that these aesthetics were directly transmitted to other voice types. The castrato techniques were adapted to noncastrated voices and were important in shaping and defining what opera singing was for all treble voice types at the beginning of opera (by the middle of the seventeenth century) through the eighteenth and early nineteenth centuries.

In addition to formal teaching situations, the castrati's presence in opera gave other singers an opportunity to "learn by example." Since the beginning of opera in the seventeenth century women (except where banned), castrati and noncastrated male singers all appeared and sang together on the opera stage. Francesca Cuzzoni (1696–1778) and Faustina Bordoni (1697–1781), arguably the two most prominent female singers in the first half of the eighteenth century, well represent this unofficial line of training. The two women sang with each other as well as side by side with castrati onstage. Their appearance together with the castrato Francesco Bernardi (ca. 1680–1759), known as Senesino and one of the most famous castrati of his day, provides a helpful example for illustrating how castrato singing closely interacted with leading female performers.[57] Cuzzoni and Senesino premiered roles in all twelve of Handel's operas written for the King's Theatre at Haymarket in London between 1723 and 1728.[58] Bordoni's London debut was in Handel's *Alessandro* in 1726, the first of six Handel operas she sang with Cuzzoni and Senesino in the late 1720s.[59] All three singers also appeared together in London in Giovanni Bononcini's *Astianatte* in 1727.[60]

It is undeniable that an informal venue for other singers to learn about the castrati's vocal methods must have occurred in such interactions over the centuries. As with Cuzzoni and Bordoni, several of the female singers who were the first interpreters of primo ottocento opera also had the benefit of singing onstage with, and learning formally or informally from, their castrati colleagues. Though for some women this might not have been a deliberate goal, many of them found themselves in the very practical situation of having to sing with castrati at some point in their careers. At the very least, this involved observing the castrato sing up close in rehearsal and performance. Frequently these women sang the prima donna characters that were romantically paired with the heroic roles assigned to the castrati in the plot. This meant that these women had to blend their voices with the castrati's, coordinate complementing embellishments, and decide where they both would breathe for the numbers where they sang together.

The final duet, "Caro, bella," in Handel's 1724 opera *Giulio Cesare* illustrates such a musical collaboration. At the end of the opera, Cleopatra (premiered by Cuzzoni) and Caesar (premiered by Senesino) are finally united as the leaders of Egypt; in their final duet, the two vocal lines weave in and out of each other. Besides being sung in close succession, the lines are written so that one line ornaments the other, and then vice versa. Additionally, there is unison singing where the two characters must breathe together and decide how to embellish the melody they share. For practical considerations of performance, the women who sang such roles needed to learn how to sing with the castrati. It is hard to imagine that these women did not internalize and, when advantageous, adapt elements of the castrato singing method for their own use.

The castrato legacy was continued on the nineteenth-century opera stage through the written transmission of their singing pedagogy. The two most famous singing treatises from the eighteenth century were written by castrati: Pier Francesco Tosi's *Opinioni de' cantori antichi e moderni, o sieno osservazioni sopra il canto figurato*, first published in Bologna in 1723, and Giambattista Mancini's *Pensieri e riflessioni pratiche sopra il canto figurato*, first published in Vienna in 1774 and revised in 1777. These studies had a wide readership; both were reprinted and translated into several languages. By the end of the eighteenth century they were translated into

English, Dutch, German, and French.[61] The two treatises were geared primarily toward the castrato voice; women's voices are mentioned infrequently, and little is written about noncastrated male voices. Nonetheless, and most importantly, these writings form the fundamentals for what was considered to be "bel canto" singing. They set the precedent for nineteenth-century treatises to emphasize connecting the singing line to the breath with proper support, techniques for performing embellishments, and the smooth transition of the voice as it passes through the full extent of its range. Even some of the same terms, such as *messa di voce* and appoggiatura, are given emphasis in both centuries.[62] One of the most widely used nineteenth-century pedagogical books, Manuel García's 1847 *A Complete Treatise on the Art of Singing*, continues the line of bel canto teaching.[63] In addition to arias contemporaneous with the time of his writing, in part 2 he also includes a few arias embellished by the last of the great castrati from the eighteenth-century operatic tradition: Giambattista Velluti and Giralomo Crescentini. In retrospect with twenty-first century sensibilities, we see castrated voices instructing the "feminization" of voice—but for the period ear (from an eighteenth-century and primo ottocento perspective) this terminology is not relevant because the castrati defined the ideal operatic voice for both the hero and the heroine.

Technique

Not only the written evidence of voice instruction, the vocal manuals from the seventeenth, eighteenth, and nineteenth centuries have preserved elements of the bel canto technique.[64] Though the treatises are not the same as the actual singing voice (however, as the early recordings made of Moreschi show, even a recorded voice can be enigmatic), they do give insight into the rhetorical construction and historical representation of the idea of the singing voice. From these descriptions we can begin to get an idea of how elements of the castrato singing tradition can be heard, modified, in later female voices of the early nineteenth century.

As testaments that document the height of opera's first exceptional singers, Tosi's and Mancini's famous treatises frame the eighteenth century. Among the first singers in opera to gain exceptional distinction, the castrati pioneered singing methods that helped define opera singing and how it was best accomplished. The unique timbre and potential in the castrati's voices are the main focus of these treatises. In both treatises an emphasis is placed on how to access the upper portion of the voice. In Tosi's first chapter, "Observations for one who teaches a soprano," he gives directions for how to sing high notes:

> On the sol-fa-ing, let him endeavour to gain by degrees the high notes, that by the help of this exercise he may acquire as much compass of the voice as possible. Let him take care, however, that the higher the notes, the more it is necessary to touch them with softness, to avoid screaming.[65]

Tosi outlines what is to become a core component in bel canto singing: the extension of the vocal range is accomplished from the middle outwards. Not only are the high notes gained "by degrees," but singers should "toccarle con dolcezza," "touch them with softness" or "play them with sweetness," so as to avoid a harsh effect. Several paragraphs later we find out more about the sound of these notes. Tosi continues: "The *voce di testa* has a great volubility, more of the high than the lower notes, and has a quick shake [= trill], but [is] subject to be lost for want of strength."[66] The *voce di testa* literally means "head voice"; however, in this treatise Tosi uses it interchangeably with falsetto.[67] In this sentence we find out that the head/falsetto voice is geared toward great flexibility, but the quality of the sound is not forceful. The top notes were more for ornamentation and effect (as well as affect) than for declaring text or carrying the main melody. The high notes were sought out and trained, but they were not weighty or overly powerful.

Instead of high decibel levels, the projection of these high notes was achieved by a light orchestral accompaniment (dramatically smaller than later nineteenth-century orchestras) and the style of vocal writing. A stylistic feature that helped the castrati voices be heard throughout the theater was the messa di voce. It is mentioned several times throughout Tosi's treatise, and Mancini devotes all of his chapter 9 to it (simply entitled "Messa di voce").[68] Literally the term means the "placement of the voice." In practical terms, it refers to starting a note very softly, gradually increasing the volume and intensity, and then slowly decreasing the volume until the sound virtually disappears. This drawn-out crescendo and decrescendo, or swelling effect, was a way to make the sound stand out and resonate through the opera house. The messa di voce displayed great virtuosity in breath control, for the longer the singer could sustain the sound, the more exciting the effect. Additionally it showcased a remarkable technique; to achieve the elasticity needed to increase and decrease the volume, the note had to be placed securely on the breath; otherwise, the tone would collapse and disappear in the soft sections and become harsh or shrill in the loud sections.

The softness and sweetness of the upper notes in the head/falsetto voice were hallmarks of the unadorned *stile spinato* (expressive or "pathetic") style of singing. The stile spinato emphasized slower and less ornamented singing than the other popular type of singing, the bravura style with lots of fioratura, that become popular later in the eighteenth century. The singing technique that supported this later bravura style required a stronger sound in the upper reaches of the range. As a result, the vocal technique needed to adapt.

Tosi's singing career was closer to the earlier style of singing that highlighted the stile spinato. He was born in 1647 and trained in Bologna, one of the most important centers for the castrati. His operatic career took him throughout Italy as well as England and Germany. His international career aided the dissemination of his treatise in England (translated into English in 1743 by John Ernest Galliard, a London theater oboist and composer) and Germany (translated into German in 1757 by John Friedrich Agricola, a student of J. S. Bach's).[69] After retiring from the stage in the 1690s, Tosi's career in the eighteenth century focused on composition and pedagogy, and from 1703 to 1712 he was the court composer in Vienna. His influential treatise *Observations on the Florid Song* was written near the end of his career in 1723, after he returned to Bologna, about a decade before he died in 1732 in Faenza. Though his treatise dates from the eighteenth century, it most accurately reflects the singing practices during his own career in the second half of the seventeenth century. This is not to imply that the brilliant melismatic bravura style with high notes and extensive ornamentation was absent, it was just practiced in moderation.

In the eighteenth century, the bravura style became the signature sound of the bel canto and switched places, so to speak, with the stile spinato. Near the end of Tosi's treatise he acknowledges, begrudgingly, this change and questions its merit in modern singers (referring to the time he was writing in 1723). In his chapter "On arias," he voices his opinion against excessive ornamentation (Galliard uses an older term, "divisions," for ornamentation and fioratura):

> Too many modern singers add so many divisions that all airs sound alike; whereas not long ago one bravura air for each singer was enough in an opera. Is it the composer or the singer who has banished the pathetic from the stage? All musicians agree that it has the greatest charm, but they praise the pathetic, yet sing the allegro. He must want common sense that does not see through them. They know the first to be the most excellent but they lay it aside, knowing it to be the most difficult.[70]

A little later on, Tosi remarks that if the best of the current singers "were but a little more friends to the pathetic and the expressive, and a little less to the divisions, they might boast of having brought the Art to the highest degree of perfection."[71]

Despite Tosi's caution against the "overuse" of the bravura style, it continued to be the trend throughout the second half of the eighteenth century. Giambattista Mancini's treatise from 1774 (and revised in 1777), *Practical Reflections on the Figurative Art of Singing*, bears this out. In chapter 12, "The Agility of the Voice," a new section that was not given a separate chapter by Tosi, Mancini identifies the "disorder" where singers not properly instructed, or gifted by nature, rely too heavily on the bravura style. Without disagreeing with Tosi's sentiments, Mancini's position later in the century gives him a different perspective that confirms Tosi's prophetic comments:

> Having thought very seriously upon this matter, I feel that the only explanation I can give as to the cause of this disorder, is that it is either due to the wrong belief of present day singers, who think they cannot be successful unless they sing with agility; or else, it is caused by their anxiety for applause, which desire induces them to make an effort to perform some sort of agility at any cost. [T]he fault lies with the teacher, who, although finding no natural disposition in his pupil, nevertheless induces him to study it, and teaches him all the rules and precepts. . . . The pupil is mistaken when he thinks that only agility can bring success to a singer.[72]

Regardless of how he felt about the prominence of the bravura style, Mancini's *Practical Reflections* provides a complementing document to Tosi's treatise in how singing developed over the late seventeenth and into the eighteenth centuries. To sustain the new emphasis on high notes with agility and more power, the vocal technique needed to evolve. For most of his treatise, Mancini uses Tosi as a starting point; in fact, he even refers to specific page numbers in Tosi's *Observations* several times throughout his *Practical Reflections*. Mancini develops concepts and adds new chapters when necessary to reflect the contemporary priorities in singing around the second half of the eighteenth century.

The key to supporting the new type of bravura singing has its roots in Tosi's technique. Mancini begins with the concept of evening out the break in the voice in the *passaggio* region, something that Tosi promoted, and then applies to the entire range. In fact, Mancini emphasizes this point to such an extent that he devotes the beginning of chapter 8 to it: "Of the Blending of the Registers, Portamento and Appoggiatura."

The basis for blending the registers is to provide a strong core throughout the voice to support the emphasis on the fioratura and bravura style of singing. Mancini outlines the new aesthetic for blending the chest and head/falsetto registers so as to carry some of the stronger register (usually the chest voice) into the weaker one (usually the head/falsetto):

> In my opinion, however, the worth of a voice will always depend upon its evenness of quality throughout the whole register and perfect intonation. The strength of the medium and chest tones must also be equivalent to those of the head, in order to form an even register. . . . It is easier and more natural to attack the low tones than the high, because they can be taken with less effort. Great care must be taken by the student to attack the high tones with the required sweetness and proportion, in order that he can command his entire range to perfection.[73]

In the case where the chest voice is weaker, he prescribes an exercise to remedy the situation. After advising the student to focus on strengthening the chest voice on its own, he then directs:

> The next step for the teacher is to dictate a solfeggio mingled with tones of the second register (head), and as we find in these cases that such tones are already good, and that the pupil possesses the facility to draw them, the matter of blending the registers will be easily accomplished.[74]

In these passages Mancini shifts the vocal paradigm from thinking of the voice in terms of two parts with an emphasis on smoothing out the meeting point (the break or passaggio) where one register ends and the other begins. Instead, he advocates a *blended voice* where the weaker notes are enhanced and supported by the stronger section of the voice. This technique affected the entire range of the voice; however, it had the most radical results in the highest notes where the formerly weak falsetto/head voice notes were now filled out with more power behind them. This technique extended the upper register to include notes that previously could not be sung. With this development, the most famous castrati singers—Farinelli, Bernacchi, and Carestini along with others—became exceedingly popular and legendary.

Bel Canto Technique Overview into the Primo Ottocento

The treatises that Tosi and Mancini wrote provide two sets of blueprints for the architecture of sound in the latter part of the seventeenth and through the eighteenth century. Though there are variances between the two treatises, they are closely related to each other. Mancini's frequent references to Tosi indicate that he thought his writings evolved out of Tosi's principles, similar to reinforcing the foundation and adding a top floor onto an original frame. As the bravura style became more popular and the demand for more power and agility in the highest range grew, singing technique evolved to reflect these preferences. The differences between the two treatises stem more from a response to the contemporary practice of their respective times than from an incongruence of ideas concerning aesthetics.

Tosi's ideal bel canto voice was one that had a smooth transition between the chest voice and the head/falsetto voice. Though there needed to be a seamlessness in the shifting between registers, the entire compass of the voice could have different sounds; for example, the higher notes were sung more gently with *dolcezza*, a soft sweetness. Tosi talks about two voices, the *voce di petto* (chest voice) and *voce di testa*/falsetto (head voice/falsetto), that a singer produces. While Mancini adapts the same terminology that Tosi uses (voce di petto, voce di testa/falsetto), he very strongly emphasizes the importance of blending the registers. Mancini's ideal bel canto voice has a consistent core throughout the range, not just an evenness between the break.

The primo ottocento continued the techniques of bel canto singing. Though the cast of singers changed, the tenor became an increasingly important voice type, and the female mezzo-soprano and contralto replaced the castrati in the heroic travesti role, the style of castrati singing was adapted for other voices. This was not an event that was new in the nineteenth century. As was illustrated in two productions of Alessandro Scarlatti's *Pompeo* at the end of the seventeenth century and Handel's *Rinaldo* in the beginning of the eighteenth century, women had long been seen and heard as acceptable substitutes for the castrati. Although the tenor had appeared in opera since the seventeenth century, it was not until the end of the eighteenth century that he finally began to emerge as a virtuosic voice type who inspired heroic roles (e.g., Anton Raaff, for whom Mozart wrote the title role in *Idomeneo*, 1781). What was different about the early nineteenth century was that the aesthetics for the sound of bel canto singing persisted even though the castrato, the pioneers of that sound, left the opera stage.

In his discussion of the development of the bel canto technique, Rodolfo Celletti refers to the technique outlined by Mancini as the *voce mista* (mixed voice).[75] Celletti argues that the castrati learned how to blend characteristics of the chest voice into the falsetto (or head voice); thus, the highest notes were combined with the power of the chest voice. I find the construction of this "mixed voice" helpful for mapping the diverse visual and aural codes that surrounded the castrati. Not only were their voices accepted as male and female characters, but the body pro thot hog the sound was believable in male and female roles. The "mixed voice" that blends two voices into one provides a helpful metaphor for illustrating the friction between gender categories. As the castrati learned to blend the chest voice into the head voice, the new hybrid sound could transgress the stratification for what was heard as male and female: a sound that encompassed the heroic, masculine, and feminine all at the same time.

As will be seen in later chapters, the women who replaced the castrati on the primo ottocento stage inherited not only their heroic roles, but also the complex codes behind the castrati's hybrid sound. As travesti singers became the ideal voice of the hero in the first decades of the nineteenth century, the combination of male and female was reconfigured. The acceptance of a woman's voice emanating from a woman's body as a male character was a stylized convention. Unlike the castrati onstage who could "pass" as women to an unsuspecting member of the audience (e.g., Balzac's Sarrasine), no one in the audience believed that the female travesti singers were men offstage. The audience saw a woman dressed as a man and heard a voice they accepted as heroic. Hence, the stylization of sound and image begun with the castrati was continued with women in the primo ottocento. Women's voices (recalling the sound of the castrati) encapsulated a hybrid sound that brought together the simultaneity of seeing a woman and, within the world of the opera, hearing a male voice.

As the castrato bel canto singing technique went through a development that privileged the bravura style with agility in the highest notes and the support of the chest voice mixed, blended, into the top register, the aesthetics of primo ottocento singing underwent a similar evolution. Around 1830 the preference for higher notes with more power (a necessity to carry over the expanding size of the orchestra) came into vogue. It was in this time when tenor Gilbert Duprez became famous for his do di petto (as we have seen, a chest voice high C), a note that Celletti asserts was produced by the voce mista,[76] and the tenor-soprano operas of Donizetti and Bellini were first coming into popularity (e.g., Donizetti's *Anna Bolena* and Bellini's *La sonnambula* and *Norma*). With this development, the new Romantic tenor effectively became the standard leading man and supplanted the female travesti hero.

The castrato bel canto (of the eighteenth century) and the primo ottocento bel canto each underwent a major shift in the aesthetic practice that was brought on by a development in vocal technique. In both cases the preference for more power in the highest range fueled the change. For the castrati, it was the blended register, the voce mista, which opened up a new sound through higher and more powerful notes. This led to the subsequent highlighting of agility through increased fioratura and a further development in the bravura style. In the primo ottocento the tenor's acquisition of strength in the highest register, being able to sing the do di petto, was one of the factors that led to a change in the sound and gender of the hero. For castrati and tenors the power of the sound led the way for modifications in performance.

For the female travesti singers around 1830 the aural change precipitated a crisis of character and role. No longer heard as the ideal heroic voice, these women either sang the few travesti roles that continued to be written (usually page roles where the female voice was heard as an appropriate substitute for a prepubescent boy), or they moved into the higher soprano repertory. Their ability to sing such repertory was due to their adaptation of the blended register (voce mista) technique that Mancini discusses. In this way these women's voices could recall the castrati timbre not only when they sang the travesti roles, but also when they sang female characters because they utilized and adapted castrati vocal techniques.

Theorizing the Castrato's Voice

Given their ability to portray either men or women both on and off the opera stage, the castrati's voices represent the reenactment of gender codes; the same voice could represent both male and female. Such a complex performance practice that marks gender and voice leads to a subsequent interrogation between vocal types and character types. In this way, the same type of voice could represent what were considered "masculine" and "feminine" characteristics. By bringing these things together, the castrati embodied many ambiguities that demonstrate how gender in opera is constructed.

The historical construction of gender and how it interacts with designating sex identity has varied over time. Thomas Laqueur has outlined "premodern" and "modern" frames for understanding writings about gender and sex from the Greeks to Freud.[77] According to Laqueur, in premodern ideologies up through the seventeenth century, male and female are understood as inversions of one another. Men's genitalia were visible on the outside and were counterbalanced (in what was considered an inferior fashion) by women's sexual organs inside the body. Hence, a single-sex model emerged where women and men were two versions of the same whole. In a premodern view,

> There was but one sex whose more perfect exemplars were easily deemed males at birth and whose decidedly less perfect ones were labeled female. The modern question, about the "real" sex of a person, made no sense in this period, not because the two sexes were mixed but because there was only one to pick from and it had to be shared by everyone, from the strongest warrior to the most effeminate courtier to the most aggressive virago to the gentlest maiden. . . . In this world, the body with its one elastic sex was far freer to express theatrical gender and the anxieties thereby produced than it would be when it came to be regarded as the foundation of gender. . . . An open body in which sexual differences were matters of degree rather than kind confronted a world of real men and women and of the clear juridical, social and cultural distinctions between them.[78]

Thus, the "one elastic sex" that everyone shared was a receptive environment for boundary crossings between what was considered male and female. Male and female were "matters of degree" because the two existed as points along a single continuum.[79] It is not surprising that within this context the castrati in Italian opera, as well as the Shakespearean boy actors on the Elizabethan stage, were accepted as female characters.

For the castrati and English boys who played women on the seventeenth-century stage, the dimension of vocal timbre is an important element. For similar reasons, the boys and castrati were able to play women: the hormonal physical changes due to an increased level of testosterone (e.g., deepening voice, the appearance of an Adam's apple, and the hardening of defined muscles) rendered the illusion believable. Moreover, for both groups, the flexible treble timbre of the voice was the aural marker of femininity. Yet the stakes for the castrati were different than for the English boys. Once the boy's voice broke, he moved out of the female roles. The orchiectomy preserved the essence of the boy's voice in the castrati throughout their careers, and, should one so desire, a castrato could make a career specializing in female characters.

Laqueur's premodern formation of a culturally gendered and biologically sexed construction works well, up to a point, for the castrati. In terms of physical appearance, their bodies could be convincingly costumed as male or female characters and made even more realistic through behavior. Their singing embodied the aesthetic ideal for both male and female voices. Whereas the body could be attired to be seen as either a man or a woman, the voice fulfills this task more directly, for it required no mediation to be heard as male or female.

Laqueur discusses the emergence of a new paradigm in the eighteenth century where women were no longer the "imperfect" inversion of men; instead, women were considered a separate opposite. What defined sex in one, represented the opposite sex in the other. This led to a two-sex model where

> The dominant, though by no means universal, view since the eighteenth century has been that there are two stable, incommensurable, opposite sexes and that the political, economic, and cultural lives of men and women, their gender roles, are some how based on these "facts."[80]

During the Enlightenment, the emphasis on scientific knowledge provided a seemingly stable way to classify the body as to biological sex. In this modern context, sex and gender lined up on opposite sides. Earlier in the premodern model biological sex was able to span across the divide of a cultured gender; men and women might behave differently, but they are still part of the same biological whole, just different versions. In the later modern view, men and women were intrinsically different.

During the time of the castrati, both ideological formulations existed. The premodern one-sex model at the beginning of their reign in opera in the seventeenth century was later joined by the modern two-sex model around the time of their decline at the end of the eighteenth century. By the nineteenth century, both ways of thinking about sex and gender were accepted. In the premodern one-sex model, the construction of sex and gender is rather fluid; men and women are different articulations of the same whole, and the overlapping of male and female is tolerated. Since the biological distinction is a matter of degree, rather than a separate category, a shared area comprised of elements from both extremes is possible. Thus, with such a construction, castrati could occupy a liminal space between male and female.

Encompassing both premodern and modern ideologies are writings that take into account hermaphrodites: persons born with both male and female sexual organs and the potential to mature into either sex.[81] While it is little surprise that, from the seventeenth century forward, the practice of choosing a sex for a hermaphroditic baby was standard, it might seem likely that a premodern ideology which saw male and female as part of the same whole would be able to find a place for a biologically ambiguously sexed person, such as a hermaphrodite or a castrato. Such a place could be positioned biologically and culturally between male and female. However, for hermaphrodites, this was not the case due to cultural dynamics contingent upon gender differences. Given the separate social, legal, and economic positions of men and women, the identifiable sex of a person was an important definition for living in society. For this reason, medical writings on hermaphrodites that go back to the Renaissance address the anxiety of this duality by explaining how to determine which hermaphroditic babies should be made male, and which ones female.[82]

Unlike the feared hermaphrodites who were born with a biological duality of sex that would destabilize the cultural construction of gender, the revered castrati were biologically altered because a cultural aesthetic enjoyed a destabilization of gender in terms of sound. As castrati were able to portray opera characters of both sexes, societal restrictions demanding singular gender identification were suspended. In a dramatic contrast to daily life, opera provided a special case to Laqueur's premodern and modern constructions of sex and gender. The castrati were able to portray male and female in a so-called hermaphroditic, or ambidextrous, way. As mentioned earlier, the castrato's body was physically altered so that it contained characteristics that were considered both masculine (e.g., generally a tall and large stature) and feminine (e.g., extra flesh around the chest and hips, and no Adam's apple). Depending upon costume, the castrato could very compellingly depict either man or woman. Intertwined with the visual presence was the voice—the aural presence—that simultaneously sounded heroically masculine and feminine. Within both of Laqueur's contextual models, the castrati straddled distinctions between male and female.

Understanding the accepted cultural and biological constructions of men and women adds a further dimension to understanding the resonating of castrati and women's voices in their time. If in the single-sex, premodern model, castrati were thought of as men by the seventeenth and eighteenth century public, then it would make sense that their voices were heard as masculine. This construction works well for the dominant type of role the castrati sang: the hero. Within such a context, female voices could be heard as imitations, albeit less-accomplished ones, of castrati voices.

The similarity in timbre and pitch between castrati and women could be aurally aestheticized and heard as different shades of the same sound. Within this cultural sonic world, women's voices could be heard as interchangeable with the castrati and assume the same cultural signifiers—a heroic masculinity. Conversely, in less frequent situations, the castrati were also convincing as female characters onstage, as the abovementioned Sarrasine and accounts by Casanova and Goethe suggest. For these situations the imitation goes the other way, and the castrati were feminized in body and sound.

With the development of Laqueur's modern sensibility, male and female were no longer connected; they represented opposites. The decline of the castrati in opera at the end of the eighteenth century and disappearance from the stage at the beginning of the nineteenth century reflects the changing sentiments of the time; as Laqueur might argue, the one-sex model was giving way to the two-sex model. However, the possibilities for what the castrati's voices meant undergoes another transformation. In nineteenth-century opera their voices were a sound of the past, and their replacements were the female travesti singers. Since women had already been performing male and female characters in the eighteenth century alongside the castrati, these female voices now became the sole representations of the multivalent relationship between voice and character that they had shared earlier with the castrati voices.

The legacy these women inherited is a voice that was heard as being gendered masculine *and* feminine without different aural markers. The voices of these women, as well as the earlier operatic castrati, were heard as sometimes male and sometimes female, depending upon the surrounding context. In looking back, it is also possible to imagine their voices as neither man nor woman in an exclusive sense, but regard them as a combination of something in between: a "third" option for gendering the singing voice.

I would like to pursue the construction of the "third" possibility further. Though it is made up of codes that are both masculine and feminine, there are different ways to interpret this interaction. This third category could be neither masculine nor feminine, but something new that results from the combination ($a + b = c$). Or, it could be both simultaneously ($a + b = ab$), invoking something new, yet a synthesis of both older elements. When I hear Alessandro Moreschi's castrato voice on the rereleased recording, at times it sounds like something close to a woman's voice with a man's voice mixed in ($a + b = ab$). Yet at other points in the recording a new and different type of voice comes through, one that sounds completely foreign and unlike any voice I have ever heard ($a + b = c$). Unfortunately, I do not know if the sound of the "new voice" is due to inadvertent distortion from the transferring process of the recording, or if it is a glimpse of the "true" sound of the historic castrato voice. The digitally processed voice of the title character in *Farinelli* reinforces this sonic ambiguity. It is a very pleasant voice to hear with its uncanny beauty: it sounds like a smooth fortified countertenor combined with the round warm timbre of a woman's voice. The familiarity of the sound illustrated in my attempt to articulate how I heard it as the voice of a countertenor crossed with a woman's voice (perhaps influenced by my knowledge of how the voice was created) could be described as an identifiable blended voice ($a + b = ab$). Yet the knowledge that such a voice was digitally created and does not actually exist in one person's throat makes it a completely new voice ($a + b = c$).

In her work on cross-dressing, cultural theorist Marjorie Garber sets the Elizabethan stage as a "privileged site of transgression" where cross-dressing was featured not only in the all-male casts where boys played the female roles, due to the ban against women onstage (similar to young castrati assuming the roles of women in Rome), but also in the "changes of costume that violated edicts against wearing the clothing of the wrong rank." [83] Such a double set of cross-dressing where interchanged class or status markers are combined with confused gender identities illustrates "the centrality of the transvestite as an index of category destabilization . . . an underlying psychosocial, and not merely a local or historical, effect." [84] Garber returns to this point about category destabilization and the cultural anxiety concerning gender codes to emphasize that *"transvestitism is a space of possibility structuring and confounding culture:* the disruptive element that intervenes, not just a category crisis of male and female, but the crisis of category itself."[85] To reframe this discourse, Garber proposes the construction of a gender designation that encompasses neither masculine nor feminine exclusively, but rather a "third" that incorporates both elements together. "The 'third' is that which questions binary thinking . . . The 'third' is a mode of articulation, a way of describing a space of possibility. Three puts in question the idea of one: of identity, self-sufficiency, self-knowledge."[86]

This "third" which occupies a "space of possibility" is similar to my earlier construction of a third which mediated between a synthesis of two familiar elements and something that is entirely new. By placing the sound of the castrati's voices and the early-nineteenth-century female travesti singers voices in what I am going to call a "third zone," both masculine and feminine can coexist and alternate at the same time. This "third zone" is a sonic space that existed before 1830. The 1830s and 1840s saw the end of the heroic travesti roles and the establishment of a bifurcated gender system where, similar to the Laqueurian two-sex modern model, the clear sonic distinction between male and female vocal sound emerges: the tenor becomes the leading heroic voice and the high soprano becomes the model of ultrafemininity.

The castrati present a special case to Garber's discussion of cross-dressing. Since their physical bodies exhibited both feminine and masculine characteristics, some could sustain the illusion of belonging to either gender outside of the opera house, despite the men's or women's clothing they wore. The relationship between the castrati and the "third zone" continued off the stage, and they embodied a realm of possibility where neither gender exclusively and aptly described who they were. Since this situation blurs the distinction between when the castrati were cross-dressing and when they were wearing their "correctly gendered clothing," the "third zone" gives them the latitude to exist in a liminal category that has a unique relationship to both male and female, but is not completely one or the other.

An available zone for various possibilities most accurately describes the castrati's special position as a group. What Garber calls a "crisis of category" when she refers to the crossed boundaries in her construction of the "third," I am recasting as a performance practice that is part of a larger aesthetic. Garber's categorical crisis that is indigenous to cross-dressing traverses time. In her model transvestitism always precipitates a rupture in social codes that causes friction. In my examination of the castrati, I am rooted in the time period they occupied in opera: the seventeenth through early nineteenth centuries. During these years the aesthetic they embody is historical. Their "space of possibility" was nurtured within a specific context that allowed sound, the singing voice, to articulate gender in a stylized way that was understood and enjoyed. When women replaced the castrati on the primo ottocento stage, the component of transvestitism was foregrounded. Unlike the castrati, the women's bodies were not ambiguously sexed; hence the identity of their bodies as women's bodies was rarely, if ever, under question. In these transi-

tional years in the beginning of the nineteenth century, the older aesthetic preferences led audiences to listen to the voices of the female travesti performers as the
reincarnations of the castrati.

The castrato's voice is coded to say several things at once. In the first decades of
the nineteenth century when female travesti singers replaced the castrati in opera
productions, female voices entered this "third zone" of aural possibility. With the
transitory nature of the primo ottocento that shunned the presence of the castrati
onstage, yet still favored the aesthetics of high flexible treble timbres for heroic
male leads, female singers performed male roles en travesti and became the most
desirable substitutes for the castrati. As Marianina embodied the vocal progeny of
her great-uncle, La Zambinella, at the great ball in the 1830s, so do the women who
sang en travesti during this same time continue the legacy the castrati left in the
nineteenth century.

Because of a lack of documented evidence, there have not been many studies
that record the activities of the castrati after their retirements from the stage. How
long they taught singing privately and to what extent they were a part of the ver-
nacular musical life of their time is virtually impossible to determine given extant
sources. Though drastically reduced in their numbers and the power of their influence, the castrato's presence in the nineteenth century had musical and ideological meaning. Emblems of a past ideal, the castrato haunted the nineteenth century
as an anachronistic and enigmatic voice that opened up new possibilities for other
voices.

3　Meyerbeer in Italy:
The Crusader, the Castrato, and
the Disguised Second Woman

The history of Italian opera in the first half of the nineteenth century is usually presented as a narrative threading together the accomplishments of four major Italian composers: Gioachino Rossini, Gaetano Donizetti, Vincenzo Bellini, and the early works of Giuseppe Verdi. For the purpose of gaining a general overview of the period, these composers work well: their operas were exceedingly popular in their own time and still continue to hold the stage today. To augment this view, Saverio Mercadante, Giovanni Pacini, Michele Carafa, Carlo Coccia, Francesco Morlacchi, and many other Italian composers who were also popular in this time period could enrich the picture. If this list were to include a few foreigners working in Italy, Giovanni Simone Mayr and Otto Nicolai would be the logical additions. Not many people have looked at early operas by Giacomo Meyerbeer to gain insight into primo ottocento opera.

Scholarship has not paid much attention to Meyerbeer's six Italian operas.[1] Nonetheless, between the years of 1816 and 1824, Meyerbeer spent eight years in Italy with the expressed purpose of learning how to write Italian opera. Immediately following his time in Italy, Meyerbeer went on to become the preeminent composer of the most lucrative genre of opera in the nineteenth century: French grand opera. While his groundbreaking works for the Paris Opéra have garnered the most attention (*Robert le diable*, 1831; *Les Huguenots*, 1836; *Le prophète*, 1849; and *L'Africaine*, 1865), his reputation in opera found its real beginning during the years he spent in Italy before he settled in Paris in 1825. These eight years in Italy presented Meyerbeer with a training ground where, as a talented young composer poised on the brink of what would become a major international career, he could assimilate the conventions of Italian opera in the late 1810s and early 1820s. His operas for Italy present an insightful microcosm of the norms of Italian opera of that time, self-consciously studied and absorbed by a foreigner learning the trade and making his mark.

Born and raised in Berlin, Jakob Liebmann Meyer Beer (1791–1864) came from a wealthy family that was able to support his interest and talent in music. His formal musical training took him to Vienna, where he studied with the leading composers and theorists of the time: Carl Friedrich Zelter, Muzio Clementi, and the abbé Joseph Georg Vogler. However, since none of these teachers specialized in writing opera, he realized that if he were serious about mastering the genre, he would need to visit Italy and Paris. Indeed, after having written a few operas and stage works in German (between 1810 and 1814), he traveled to Paris before deciding to start what can be thought of as his independently organized opera apprenticeship in Italy in 1816.[2]

Giacomo Meyerbeer's (in Italy he Italianized his name) years in Italy were self-consciously a critical training period during which he worked toward his goal of mastering the art of writing opera. Prior to his trip to Italy, during his eighteen-month stay in Vienna in 1814–15, he expressed these sentiments in a letter to his father. Feeling his father's pressure to return to Berlin and accept a position as a second director at the Königliche Schauspiele (the new opera house in Berlin that was created through the merger of the Royal Opera House and the National Theater companies in 1807), Meyerbeer was adamant about learning French and Italian national operatic styles:

> But you know that I have always considered familiarity with the French and Italian theater to be indispensable. This is why I cannot, under any circumstances, return to Berlin until I have made both of these journeys. I believe this to be of the utmost importance to my musical training and would not let anything in this world prevent me from going, even if I had to set out on foot and wage battle against the raging elements.[3]

After spending much of 1815 in Paris, Meyerbeer arrived in Italy in 1816. Caught up in what he referred to as the "sweet ecstasy" and "paradise" of Italy during the height of Rossini's popularity, Meyerbeer fully immersed himself in the musical life of Italian opera.[4] Writing about this time in retrospect to his German biographer, Dr. Jean F. Schucht, in 1856, he said:

> I was as one bewitched in a magic garden. I did not want to go into it, but I could not avoid it. All my feelings, all my thoughts, became Italian. After having lived there for a year, I felt like a real Italian. I had become so completely acclimatised to the magnificent splendor of nature, through Italian art and cheery friendly living, that I could, as a consequence, think like an Italian, feel and experience like an Italian. It is understandable that such a complete transformation of my inner life would have to have a basic effect upon my style of music. I did not want, as is commonly supposed, to imitate Rossini or to write in the Italian manner, but I had to compose in the style which I had adopted under the compulsion of my state of mind.[5]

In this much-quoted letter, Meyerbeer presents an engaging, if somewhat contradictory, account of his compositional style during these Italian years. While he insists that he was not trying to "imitate Rossini" or even "write in the Italian manner," his memory for experiencing an overwhelming immersion in all things Italian is revealed in his comments. Regardless of whether, in retrospect, he was imbuing this period with nostalgia, the strength of his reminiscences—he "felt like a real Italian" and could "think . . . feel and experience like an Italian"—illustrates the powerful encounter he experienced with things Italian. During his eight-year stay Meyerbeer traveled and saw operas all over the Italian peninsula and even included an extended trip to Sicily.[6] With these experiences, his compositional style was influenced by his so-called Italian "state of mind" and reflected his desire to acquire elements of this operatic world that would improve his technical skills and bring him financial and artistic success. With the demeanor of an apprentice, Meyerbeer wrote what he considered to be "Italian" operas.

For the birthplace of opera, the early nineteenth century in Italy was a transitional time; the years Meyerbeer spent in Italy, 1816–24, give us a particularly helpful view into the different practices that were popular in various regions. When Meyerbeer arrived in Italy, Rossini was the rising star. Earlier works such as *Tancredi,* which premiered at La Fenice in Venice (February 1813), and *Il barbiere di Siviglia,* which premiered at the Teatro Argentina in Rome (February 1816), had been very successful and established Rossini as a leading composer of both serious and comic opera. In 1815, the year before Meyerbeer arrived in Italy, Rossini signed a contract with impresario Domenico Barbaja to become the musical director of the Teatro San Carlo in Naples (one of Italy's most prestigious opera houses). Prior to this contract, all of Rossini's operas had premieres in northern Italy (Milan, Venice, Ferrara, and Bologna), not surprisingly given his birth in Pesaro and his northern relatives and connections from that area. Though his contract with Barbaja did not preclude his writing for other venues, Rossini concentrated his efforts on the serious operas he wrote for Naples. From 1815 onwards, he composed a total of nineteen operas for Italy: fifteen operas written for theaters in the south (Naples and Rome), and the remaining four operas commissioned by houses in the north (Venice and Milan).[7] After 1822 Rossini traveled to Vienna, London, and Paris, where he eventually settled in 1824.

By contrast, although Meyerbeer traveled throughout Italy, he settled in the north, and all six of his Italian operas were written for northern theaters (his first two for Padua and Turin, and then two each for Milan and Venice). After 1815, when Rossini was primarily working in the south and traveling across Europe, Meyerbeer became one of the leading opera composers in Italy until his departure in 1824; his popularity in northern Italy was especially strong.[8] In a time when the concept of repertory opera (operas performed for subsequent seasons rather than for one house, cast and season) was new, most of Meyerbeer's Italian operas had revivals in successive seasons in Italy. Moreover, they found audiences in Germany, Austria, and Paris with increasing frequency. Additionally, Meyerbeer's Italian operas made money—a difficult feat at a time when the business of the opera industry was still very much a risky venture.[9]

Meyerbeer's six operas for Italy were collaborations with many of the most prominent figures in the opera industry working in northern Italy during that time. He was able to work with two leading librettists: Gaetano Rossi (1774–1855) and Felice Romani (1788–1865).[10] Rossi, who had collaborated with Rossini on *Tancredi* in 1812–13, and Meyerbeer collaborated on four of his six Italian operas. Romani, who later went on to become Bellini's principal librettist, was at the very beginning of his career and collaborated with Meyerbeer on the other two.[11]

In addition to the leading librettists, Meyerbeer also worked with many of the star singers who had already, and continued to, interpret roles by Rossini, Mercadante, Pacini, Donizetti, Bellini, and other composers whose works shaped the primo ottocento. His first five Italian operas featured such leading singers as Rosamunda Pisaroni, Carolina Bassi, and Adelaide Tosi. The casts for the premiere and sub-

Table 3.1. Principal Roles for Women's Voices in Meyerbeer's First Five Italian Operas

Second woman is italicized   * Travesti role   ** Spends time in disguise

1817 *Romilda e Costanza* (Gaetano Rossi, Padua, Teatro Nuovo)	
*Romilda***	Rosamunda Pisaroni
Costanza	Caterina Lipardini
1819 *Semiramide riconosciuta* (Gaetano Rossi, Turin, Teatro Regio)	
*Semiramide***	Carolina Bassi
Tamiri, daughter of the King of Bactria	Teresa Cantarelli
Scitalce,* prince of India and former lover of Semiramide	Adelina Dalman-Naldi
1819 *Emma di Resburgo,* (Gaetano Rossi, Venice, Teatro San Benedetto)	
*Emma di Resburgo***	Rosa Morandi
Edemondo,* exiled Earl of Lanark and husband to Emma	Carolina Cortesi
Etelia, Olfredo's daughter	Cecilia Gaddi
1820 *Margherita d'Anjou* (Felice Romani, Milan, La Scala)	
Margherita d'Anjou,** widow of Henry VI of England	Carolina Pellegrini
Edoardo, her son*	Gaetana Carcano
*Isaura, wife of the Duke of Lavarenne***	Rosa Mariani
1821 *L'esule di Granata* (Felice Romani, Milan, La Scala)	
Almanzor, King of Granada*	Rosamunda Pisaroni
Azema, daughter of King Sulemano, exiled King of Granada	Adelaide Tosi

sequent productions that Meyerbeer oversaw of *Il crociato in Egitto,* his last and most successful Italian opera, were his most impressive. They included singers he had worked with before, Carolina Bassi and Adelaide Tosi, as well as other singers whose names have gone on to become synonymous with the sound of primo ottocento singing: Henriette Méric-Lalande, Ester Mombelli, Maria Malibran, and Giuditta Pasta. *Il crociato* also presents a dramatic narrative for the primo ottocento's new concern for male voices. For the male characters of Armando/Elmireno (castrato, heroic travesti), Adriano (tenor), and Aladino (bass), Meyerbeer worked with the castrato Giambattista Velluti, tenors Nicola Tacchinardi and Domenico Donzelli (for two different productions), and bass Prosper Levasseur. Hence, more than a sole reliance on his letters affirms his mastery of the Italian operatic style, the stature and number of collaborators he worked with who were central to the core repertory of the primo ottocento situate Meyerbeer's six operas firmly within the Italian tradition.

Table 3.1 lists the roles for women for the premieres of Meyerbeer's first five Italian operas (this information for his last Italian opera, *Il crociato in Egitto,* will be presented later in the chapter). As can be seen from the table, all of these operas have multiple roles for women's voices. Meyerbeer employed the heroic travesti role only twice: Edemondo (*Emma di Resburgo*) and Almanzor (*L'esule di Granata*).[12] The other cross-dressed role is Edoardo (*Margherita d'Anjou*), whose character references the pageboy type of travesti role where a woman's voice represents a young boy's voice before puberty.

In four of these five operas the second woman (always a female character in the plot) spends some time in the opera in disguise cross-dressed as a male character; hence, through various twists of the plot within the opera, a female character assumes the identity of a man. This plot device of disguise becomes a central feature of Meyerbeer's second woman. Unlike the travesti roles where a woman assumes a male character throughout, these disguised roles are when a female character temporarily pretends to be a man within the plot of the opera; near the end of the opera, she is revealed as a woman.[13] Sometimes it is because her character needs to travel alone, and dressing as a man ensures her safe passage and ability to function in worlds that did not allow women such independence: Romilda in *Romilda e Costanza,* Emma in *Emma di Resburgo,* and Isaura in *Margherita d'Anjou.*[14] In all three of these operas, this second woman in disguise is righting some injustice, and her male persona enables her to "rescue" and/or be reunited with the hero.[15] The title character in *Semiramide reconosciuta* follows the Semiramide story as Rossi adapted it from Metastasio's eighteenth-century libretto. Semiramide spends most of the opera disguised as her own son (Nino) and reigns as the King of Assyria. Like the other three operas with the use of cross-dressing for disguise, by the end the second woman is unmasked, resumes her female persona, and is romantically paired with the hero.

With the use of this device of the disguise, the possibilities for women on the opera stage continued to expand. In all of Meyerbeer's Italian operas at least one female voice was given the opportunity to hover between genders through cross-dressing. This practice allowed a female voice to represent, at least for a portion of the opera, a male character. The two heroic travesti roles and Meyerbeer's five second women all illustrate how "heroic" associations were elicited by the female voice; in the case of the second women's use of disguise, the heroic voice was now brought to the heroine. On one level, Meyerbeer's use of disguise with the second woman could be seen to overlap with the heroic travesti tradition and seem to produce the same effect; in both cases women's voices stand in for male characters. Yet the situation is made more complex given the surrounding contexts. As each woman sang her respective character, the audience "heard" the two characters (and their voices) differently. In the heroic tradition the travesti voice was marked by the gender of the character—the opera role—she portrayed: the hero. While listening to the cross-dressed female singer as the hero, the audience heard an evocation of the castrato voice. Hence, the heroic travesti singer's voice became the sound of heroism; her voice was the idealized voice of the castrato hero.

With the use of the second woman in disguise, Meyerbeer begins to blur the line between the sound of the hero's voice and the sound of the heroine's. The suspension of belief that the audience was accustomed to accepting for travesti roles was brought to the forefront and given a deliberate position in the drama. The audience was now forced to become consciously aware that a woman's voice was pretending to be a male character. Instead of women's voices being "naturally" heard and accepted as that of men, attention was now drawn to the artifice of this practice at the level of the plot. In a covert way, the cross-gender disguise could be seen as a way to wean audiences off of having women's voices represent male characters. By giving the voice of the second woman a disguise that she used only temporarily to accomplish some "male" business in the plot (e.g., traveling alone, finding out hidden information, or doing something that was not considered appropriate behavior for women at the time), the association of this voice with a male character took on the status of a feigned identity. This disguise might "fool" the other characters onstage, but the audience knew what was going on and was "wise" to this pretense. At the opera's conclusion, no one watching the opera was surprised when the young "valiant hero" was unveiled in the plot as the heroine.

In the male disguise, Meyerbeer's second woman reminded the audience of the dual possibilities in this voice. His operas provide a stepping stone for revealing what could be wrapped inside a character's voice: here is a woman, but she can also easily cross over and become a man. Such distinctions are subtle, yet instructive, because they illustrate the different simultaneous meanings women's voices generated. Depending upon the context, the period ear of the audience was accustomed to deciphering these coexisting codes concerning gender and character.

Il crociato in Egitto

Meyerbeer's final Italian opera, *Il crociato in Egitto* (*The Crusader in Egypt*), his fourth and final collaboration with Gaetano Rossi, was his greatest success in Italy as well as abroad.[16] Though *Il crociato* is not well known today, it is the only one of Meyerbeer's six Italian operas for which a full score, in a facsimile edition, is published in a modern edition and readily available.[17] This two-act *melodrama eroico* (heroic melodrama) had its premiere at La Fenice in Venice on March 7, 1824, and was revived several times in its first few years. Not only did the opera gain great popularity in Italy, it was also widely performed throughout Europe and became Meyerbeer's entrance into the operatic scene in Paris when Rossini invited him to mount a production at the Théâtre Italien in September 1825. This success of *Il crociato* at the Théâtre Italien led to a Parisian staging of *Margherita d'Anjou* the next year and eventually a commission from the Opéra Comique for *Robert le diable;* which was ultimately given by the Opéra in 1831 and was the first of Meyerbeer's enormously successful French grand operas.

Meyerbeer's final opera for Italy was not only his transition into the international opera scene of Paris, but it was also a special amalgam of the features in his

Italian period. Looking back, the popularity of *Il crociato* was most likely due to the fact that it contains so many of the elements that contributed to the "essence" of the primo ottocento: complicated twists in the plot, a variety of roles for women, the eventual working out of the imbroglio, and a vocal style of singing that emphasized long, legato, spun-out, melismatic vocal lines. Looking ahead to the aesthetics of French grand opera, there were also opportunities to highlight the spectacle of scenery (e.g., the grand boat entrance in act 1) and pageantry (e.g., the act 1 finale with the double bands for the Knights of Rhodes and the Egyptians). The Egyptian locale also provided opportunities for Orientalized "exotic" situations. In terms of this study, its exoticism stems both from its setting in Egypt as well as the sophisticated pairings of voice and character in the deployment of the plot.[18]

Like two of Meyerbeer's other operas, *Semiramide riconosciuta* set in ancient Babylon and *L'esule di Granata* set in medieval southern Spain (Granada), the setting for *Il crociato in Egitto* is in an eastern "exoticized" locale during the Christian crusades. Unlike his earlier operas, whose plots dealt with a full cast of foreign personae, Meyerbeer's *Il crociato* introduces a strong juxtaposition between the "Other," the Egyptians, and the West, the Knights of Rhodes from Provence.[19] Armando, the central protagonist, is caught within a web of intrigue involving honor to his country, religion, and moral beliefs. Teetering with precarious balance, his position in the opera comes to embody both the "Other" and the West simultaneously.[20]

In terms of vocal sound, Armando is uniquely positioned to represent both the foreign "Other" and the familiar Western voice to his early-nineteenth-century listeners. Distinguished as the last role by a major composer for a castrato, Armando's voice was coded to say two things at once to his audience. As a holdover from the previous century's aesthetics, the castrato voice could still resonate as the hero. However, this was an old-fashioned practice and not a common occurrence in the 1820s. By this point the female travesti singers had already taken over the heroic roles; in fact, these female voices were in the process of being replaced by the tenor. Less familiar than foreign, the exoticism of Armando's vocal costume in the sound of his voice allowed him to encompass his dramatic role as a Knight of Rhodes from Provence (the West) who has assimilated to the Saracen ways of Egypt (the exotic).

In the prehistory to the beginning of the opera, Armando was the sole survivor of a Christian crusade to Egypt. Disguising himself in the uniform of a fallen Egyptian solider, he is taken back to Damietta, where he assumes the name Elmireno and lives as an Egyptian. Having saved the life of the Sultan of Damietta, Aladino, Armando is then treated like the Sultan's son. Meanwhile, in secret, Armando and Aladino's daughter, Palmide, have fallen in love, gotten married, and had a son.

At the beginning of the opera, a delegation of the Knights of Rhodes arrives to celebrate peace with Egypt. Leading this Western assembly is Adriano, the Grand Master of the Knights of Rhodes (who also happens to be Armando's uncle). Traveling in this group is Felicia (Armando's betrothed from Provence), who, along with the others, believes Armando to be dead and wishes to pay respect at his grave. Not only has Felicia traveled with the Knights of Rhodes, she is also dressed in their

Giambattista Velluti in 1821, three years before he premiered the title role in Meyerbeer's *Il crociato in Egitto,* in an operatic costume at the Teatro del Torino in Regio. His pose with the harp is extremely unusual for a male character; the harp is usually reserved for women (see the figure in the Interlude with Maria Malibran as Rossini's Desdemona). *The Harvard Theatre Collection, The Houghton Library.*

male attire as a Knight.[21] Like the second women in four of Meyerbeer's earlier operas (Romilda, *Romilda e Costanza;* Emma, *Emma di Resburgo;* Isaura, *Margherita d'Anjou;* and Semiramide, *Semiramide riconosciuta*) it makes sense that Felicia is dressed in male clothing because she is traveling with a group of men. Nothing in the plot acknowledges that she is dressed inappropriately. However, unlike the earlier cases, one unusual feature with Felicia's disguise is that she is never "unmasked": there is no direction or indication that she ever changes back into female clothing at the end of the opera.

In two separate scenes, Adriano and Felicia each see Armando and learn of his new Egyptian identity and situation. Though both Adriano and Felicia are betrayed by Armando's new identity, they react differently. Felicia first encounters Armando indirectly; before she sees him, she comes across Palmide and Mirva (the five-year-old son of Palmide and Armando/Elmireno). Through her recognition of Armando's features in the boy, Felicia realizes that Armando did not die in the Crusade, and his love is now with Palmide. Though Felicia continues to love Armando, she relinquishes her claim on him when she realizes the magnitude of his commitment and obligation to Palmide—as the father of her son. In contrast to Felicia's compassionate understanding, when Adriano first sees Armando in Egyptian dress, he curses his nephew for betraying his honor as a Knight of Rhodes. It is only when Armando resolves to reassume his original identity that Adriano forgives him. Through various machinations of the plot, the opera ends happily: Felicia gives her blessing to Armando and Palmide, and Adriano and Aladino ultimately forgive the couple for the secrecy of their marriage and son.

Though the basic plot of *Il crociato in Egitto* remained the same, the opera was given in several different versions under Meyerbeer's direction.[22] Despite the adjustments for the different versions of the score, the presence of castrato Giambattista Velluti in the opera recasts some of the same issues surrounding vocal type, character, singer, and disguise that were seen in Meyerbeer's earlier Italian operas. Velluti was the voice of the central hero, Armando, for the premiere and two subsequent major revivals: the first two months later at the Teatro della Pergola in Florence on May 7, 1824, and the second for the London staging that took place in June of the following year. Meyerbeer made changes in Armando's role (as well other changes) for both of these productions. In other revivals, which Meyerbeer supervised and revised, he reworked the role for different women's voices. Table 3.2 lists the five casts of the opera for which Meyerbeer oversaw the production.[23]

The two women who sang Armando in the casts Meyerbeer supervised were well-known travesti singers. Carolina Bassi (who sang the role in Trieste) had worked with Meyerbeer before, and Giuditta Pasta (who sang the role in Paris) was one of the leading singers of the time. As Bassi had premiered the title role in Meyerbeer's *Semiramide riconosciuta,* she was also the original voice behind the title travesti role of Almanzore before the project became *L'esule di Granata* and moved to La Scala with Rosamunda Pisaroni in the lead role. Like Bassi, Pasta's repertoire also included both heroic travesti roles and female characters; two of Pasta's signature roles were Rossini's Tancredi and Desdemona.

The highest soprano—and first woman—role in *Il crociato,* Palmide was performed by several sopranos who rarely, if ever, performed en travesti. Among those who went on to become leading singers were Adelaide Tosi and Henriette Méric-Lalande.[24] These two singers shared another role, the female lead, a few years later in Bellini's first professional opera, *Bianca e Gernando.* After the success of his student opera *Adelson e Salvini*—performed with an all-male student cast at the Real Collegio di Musica di San Sebastiano in Naples (Bellini's school)—Bellini received a commission from the prestigious Teatro San Carlo in Naples, which led to *Bianca e Gernando.* The part of Bianca was written for Adelaide Tosi; however, due to the delays in production, Tosi had to fulfill other commitments made earlier, and Bianca was premiered by Henriette Méric-Lalande in 1826. In 1828, when Bellini was asked to write an opera for the opening of a new theater in Genoa, the Teatro Carlo Felicia, he was given permission to adapt the earlier work. In his first (of what would become many) collaboration with librettist Felice Romani, the opera became *Bianca e Fernando,* and Tosi sang the leading female role.[25]

Table 3.2. Five Cast Lists of *Il crociato* that Meyerbeer Supervised

Role	Voice Type
Armando	Castrato/Travesti
Palmide	High soprano
Felicia	Lower soprano
Adriano	Tenor
Aladino	Bass

Premiere, La Fenice, Venice, March 7, 1824

Armando	Giambattista Velluti
Palmide	Henriette Méric-Lalande
Felicia	Brigida Lorenzani
Adriano	Gaetano Crivelli
Aladino	Signor Zuccoli

Florence, Teatro della Pergola, May 7, 1824

Armando	Velluti
Palmide	Adelaide Tosi
Felicia	Carolina Biagelli
Adriano	Domenico Reina
Aladino	Luigi Biondini

Trieste, Teatro Grande, October 1824

Armando	Carolina Bassi
Palmide	Caterina Canzi
Felicia	Signora Villa
Adriano	Nicola Tacchinardi
Aladino	Luciano Bianchi

London, The King's Theatre, June 30, 1825

Armando	Velluti
Palmide	Rosalbina Caradori-Allan
Felicia	Maria Malibran
Adriano	Alberico Curioni
Aladino	Raniero Remorini

Paris, Théâtre Italien, September 25, 1825

Armando	Giuditta Pasta
Palmide	Ester Mombelli
Felicia	Bianca Schiasetti
Adriano	Domenico Donzelli
Aladino	Prosper Levasseur

Felicia

Felicia was not a typical primo ottocento type of role. In fact, going back to the genesis of the opera, her character was a relatively late addition to the plot as Rossi was working on the libretto. Originally considered for Trieste, *Il crociato* (under its original title of *I cavalieri di Rodi*—The Cavaliers of Rhodes) was later moved to La Fenice in Venice. To fit the plot to the singers engaged at La Fenice, Rossi wrote to Meyerbeer, "you have at La Fenice [Brigida] Lorenzani for whom I cannot find a part in our book."[26] A few days later, Rossi wrote back:

> Thinking of our *Cavalieri,* for which there was no part to be found for Lorenzani. Bright idea! We could have Felicia, a young lady betrothed to Armando, now in the dress of a man in the company of the Gran Maestro—now *Cavalieri* is adapted for the company. With the addition of interest, passion, and a contrast to Armando . . . I've found a way for you to give our *Cavalieri*. It will be sublime.[27]

Though Meyerbeer and Rossi's contract with La Fenice required that all of the leading members of the company had to be given roles, this letter demonstrates the conventions of the time which warranted that a new role be created to accommodate Brigida Lorenzani, a singer who specialized in heroic travesti roles. This was true even with, or despite, the presence of Velluti—the castrato voice that the female travesti singers were replacing (more on this topic later in this chapter).

Rather than a straightforward female character or a full travesti role, Rossi constructed an in-between character that combined elements of both: a female character who performed en travesti. Such a configuration in the plot implies that Lorenzani most probably had the voice of a second woman who also frequently sang heroic travesti roles. This supposition is confirmed in the casting of Donizetti's *Elvida* two years later in 1826 at the Teatro San Carlo in Naples when Lorenzani and Méric-Lalande (*Il crociato*'s first Palmide) were paired up again.[28] Méric-Lalande performed the title role, and Lorenzani performed the travesti role of Zeidar, the son of the Moorish chieftain, who tries to woo the captured Elvida before she is rescued by her fiancé, Alfonso, a tenor role.

As a female character who rivals the other soprano and spends time in disguise, Felicia almost fits the model of the second woman we saw in Romilda and Isaura in Meyerbeer's earlier operas. Yet Felicia's "disguise" as a Knight of Rhodes works differently from the disguises used by Romilda and Isaura. Like her two predecessors, Felicia's disguise could be explained as a convention for her to be able to travel as a single woman—in Felicia's case, with the male delegation. In the same vein as Isaura who successfully fights as a soldier, Felicia's male impersonation is a convincing disguise that allows her to "pass" as a man, even among women, as we see in act 1. In Felicia's first encounter with Palmide and Alma (Palmide's confidant), Alma refers to Felicia with the masculine ending on the word for stranger ("straniero" and "stranier"), and it is clear that she thinks Felicia is a man: "Quì lo *straniero!*" (Here the *stranger!*) When Palmide sees her son Mirva in Felicia's arms,

Alma replies: "Lo *stranier* mel trattenne, e vedi come lo contempla, lo bacia: e stringe al petto!" (The *stranger* took him from me, and see how he looks at him, kisses him and holds him to his chest!)

Felicia's "unmasking" as a woman in the opera is handled differently than in Meyerbeer's earlier operas. All of the other second women use disguise as a means to an end—to be reunited with their husbands (in the cases of Emma and Isaura) or to win the affections of the hero (in the case of Romilda). Even Semiramide, who is masquerading as King Nino so that she can be the ruling monarch, at the end of the opera unmasks herself so that she can be reunited with Scitalce, her former lover. Like Semiramide, Felicia's disguise is in place from the beginning of the opera: we first see each of them in their male persona. Moreover, at the beginning of the opera there is no obvious reason for either to reveal her true identity in the course of the opera: Semiramide is interested in maintaining her position as the "King," and Felicia is traveling with the knights of Rhodes to Egypt so that she can pay her respects to her betrothed, who is believed to have been killed. When Semiramide unmasks herself at the end of the opera, she joins the ranks of the other second women who undergo disguise and end up coupled. However, Felicia's disguise takes a different turn; for all intents and purposes, she maintains her disguise throughout the opera. She is never officially "unmasked" as a woman, nor does she end up with the hero. She very selectively reveals her true identity to Palmide; yet rather than asserting her claim on Armando, Felicia sees that Mirva's presence changes things, and she rescinds her status as Armando's betrothed. Even when she has the opportunity to officially claim Armando as his rejected beloved publicly, she calls herself his brother.[29] Except for those who know Felicia's real identity—Adriano, Armando, and later Palmide—within the world of the opera, Felicia's disguise is taken at face value. She travels with a group of men, dresses like them, carries a sword, and, in the second act, is imprisoned with them. For all other purposes, within the action, Felicia becomes an honorary man.

The size of Felicia's role changed in the different performances and versions of *Il crociato.* The nearly archaic practice of casting Velluti as the hero in an opera written in 1824 would practically guarantee needed adaptations in subsequent revivals because operatic castrati were no longer readily available. In fact, besides Velluti, no records have surfaced that indicate another castrato performed the role of Armando. In productions with Armando sung en travesti by a woman, Felicia's role was made smaller.[30] Yet even in later performances which Meyerbeer oversaw and which still featured Velluti, the role of Felicia was modified.

The part of Felicia was the largest in the opera's premiere in Venice. Felicia's entrance was spectacular as she disembarked in the Damietta harbor from the boat bringing her with the Knights of Rhodes to Egypt. With the chorus and onstage *banda* (small instrumental ensemble) announcing their arrival, Felicia sang a showpiece double aria (cantabile: "Pace io reco, a noi più grata"; and cabaletta: "Ah! più sorridere labbro d'amore"). In addition to this grandiose entrance, she also participated in two ensembles (the act 1 trio "Giovinetto cavalieri" and the act 2 benediction quartet "O cielo clemente") and the act 1 finale (where she saves Armando by intercepting Aladino's sword). Near the beginning of act 2 she had another substantial aria: in the cantabile ("Ah! ch'io adoro ancor") her melancholy is expressed when she unhappily admits to still loving Armando; however, in the cabaletta ("come dolce a lusingarmi") she is revived by the thought of helping him survive the Sultan's wrath.

In the Florence production two months later, the spectacular first act entrance of Felicia's aria on the boat with the chorus and banda was given to Velluti, the original aria replaced with the newly composed rondò "Cara mano." Such dramatic entrances were a hallmark of the castrati in the eighteenth century, and, given Velluti's presence in the opera, it was a little odd that it originally had been given to Felicia. Most likely Velluti thought this as well and had a hand in getting Meyerbeer to rewrite the entrance for him and reinforce his status as the leading character. In this revised scene for Florence, Armando (in his Elmireno disguise) disembarks from the royal ship entering the Damietta harbor, having returned victorious after defeating the enemies of the Sultan Aladino. The grand arrival of Felicia, Adriano, and the other Knights of Rhodes was cut, and Adriano and Felicia are now first seen at the Hospice of the Knights on the banks of the Nile.[31]

In the Trieste version, with Carolina Bassi taking the role of Armando, Felicia is stripped of all of her solo arias and sings only in the ensembles. This drastic reduction in Felicia's role has less to do with her effectiveness in propelling the plot than the complications that arise from having two very similar timbres in similar types of leading roles. Though Bassi is the heroic role en travesti and Felicia is the second woman, Felicia's character acts less like a woman and more like a second travesti role. This Trieste production further reveals the changing aesthetics of the time in the boat scene, which was revised yet again. Instead of maintaining the dramatic opening as a feature of Armando's role (from the Florence production five months earlier), now sung by Bassi, it was given to a third character: Adriano. Sung by Nicola Tacchinardi, a veteran tenor whose fame was already well established, Adriano becomes more of a heroic lead with his seminal entrance and the increasing importance given to the tenor voice.[32] With Armando sung by Bassi, the role of Felicia was greatly reduced in importance and given to a less prestigious singer, a "Signora Villa." Both Bassi and Tacchinardi were leading singers of the time; however, without a castrato, Meyerbeer chose to rewrite the most spectacular entrance for the progressively more favored vocal type of the heroic Romantic tenor.

As with Meyerbeer's other Italian operas, the theme of alternative and hidden identity in treble timbres is featured prominently. As in *Margherita d'Anjou* with Margherita and Isaura, two characters in *Il crociato* undergo an alternative identity, Felicia and Armando, and only one involves explicit cross-gender dress, Felicia. As mentioned above, Felicia's female identity is not fully hidden in the usual travesti manner. Moreover, her disguise hovers between the two constructions of the full travesti roles and the cross-gender disguise. Also mentioned above, though Felicia is a female character, when she is not "unmasked" at the end as a woman, she breaks the pattern established by Meyerbeer's four other second women in cross-gender disguise (Romilda, Semiramide, Emma, and Isaura). Instead, Felicia spends the entire opera dressed in male attire. Hence, even though she does not portray a male character, she seems to have much in common with the travesti roles. Yet contrary to the three other heroic travesti roles in Meyerbeer's Italian operas (Sciltace, Edemondo, and Almanzor), Felicia is not paired with the high soprano; instead, she starts out as Palmide's competitor for Armando.[33] Not only does Felicia become Palmide's friend, she ends up being Palmide and Armando's strongest advocate when she supports the lovers' relationship in face of the opposition from Aladino and Adriano.

The device of having Felicia dressed as a travesti role allows her to "look the part" that accompanies her bold actions. Her role was the largest in the opera's first incarnation at its 1824 Venetian premiere. With such an entrance, when she arrived into the Damietta harbor in her grand boat scene, she participates in state affairs. Bearing an olive branch of goodwill, which she presents to Aladino, she acts as an envoy offering the official proclamation of peace between Provence and Egypt. Additionally, in the first act finale, she has the opportunity to show her valor as she heroically thrusts herself between Armando and Aladino's sword, thus saving Armando's life, when the Sultan finds out that Armando is not really Elmireno. At the end of the opera Felicia's bravery is once again demonstrated when she is imprisoned with Adriano and the rest of the Knights of Rhodes; she is given no special dispensation because she is a woman, and she bears a sword like the other Knights. With access to the world of men, Felicia's "disguise" as a Knight of Rhodes transforms her feelings for Armando into an idealized love that inspires her to act courageously and make honorable decisions.

Armando

Like Felicia, Armando's character is disguised within the opera. However, Armando's disguise does not overtly address the issue of gender, and his two identities are male characters: Armando, the Knight of Rhodes, and Elmireno, the Egyptian persona he assumed to survive in enemy territory. His character encompasses the "masculine" hero in two very different worlds. As Armando, he is the warrior fighting in the Crusades to bring Christianity to the Muslim Egyptians; Felicia, his betrothed, is faithfully waiting for him back in Provence. Yet this persona has given way to Elmireno, who has established an Egyptian life for himself. Rather than fighting the Muslim world of the Egyptians, he has won the favor of the Sultan. Where his valor on the battlefield was lost, the "virility" he forfeited as a warrior was transferred to a personal realm. He fell in love with Palmide, secretly married her, and fathered a son—a rather odd plot device for a castrato, but not without precedent.[34]

However, there are also other dynamics at work: his two identities juxtapose the Western known with the foreign Egyptian unknown. As Elmireno, he is associated with the exotic Other; the enemy he arrived to conquer and convert has subtly claimed him as one of their own. Within the plot of the opera these two worlds (the Muslim Egyptians and the Christian Knights of Rhodes from Provence) are set in sharp contrast. Inasmuch as the opera opens with the two groups at peace (the delegation from Rhodes traveling to Damietta to officially acknowledge their

ARMAND D'ORVILLE. Général Surrazin
1 Costume.   } Mᵐᵉ Pasta.
dans Il Cruciate Opéra en 3 actes. (Acu. Rᵉ de Musique.)

Giuditta Pasta as "Elmireno,"
Armando's Saracen disguise,
with his sword prominently
displayed. From the Paris premiere of Meyerbeer's *Il crociato
in Egitto* in 1825. Lithograph
by Engelmann. *The Harvard Theatre Collection, The Houghton Library.*

Pasta rôle en Armando
Il crociato in Egitto

Another image of Giuditta
Pasta as "Elmireno," in Meyer-
beer's *Il crociato in Egitto.*
Lithograph by Langlumé.
*The Harvard Theatre Collection,
The Houghton Library.*

reconciliation after the earlier conflict), the potential for trouble is never far from the surface.[35] For Armando, the predicaments begin in the first scenes of the opera when Aladino offers Palmide to Armando in marriage and thus threatens to expose their secret marriage and child together; a short time later Adriano recognizes Armando as his nephew and rebukes his Egyptian disguise.

The conflict fully erupts in the first act finale when Armando attends the official peace proclamation ceremony dressed as a Knight of Rhodes, thus revealing his true identity. With this revelation of deception Aladino draws his sword against Armando, only to be stopped by Felicia, who fearlessly risks her life to save him by jumping between the two men. As war is declared, Meyerbeer musically represents the sides of the conflict in his dramatic use of two onstage bandas. He writes quarter-note arpeggios and chords in four-part harmony for the traditional "Western" brass banda made up of trumpets, horns, and trombones. For the "Banda seconda degli Egitiani" (Second band of the Egyptians), he writes in a contrasting *musica turca* (Turkish music) style: more chromaticism with repetitive, short, sinuous sixteenth-note figures. (This "Egyptian" banda includes several wind instruments—such as the quartino and piccolo clarinetto along with clarinets, oboes, and bassoons—along with trumpets and a trombone.)[36] While Aladino and Adriano lead the Egyptians and Knights, respectively, Felicia, Palmide, and Alma form a third group. Made up of characters from both sides, this last group pleads with the two leaders to show mercy to Armando, albeit, to no avail. In the score of the Venetian premiere, Armando is silent in this final section. As Palmide, Felicia, and Alma sing for his life, his configuration in the music drama reflects his straddled position of being in both worlds.[37]

At the end of the opera, peace is established with the final reconciliation between the Knights of Rhodes and Egypt. Both the Sultan (Aladino) and the Grand Master of the Knights of Rhodes (Adriano) accept the union of Palmide and Armando. A sense of final order is established with the discovery of Palmide's earlier conversion to Christianity when she had secretly married Armando (in the opera's prehistory). Along with the other Knights and Felicia, Palmide returns with Armando to Provence and agrees to raise their son as a Christian. While Armando claims to have been under an "exotic spell" during his period of false identity as Elmireno, everything is ultimately resolved at the end.[38] In the wake of Napoleon's Egyptian campaigns that had begun in 1798, the spirit of exploration has been sated. The "Other" in Armando, as well as in the opera as a whole, has been tamed.

The dual identities of Armando that propel the plot have a deep resonance in the Italian operatic culture of the time. As a locus for the convergence of contrasting personae, Armando's character can be conceptualized as a continuum upon which divergent elements coexist. On one end we have Armando, the crusading Knight of Rhodes, the heroic castrato, betrothed to Felicia, and the imperial representative who brings Christianity to the nonbelievers. On the other side we have the Orientalized Elmireno, who, in secret, has married the Sultan's daughter, converted her to Christianity, and fathered a son.

As the Sultan's favorite, Elmireno is portrayed by a now "exoticized" castrato voice. While the castrato voice itself was not commonly heard on the opera stage in the 1820s, it was close enough historically to hover in the background as the legacy to the still-current practice of female heroic travesti roles. Hence as Armando, the castrato voice retained its heroic associations. Yet as Elmireno, the disgraced Crusader hiding in the clothes of the heathen enemy, the nearly foreign quality of the castrato timbre was masquerading in a less-than heroic situation. Such dissonant juxtapositions between vocal sound and character type created a conflict that needed resolution within the course of the opera. This dilemma is brought to the foreground as the opera begins with the arrival of the delegation from Provence and the very real possibility that someone could recognize him.

In fact, it is the revelation of Armando's true identity that becomes a vital theme in the opera. In two central recognition scenes, Armando's disguise is revealed when his voice is unmasked: first by his uncle, Adriano, and then by his former fiancée, Felicia. In these two dramatic meetings Armando's visual and aural personae collide. Both scenes highlight the importance of Armando's sounding voice that provides the decisive factor in determining his identity. Though his Saracen costume might have been able to hide his visual features, in each confrontation he cannot escape the distinctive quality of his voice that is eminently recognizable to Adriano and Felicia:

Adriano and Armando Recognition Scene and Duet, *Il crociato in Egitto*

Scena (excerpt)

Adriano
Del soldano a noi s'avvanza un'altro Emiro.

Another emir from the infantry approaches.

Armando
A voi salute, illustri Cavalier

Greetings noble knights.

Adriano
Gran Dio! Questa voce!

Great God! That voice!

Armando
Che veggo!

What do I see!

Adriano
Egli!

Him!

Armando
Mio zio! (Ciel! Qual fulmine!)

My uncle! (Heavens! What a disaster!)

Adriano
Caro Armando! . . . Dolce nipote! Tu vivi? Qh ¢ji l' Clir iʀʋʋ⁰ʳ ⁴ ʳⁱᴀᵍᵘⁱᵘⁱᵘ! Che festi in quali spoglie!

Dear Armando! Beloved nephew! Iou live! Oh Heavens! What do I see? Scoundrel! What are you doing in those clothes!

Armando
(Aprite, o terra!)

(Open up, oh Earth!)

Adriano
[*crossed out:* Il figlio di mia sorella!]
Tu del mio sangue. Un cavalier di
Rodi! Che orror! Perfido! Parla: e
come!

Armando
Il caso, e la necessità. Io, là sul campo,
ferito e sangue rimasto sol de' miei
compagni estinti le indossai per sal-
varmi.

Adriano
E abbandonasti Le auguste insegne
dell'onor! Sapevi ch'era viltà delitto!

Armando
Io ne serbai fido ognora la spada. E tu
non sai quanto più cara a me divenne
. . . e quale . . . qual prezzo v'attaccai.

Adriano
(*severo*) Porgila.

Armando
Ma . . .

Adriano
Obbedisci.

Armando
Eccola.

Adriano
(*solennemente*) In nome del nostro
ordine augusto, io, Gran Maestro,
riprendo a te, Armando, questa spada
che tu disonorasti. E . . . la spezzo.

Armando
(*oppresso*) Ah! (*poi con vivacità*) Mi
rendi . . . rendi a me quell'acciaro.

Adriano
E che protendi

TEMPO D'ATTACCO

Adriano
Va: già varcasti, indegno,
Della perfida il segno:
Scordasti patria e onore,

[The son of my sister!] You of my
blood, a Knight of Rhodes! What horror! Traitor! Speak, and how did this
happen?

This is a case of dire necessity. I was
there on the field alone, wounded,
bleeding. I was the only one of my compatriots alive; I put on these garments
to save myself.

And you abandoned the august standards of honor! You knew that it was
cowardice, a crime!

I always kept my sword true. And you
do not know how dear to me it became
. . . and what . . . what price I held on
to it.

(*severely*) Give it to me.

But . . .

Obey me.

Here it is.

(*solemnly*) In the name of our august
order, I, Grand Master, take back from
you, Armando, this sword which you
have dishonored. And . . . I break it.

(*oppressed*) Ah! (*then with vitality*)
Give me . . . give me back that sword.

And what do you expect?

Go, unworthy man, you have
Already exceeded the limits of treachery.
You have betrayed and forgotten

Tradisti la tua fè . . .
Ti lascio al tuo rossore,
Fremo d'orror per te.

Armando
Ah! Dai rimorsi oppresso
Orrore ho di me stesso:
Perdona, oh Dio! l'errore,
Abbi pieta di me
[with dignity]
M'avvampa ancor nel core
Fiamma d'onore di fè.

Adriano
Vuoi aspirar perdono?

Armando
Posso aspirar? Imponi.

Adriano
Le insegne ree deponi:
Sappia Aladin qual sei:
Meco partir tu dei . . .

Armando
Partire! . . . (Oh ciel! . . . e
Palmide! . . .)

Adriano
Sposo a Felicia omai . . .

Armando
Io sposso di Felicia! . . .

Adriano
Tu fremi? Ohimè! . . . Se mai! . . .
Fremi. . . . I tuoi guiuri! . . .

Armando
Svenami: io tradi tutto.

Adriano
Perfido! E per chi mai! . . .

Armando
Odi . . . Qual nuovo orror!

Adriano
Taci . . . Qual nuovo orror!

CANTABILE

Armando
Non sai quale incanto
Quest'alma sorprese:
Colei che m'accese

Your country, your honor, your faith . . .
I leave you to your shame,
I shudder with horror for you.

Ah! Stricken with remorse
I feel a horror of myself:
Pardon, oh God, my crime,
Have pity on me.

The flame of honor, of faith
Is still alive in my heart.

Do you wish to earn forgiveness?

Can I hope to? Tell me what to do.

Cast aside that evil insignia:
Tell Aladino who you are.
Afterwards you must depart with me . . .

Leave! . . . (Oh heavens! . . . and
Palmide! . . .)

Now you will marry Felicia . . .

Marry Felicia! . . .

You tremble? Alas! . . . Could it be! . . .
Beware . . . Remember your vows! . . .

Kill me: I have betrayed everything.

Traitor! And for whom then! . . .

Listen . . . there is a new horror!

Tell me . . . there is a new horror!

You do not know what a spell
Was cast over my soul:
She who set me aflame

Mortale non è.	Is more than mortal
Di grazie, e candore	A heavenly combination
Compleso celeste	Of grace and innocence.
Nel solo mio core	She found understanding
Trovava mercè . . .	In my heart alone . . .
La misera or muore . . .	Now the unhappy one will die . . .
E muore per me.	And dies for me.

Adriano

Nel duolo, nel pianto	In grief and anguish
Tua madre gemeva:	Your mother mourned:
Io seco piangevo,	I wept with her,
Ingrato, per te.	Ingrate, for you.
E in seno all'amore	But you meanwhile
Tu intanto languivi!	Languished in loving dalliance!
Tradivi l'onore,	You betrayed your honor,
I voti, la fè! . . .	Your vows, your faith! . . .
Tua madre or muore	Your mother is dying now . . .
E muore per te!	And dies for you!

TEMPO DI MEZZO

Adriano

| Scegli dunque—Un cieco amore! . . . | Choose then—a blind passion! . . . |

Armando

| Vincerò. | I shall conquer it. |

Adriano

| Virtude . . . onore! | Or virtue . . . honor! |

Armando

| Seguirò | I will follow you. |

Adriano

Su questa spada . . .	Upon this sword . . .
Fu la spada di tuo padre,	Which belonged to your father,
Or lo giura.	Now swear it.

Armando (*taking the sword*)

| Ah! Porgi: chio | Ah! Give it to me: thus |
| Or la baci. | Now I kiss it— |

(*SWEARS THE OATH*)

Padre mio!	My father!
Io te invoco . . . per te guiro,	I invoke you . . . by you I swear,
Di te degno tornerò,	I shall be worthy of you again.

CABALETTA (*FIRST ARMANDO, THEN ADRIANO, THEN SECTIONS TOGETHER*)

Il brando invito	The invincible sword
Del genitore	Of my/your father
Io mio/tuo valore	My/your valor
Accenderà.	Will awaken.

70   *Voicing Gender*

D'ogni nemico,	Over every foe,
D'ogni periglio,	Over every danger,
Con esso il figlio	With it your son
Trionferà.	Will triumph.

When Adriano first sees Armando (whom he thought to be dead), Adriano does not recognize him by his appearance alone. Instead, it is an aural marker—his voice ("Gran Dio! Questa voce!")—that signals who he really is. When Adriano identifies the familiar voice, he wants to embrace his long-lost nephew; however, he is horrified at the Saracen costume Armando is wearing. He rebukes Armando for betraying the honor the Knights of Rhodes and orders him to hand over his sword. Though Armando states that he has always kept his sword true and preserved its honor, Adriano is disgusted with Armando's Egyptian appearance and disregards his nephew's explanation. Just as Adriano is about to break the sword and symbolically sever all of Armando's connection to the Order, Armando pleads with him to wait. In their subsequent duet Adriano further rebukes his nephew, who expresses remorse, until Armando finally begins to sway his uncle's opinion and regain his favor. To be fully restored, Armando agrees to reassume his rightful identity and surrender his sword. At the end of the scene Adriano draws his own weapon, the sword that had belonged to Armando's father. As Armando pledges his oath to the Knights of Rhodes, he kisses his father's sword—the symbol of the Order's invincibility—awakens his valor, and regains his honor.

If we take a moment to step outside of the opera and into the early-nineteenth-century audience, this scene can easily transcend the details of the plot. Another layer of the narrative becomes audible if we remember that this encounter occurred between a castrato and a tenor. As a drama within the drama, a meta-commentary has been staged for the contemporary audiences. Armando, written for and performed by Velluti, sings about being the last living Knight stranded alone in a foreign place where all his compatriots have perished. He is the last practitioner of a code that has disappeared from around him, and his exotic disguise was not a matter of choice, but one of pure survival. As a tenor, Adriano embodies the newly arrived "Grand Master." His stern reproach for abandoning the "august badge of honor" moves from irony to a poignant symbolism when he demands that Armando turn over his sword to him. Though Armando is able to convince Adriano not to break his sword, by the end of their ensuing duet it is clear that Adriano, the emerging Romantic tenor, is the new voice on the scene giving the orders.

The sword's phallic imagery works on two coexisting planes. As a symbol of dominance, Adriano asserts his power over Armando by setting the terms under which Armando's valor is judged: either continue to renounce your true identity by living as an Egyptian and having your sword broken, or atone by returning to the Order and giving up your sword. In either case, Armando loses his sword to Adriano, the Grand Master. On a second level, the sword symbolizes the continuance of the Order. It is telling that it is Adriano, not Armando—the biological heir—who acquires the sword.

The score from the first performances in Venice adds further information about the original dynamics between Armando and Adriano in this recognition scene. In this facsimile score, Adriano's line "Il figlio di mia sorella" (the son of my sister) is crossed out; written in a different hand above Adriano's part is a different text, "Tu del mio sangue" (you of my blood). Though this change does not greatly alter our understanding of the main gist of the plot, it can be helpful for clarifying kinship relationships. In what appears to be the earlier version (the line crossed out and underneath the text above the staff), we find out that Armando's father was not Adriano's brother, a blood relation, but rather an in-law; Armando's father had married Adriano's sister. Hence, Adriano is not from the same lineage, but a relative by marriage. One interpretation that follows this rationale is that the added line, presumably used in later performances without Velluti, was changed (to "Tu del mio sangue") and the blood connection was emphasized. In either case, for both of these relationships the invincible sword that is passed on to the Grand Master symbolizes not only the right to power, but also vocal prowess. A woman singing Armando en travesti was in a similar, somewhat removed, relationship to the heroic castrato tradition as was Adriano, the tenor. Hence when "you of my blood" is sung by a tenor to a female travesti singer, their connection is strengthened: both come from the subsequent generation that replaces the castrato as the hero.

When Adriano sang these lines to Velluti, the situation was different. Although Adriano is the undisputed Grand Master, Armando's claim to the sword is reinforced by heredity; his father once owned the invincible sword. Thus, the conflict between the two leading male characters, Adriano and Armando, resonates deeply with the tensions of the changing times. Sung with the original cast, the tenor Gaetano Crivelli metaphorically takes over the castrato heroic legacy that Velluti embodied. In the later casts with Armando sung by a female travesti singer, as with Carolina Bassi six months after the premiere in October 1824, the tenor has taken over what turned out to be the transitional temporary replacement of the castrati roles by women's voices. In both cases the nineteenth-century Romantic bel canto vocal style is dramatically symbolized through the sword. With the blatant visual imagery of the potency of the sword, the tenor, more so than the castrato or female travesti singer, emerges as the one most capable for carrying this legacy forward.

Musically the dynamics of these power relationships are elegantly reinforced by the structure and singing styles employed in the duet. In the conventional form of duets for Italian opera of this time, *la solita forma* ("the usual form," the conventional forms for numbers in the early to mid nineteenth century), duets were typically preceded by an opening *scena* (scene) and then continued in four sections: the *tempo d'attacco, cantabile, tempo di mezzo,* and *cabaletta*.[39] While employing the conventions, Meyerbeer also learned how to infuse the standard formula with the drama of the situation. In the recognition scene, the opening scena leading up to the beginning of the duet, Adriano has identified his nephew (in Saracen clothing) and is just about to break Armando's sword in reproach when Armando is able to persuade his uncle to hold back.

In the opening of the duet (tempo d'attacco), Adriano's six-line stanza unfolds in a vocally demanding virtuosic display as he chastises his nephew's breech of honor. Replete with ornamented cadences (similar to written-out cadenzas),

Example 3.1. Adriano-Armando duet, act 1, *Il crociato in Egitto*. Adriano's entrance in the tempo d'attacco (example of melismatic and syllabic style).

Adriano's rhetorical gestures are highlighted through the use of the fully orchestrated chords that punctuate the vocal line and the repetition of his text. In a dramatic alternation between declarative syllabic phrases and melismatic vocal runs that span nearly an octave and a half of his range through scalar passages and wide leaps, Adriano's music showcases his command of the florid vocal style of the time. His singing provides a pointed reproach as well as an intimidating sound to follow. Armando's reply is musically strategic; he starts out with a very simple, syllabic melody as he expresses his heartfelt remorse. Stripped of his pride, his straightforward vocal phrases reflect the directness of his penitent position. In his first two lines he agrees with Adriano's assessment: Armando is stricken with contrition and is horrified at what he has done. Yet in the third line, his tone changes. Rather than dwell on his past actions, he focuses on forgiveness and asks for mercy.

As Armando implores his uncle to forgive him, he begins to rely on the affective style of his singing and a string of striking modulations away from the home key of E♭ major to make his point. Starting on the phrase "Perdona oh Dio!" (example 3.2, mm. 44–45) with the additional expression markings above his music of *a piacere* and *dolce* Armando repeats his text (the text of his opening syllabic lines was not repeated).[40] He sings these words four times with each statement becoming more musically emphatic than the last. Within a harmonically shifting context, the

Example 3.2. Adriano-Armando duet, act 1, *Il crociato in Egitto*. Armando's entrance in the tempo d'attacco (first very syllabic, then a little more melismatic).

phrase initially appears stepwise syllabically, then twice with a dotted rhythm, and finally with increasingly larger ascending leaps (moving out from a perfect fourth, fifth, and sixth on up to the octave). Throughout the rest of this stanza there is more repetition (especially of the word "pietà," mercy), and the vocal line continues in a florid style similar to Adriano's corresponding section of his verse.

Just when things seem as though they could work out to restore Armando's honor—Adriano tells him to assume his correct identity, return to Provence, and marry Felicia—Armando reveals that he has one more confession to make, thus providing the impetus for the lyrical slow section of the duet. In the cantabile section Armando declares that he has been the victim of a spell ("incanto"); if he were to leave, an honest and innocent woman would die (referring to Palmide). Faced with Armando's forsaken honor as a Knight of Rhodes, and betrayal to both his

Example 3.3. Adriano-Armando duet, act 1, *Il crociato in Egitto*. Armando swears the oath within the tempo di mezzo (slow, solemn).

country and commitment to marry Felicia, Adriano responds to this last revelation with a potent image: Armando's mother grieving for her son whom she thinks dead. The mood shifts away from the lyrical phrases of the cantabile to the declamatory character of the tempo di mezzo. Adriano makes Armando choose between his blind passion ("un cieco amore") and his virtue and honor, which now encompass his identity as a son and filial duty. With this argument, Armando finally capitulates. In the tempo di mezzo Adriano seals his promise by having Armando swear an oath on his father's sword. Armando, anxious to show his new conviction, eagerly kisses the sword, invokes his father's spirit, and promises to once more be worthy to be his son.

In the four measures of the oath as Armando solemnly pledges his vow, another sonic world is evoked. The key signature moves from A minor to C minor, and a somber tone is achieved through a change in orchestration. From the earlier string texture of the tempo di mezzo, the timbre deepens as trombones, horns, bassoons, and clarinets solemnly intone sustained chords. Everything slows down. In addition to the prolonged notes in the low brass and woodwinds, the tempo suddenly shifts from Allegro to Più lento, and Armando's vocal line focuses on half notes punctuated with shorter note values outlining downward octave leaps.

As soon as Armando kisses the sword and sings his invocation to his father, his voice is set free. His music in the cabaletta newly marked Allegro and the opening highlighted with a full orchestral chord, takes off as he repeats the last line of his oath with fast triplets that mark his highest and most florid singing thus far in the duet. Once Armando has been restored to his "true" identity, the noble Knight of Rhodes and not the Egyptian imposter dressed in Saracen clothes, his voice is released. He emerges as the heroic castrato: his voice is finally allowed to fulfill its

Example 3.4. Adriano-Armando duet, act 1, *Il crociato in Egitto*. Beginning of the cabaletta (virtuosic showcasing of the voices).

proper function and soars with melismatic freedom. In the solemnity of the oath scene, he breaks the "spell" under which he had fallen.

The cabaletta is a vocal tour de force in which both characters' voices are showcased. As Armando leads with virtuosic sextuplets, dotted rhythms, and spun-out melodies that span more than an octave in one breath, Adriano matches Armando's phrases note for note. In their shared text they praise the ancestral sword that triumphs over every enemy and danger. In the quatrains of the cabaletta, a subtle shift in the legacy is revealed through a close reading of the text and listening to the vocal drama. As Armando and Adriano sing of the invincible sword of their parents ("il brando invito del genitore"), they both conclude the cabaletta "Con esso il figlio trionferà" (with it [the sword] your son will triumph). Here the two singers, the castrato and the tenor, claim equal legacy to the tradition of the sword.

Though Adriano, Grand Master of the Order, is in possession of the sword at the end of the duet, the cabaletta provides another hearing of the drama nested within the general plot line to have Armando return to the Knights of Rhodes. Armando, the embodiment of the castrato tradition, must submit to the new aesthetics that favor the tenor as the virile heroic voice. In the recognition scene immediately preceding the duet, Armando turns over his sword to the new vocal Grand Master. However, it is not until the cabaletta at the end of the duet when, after he reaffirms his honor with the oath, Armando's voice is liberated from the burden of his transgression and sings in its true heroic form, that Adriano shows himself to be the worthy vocal successor of the older bel canto tradition of his nephew. At this point Adriano embraces the legacy by proving that he has mastered the vocal technique of Armando's complicated vocal line. At the end of the duet, Adriano has the sword and claims equal ancestry to the singing tradition it represents.

The Voice of the Young Cavalier

As Adriano and Armando are given a scene that showcases the vocal drama between their two voice types, the first vocal encounter between Armando and Felicia is also imbued with multiple layers created by the sounding of their voices. Rather than a one-on-one confrontation, as in the duet between Armando and Adriano, Meyerbeer and Rossi stage a trio that takes full advantage of the narrative potential and sonic possibilities in the three treble voices of Armando, Felicia, and Palmide. Especially proud of this number, Rossi considered it one of the best in the opera and specially mentions the novelty of the three "white" voices; a reference to the treble timbres of two women and a castrato. In a letter to Meyerbeer of August 28, 1823, while working on the libretto, Rossi exclaimed: "The trio, in the opinion of this old theatre person, is the finest piece in the opera, for the impression it will make on the public, a completely original music-theatre situation. . . . Everyone in Venice—in Europe—will be talking about the novelty of three white voices united in this manner. . . . A triumph!"[41]

The trio for these three treble voices was indeed innovative for this time and presented an unusual situation for the early nineteenth century. In terms of the conventions surrounding voice pairings, two romantic voice couplings are overlapped. We first hear the primo ottocento aesthetics of the heroic female travesti role (Felicia dressed as a man) and the soprano (Palmide). Yet with the entrance of Armando (first through a vocal entrance offstage), we are sonically brought back to eighteenth-century aesthetics with a castrato timbre intertwining with the soprano voices. In this way, the trio is more like three interconnected duets—Felicia and Palmide, Felicia and Armando, and Palmide and Armando—with both Felicia and Palmide singing about their love for Armando.

In a scene that begins with Palmide and Felicia onstage, Felicia starts the trio with the first of three strophic verses comprised of two quatrains plus a couplet refrain. She sings her verse, "Giovinetto cavalier," as a solo:

Felicia's Stanza, "Giovinetto cavalier" Trio, *Il crociato in Egitto*

Giovinetto cavalier	A young knight,
Di bel giorno al tramontar,	As twilight fell one beautiful day,
Colla Dea de'suoi pensier	With the Goddess of his thoughts
Sotto un salcio s'arrestar.	Rested beneath a willow tree.
Tacque un pò—su lei fissò	He was silent for a while—
Poi lo sguardo, e sospirò.	Then gazed at her and sighed.
La sua mano potrò al cor . . .	He placed his hand upon his heart . . .
E quì, disse, quì v'è amor . . .	And here, he said, here is love . . .
Non fidarti, o giovin cor,	Do not trust, oh youthful heart,
Dell'accento dell'amor.	Words of love.

The narrative content of Felicia's verses is told from the standpoint of the "giovinetto cavalier." Told in the third person, Felicia delivers this tender melody as a reporting to Palmide of how she was wooed by Armando. Despite Felicia's own appearance dressed as a Knight of Rhodes, we know that the young knight in her narrative is Armando from the recitative that immediately preceded this stanza when she said that this is the song Armando had sung to her when she was a "young girl with an innocent heart beneath the beautiful sky of her native Provence." He was a "tender troubadour" who came to her in the moonlight and awakened her love for him.[42] This melody of gentle seduction is presented with a wistful tinge, for we know that it is Felicia's way of remembering the beginning of her relationship with Armando, a relationship that she has just relinquished after having met Palmide and having seen Armando's features in their son, Mirva. For Felicia, the refrain illustrates a youthful love no longer valid.

However, if someone were to have walked into the opera house at the beginning of her stanza, looked onstage and listened, it would not at all have been unusual to assume that this was the beginning of a love duet between the cross-dressed Felicia and Palmide. As Palmide recognizes the song, for Armando had also sung it to her, she waits for Felicia to finish the refrain and then continues with the second stanza:

Palmide's Stanza, "Giovinetto cavalier" Trio, *Il crociato in Egitto*

Cloe d'età nel bell' april	Chloe, in the fair April of her years
Era giglio di candor;	Was a lily of innocence;
Sorrideva al suo gentil,	She smiled upon her gentle suitor,
In un tenero languor.	Tenderly dreaming.
Ma balzar quell cor sentì,	But she felt her heart leap,
E il suo tutto s'agito.	And her whole being stirred.
Un sospiro le sfuggi	A sigh escaped her
Ei l'intese . . . e l'abbracciò .	He heard it . . . and embraced her . . .
Non fidarti, o giovin cor,	Do not trust, o youthful heart,
Dei sospiri dell'amor.	The sighs of love.

That person who had just walked in to the theater at the beginning of Felicia's stanza would logically think that as Felicia had sung about herself in the opening line, a "giovinetto cavalier," for she looked the part, Palmide was now identifying with the innocent young Chloe in her opening line.[43] As Felicia referred to the young knight in the third person, Palmide also uses the third person to tell Chloe's story. However, unlike Felicia, who had explained in the preceding recitative that these were not her own words, Palmide's text tells Chloe's tale as a real stand-in for her own seduction by Armando.

Felicia's stanza is one of betrayal and deceit. On one level there is Armando's infidelity to her in his relationship with Palmide. On another level, Felicia's singing of this music presents a dual-layered visual deception on the stage. Within the narrative, this moment highlights the complications of her own status as a female character dressed as a Knight of Rhodes; she is a cross-dressed as a male character who also happens to be pining for another "young cavalier." To the audience Felicia's visual and aural presence perform another duplicity. As mentioned above, for the person who had just walked into the theater, Felicia is not as she seems: she is not a travesti hero wooing the soprano in a love duet. Instead, the real situation seems almost less plausible. Felicia is a female character dressed as a Knight of Rhodes so that she may enter the world of men to find her beloved and pay tribute to his grave. Unlike in the so-called rescue opera tradition, when she does find her beloved (and he is alive), he is no Florestan to her cross-dressed Leonore (as in Beethoven's *Fidelio*, first performed ten years earlier).[44] Instead, to continue with the example of Beethoven's opera, it is as though Florestan has fallen in love with Marzelline, his jailor Rocco's daughter. Meyerbeer's trio recalls Beethoven's "canon quartet" ("Mir ist's so wunderbar," act 1) where the cross-dressed Leonora is perceived to be Fidelio, her male persona, as she tries to rescue her wrongly imprisoned husband (Florestan). Like "Giovinetto cavalier," Beethoven's ensemble involves deceit and betrayal, in different configurations, regarding who loves whom and cross-dressed voice types.[45] One difference in Meyerbeer's trio is that the characters are all aware that Felicia really is a female character underneath her knight's armor (unlike Rocco, Marzelline, and Jaquino, in Beethoven's opera, who believe that Fidelio is really a young man). Yet the biggest difference is in the way these two German composers reference the vocal aesthetics of vocal gender crossings. For Beethoven, Leonore's "male voice" is a means unto an end for bringing the soprano and tenor together by the end. For Meyerbeer, the delight is more in the process of listening: as Palmide listens to the cross-dressed Felicia, she is reminded of Armando's voice. When Palmide sings in response, Armando's voice is conjured up from offstage.

The seeming love duet becomes a trio when Armando enters the scene vocally; as he sings the third stanza, Armando's presence is only heard, not seen, through his voice offstage. To draw further attention to the sound of his voice, Palmide makes a special reference to it: "Ah! la sua voce!—Oh cielo!" (Ah, his voice—oh heavens!). While Felicia tries to figure out what to do, Palmide, as if transfixed and unable to do anything else, anxiously listens to Armando sing; she implores Felicia to listen ("Odi!") to his offstage voice finish the song they had begun. As Armando sings his two quatrains, he is continually "interrupted" by aside interjections that Felicia and Palmide make in response to hearing his voice.

Armando's Stanza (Numbered Lines) with Interjections by Palmide and Felicia, "Giovinetto cavalier" Trio, *Il crociato in Egitto*

1. Tutto armato a lei venir . . .   One day she saw her beloved . . .

Palmide
Odi !   Listen!

2. Miro un giorno il suo tesor: Come to her in full armor:

Felicia
Qual momento!   What a moment!

Palmide
Fier cimento!   What a dreadful situation!

3. Cara, addio, con un sospir,   Dearest, addio, said he, with a sigh,

Felicia
A qual sospir.   Ah, what anguish.

**4. Son crociato, son crociato disse,   I am a Crusader, I am a Crusader
ohimè! Ohimè!**   alas! Alas!

Palmide
Oh dolor!   Oh misery!

Felicia
Oh languir!   Oh anguish!

5. Cloe gelarsi il cor senti . . .   Chloe felt her heart freeze . . .

Felicia
Così Felicia . . .   So Felicia must suffer . . .

Palmide
L'istessa pena   The same pain I feel . . .

6. Quasi estinta al suo piombò   Half dead she sank to the ground:

Palmide
Io reggo appena . . .   I can hardly bear it . . .

Felicia
Stato crudele . . .   What a cruel situation . . .

7. Ei la fredda man bacio . . .   He kissed her cold hand . . .

Palmide
S'ei mi lascia . . .   If he leaves me . . .

Felicia
Quall'ambascia.   What distress

8. Su lei pianse, e . . . spari.   Wept over her, and . . . went his way.

Mai provar, o giovin cor,   Oh, may your young heart never experi-
                                         ence,
I martiri dell'amor.   The pangs of love.

Example 3.5a. Felicia's first stanza, "Giovinetto cavalier" trio, act 1, *Il crociato in Egitto.*

On the page, Armando's stanza looks comparable, despite the interjections by Felicia and Palmide, to the two strophes sung before. Felicia and Palmide had each sung parallel double quatrains with similar *ottonario tronco* lines. Their stanzas have complementing, but not the same, rhyme schemes. For Felicia, her quatrains, abab ccdd, contain one in *rima alternata* (abab) and one in *rima bacciata* (ccdd). Palmide's quatrains, abab, cdcd, are both in *rima alternata*. Additionally, both stanzas employ a couplet in *ottonario tronco, rima bacciata* that functions as a refrain.[46]

Armando's text comprises of two quatrains with a refrain. While the refrain is the, now familiar, couplet of *ottonario tronco* in *rima bacciata*, the two quatrains do not follow the earlier model. The text of the first quatrain begins predictably with three lines in *ottonario tronco* and sets up the expectation for a rhyme scheme of *rima alternata* (aba-). However, the fourth line elongates the last verse with internal repetitions on the admission of guilt: "Son crociato, son crociato, disse ohimè ohimè," which breaks both the metric structure and rhyme scheme.

More than a simple versification change, the real textual breakdown happens in the shift from the third person to the first person speaker. Like Palmide before him, Armando starts the stanza as a third person narrative to illustrate his own situation: to uphold his oath to Adriano, Armando sings of his new responsibility to reassume his true identity as a Knight of Rhodes (and not continue his feigned identity as Elmireno, the Saracen Egyptian). In the first three lines of his opening quatrain, Armando takes up the story of the knight as he appears to the beloved in full armor. The fourth line's revelation and repetition of "I am a Crusader, I am a Crusader" signals a rupture in the verbal content and form. Even Palmide, in her autobiographical stanza about Chloe, did not allow her personal voice to bleed through in a change to the first person verb tense. Neither Felicia nor Palmide re-

Example 3.5b. Palmide's first stanza, "Giovinetto cavalier" trio, act 1, *Il crociato in Egitto*.

peat the text of their stanzas until the last line of the second quatrain, which leads into the refrain.

As Felicia and Palmide listen to Armando's voice offstage, they both react to his narrative. They hear his confession and respond as though they were aware of his struggle with the poetic form at the end of his first quatrain; both come to his aid in the rhyme scheme of the fourth line. Like the women's first quatrain, Armando's is set up to be in *rima alternata;* however, with his "ohimè," he has missed the correct rhyme that should match "tesor." Without missing a beat, Palmide supplies the missing sound with her interjection, "Oh, dolor." Felicia jumps in a moment later with the "wrong" rhyme, as though she were trying to complete a quatrain in *rima bacciata,* with "languir" (which would still be an incorrect match for the fourth line, because line 1—"venir" matches line 3—"sospir").

Both women sing the melody that Armando used to woo them. However, when Armando enters the trio, his stanza is set to new music. Instead of the lilting $\frac{6}{8}$ meter with gently undulating lines, his music continues the duple meter of the intervening recitative. With measured accents, his first three lines move in equal quarter notes with the occasional dotted-quarter–eighth-note dotted rhythm. In a practical move, this use of the duple meter easily allows Palmide and Felicia to make their comments in recitative interjections that act as asides. Dramatically, the offstage placement of Armando and his different music juxtapose his voice with the voices of the two women. After he sings his stanza, he finally appears onstage for the refrain, which he sings alone at first and then is joined by the two women.

Visually, the staging of this trio adds a third dimension to the text and music. In an ironic twist of history, Armando replaces Felicia both vocally and visually in this scene. A perfectly plausible hearing of this number would be to understand Felicia as an unsuccessful rival to Armando. Throughout the trio, the visual image

Example 3.5c. Armando's first stanza (along with interjections from Felicia and Palmide), "Giovinetto cavalier" trio, act 1, *Il Crociato in Egitto*.

Continued on the next page

Example 3.5c. *Continued*

of young lovers remains onstage. At first this is fulfilled by Felicia (en travesti) and Palmide. Shortly after Armando appears, Felicia moves into the background, barely visible, yet audible.[47] However, Felicia as a cross-dressed female character fulfills the travesti position only partially, visually and aurally, but not dramatically. Felicia is an echo of an originating sound—the castrato heroic voice—that is ultimately made visible in Velutti. The trio stages the drama behind the expectations of these three voice types.

The presence of Felicia in the plot adds complexity to the sonic and visual codes of the 1820s. A woman, dressed as a man, presents an unusual rival to the soprano for the castrato or, as Armando was recast for subsequent revivals, another travesti woman. Since Felicia immediately releases her betrothal with Armando to Palmide when she finds out about their secret marriage and son, Felicia's role in the opera extends beyond competition. In this role a woman's voice sounds and evokes the heroic ideal of the castrato. Alongside the "true" heroic voice of Armando (as a castrato or a female travesti singer), Felicia, a woman's body cross-dressed as a female character disguised as a Knight of Rhodes appears onstage. What was going on?

Disguise and Nobility

In *Il crociato* the issue of disguise attains a new level. Far exceeding a plot device ensuring that the right characters end up together, the question of identity directly involves the function of how the voices interact with each other. With the insertion of the castrato into the cast of a primo ottocento opera, the position of the second woman is called into question, and the roles of Armando and Felicia stand in direct counterpoint to each other. On the primo ottocento stage, both types of voices were nearly synonymous in terms of the practice of having the female travesti substitute for the heroic castrato role. Hence, both roles present two sides of the same function, almost acting as foils to each other. Heard in this relationship, the two types of roles appearing together in the same opera subvert the position of the heroic leading male role.

The characters of Armando and Felicia destabilize the interaction between sound and appearance. In the 1820s both vocal timbres shared many of the same codes—the noble hero who recalls the sound of the eighteenth century. In some ways Felicia fulfills this function better than Armando. Dressed in male attire and a member of the Knights of Rhodes delegation, she consistently carries herself with the decorum of this position. In fact, in the Venice premiere of the opera, her first appearance (her aria in the grand boat scene announced by the chorus and banda) invoked the spectacular entrances of the castrati in the eighteenth century. Ever the heroic model, Felicia participates in official capacities (bearing the olive branch of peace to the Egyptians in her original entrance) and twice demonstrates her ability to act courageously (when she instinctively jumps in front of Aladino's sword to save Armando in the act 1 finale and at the end of the opera when she is taken prisoner along with the rest of the Knights of Rhodes). As a woman, Felicia continues to assume the beneficent role; she sacrifices her love for Armando and acts honorably toward Palmide and Mirva

Whereas Felicia brings the nobility and idealized masculinity of a heroic travesti to a female character, Armando is given a different depletion, one that could be characterized as more "human," complete with foibles and weaknesses. He abandons the code of the Knights of Rhodes and lives assimilated as an Egyptian. His secret marriage to Palmide and their child is at the expense of his betrothal to Felicia, who waited for him faithfully in Provence. Within the terms of the opera, these deeds are morally reprehensible, and we see him chastised by Adriano at their first meeting. By assuming the persona of the Egyptian Elmireno, Armando's disguise works against the nobility of his character. Unlike Felicia's aestheticized masculinity in her men's clothes and courageous acts, Armando's feigned identity "Orientalizes" him and feminizes his persona. At least in part, he is characterized as an exotic Other.[48]

For Meyerbeer, the roles of Felicia and Armando were less innovative in who they were and what they did than in how they were each configured in the plot. By portraying Felicia as a quasi-travesti role (a female character, yet dressed in male attire with noble and courageous actions) alongside a castrato, Meyerbeer was stretching the bounds of what was conventional and innovative. Each one had a double identity: one feigned and the other "real." According to primo ottocento norms Felicia, the woman under men's clothing, was given an honorable and noble character and treated like a Knight of Rhodes by everyone, including those who knew about her disguise. The *primo uomo* (first man) role, written for the castrato Velutti, inherited the true heroic role; yet the conventions surrounding what was heroic in voice and character were in the process of evolving. Armando as a Knight of Rhodes fits neatly into the typical eighteenth-century characterization. Yet Armando as the defeated Crusader who has assimilated into Egyptian ways is weakened when he appears in exotic clothing as Elmireno. With an eighteenth-century nobility colliding against nineteenth-century adventure and a different type of realism, the deceit about his real identity undercuts the dignity of his character. Elmireno, his Egyptian persona, is a negative characterization from which he needs to be roused and brought back into the right cause by a stern censure from his uncle Adriano, the Grand Master. Velluti, one of the last castrati to survive in opera, was left to uphold the grand vocal tradition of bel canto. Yet his character had to make amends to the tenor role, and the cross-dressed female singer was showing him up as a man of her word.

Both Felicia and Armando looked backwards and forwards in operatic history. As heroic timbral holdovers from the eighteenth century, their individual characterizations interact with newer currents of the time. The Romantic hero was a new type of character who can show weakness that leads to either defeat or triumph. Not a common plot device in eighteenth-century opera, the creation of a fallible protagonist who emerged heroic was uncommon before the formation of the revolutionary politics that followed in the aftermath of the French Revolution at the end of the eighteenth century. Audiences witnessed new plot directions in Romantic opera. Elmireno/Armando embodies a new type of conflicted hero; Felicia provides the traditional strength and honor, as well as the flexible treble voice, which were associated with the heroic travesti roles. Yet Felicia, though she dresses and behaves like this type of role, remains a woman. Though Armando redeems himself by returning to his true identity in the first act finale, in some ways it is Felicia who emerges as a more valiant hero than Armando for consistently staying true to the goals and honor of the Knights of Rhodes.

In a transitional time when the aesthetics of the eighteenth century coexisted with the early directions of what would eventually lead into nineteenth-century Romanticism, Meyerbeer's desire to assimilate the Italian style into his operas for

Italy combined with the popular and financial success these operas received provides a revealing view into the norms of primo ottocento opera in the late 1810s and early 1820s. As the aesthetics for pairing the sound of voices with specific character types was under flux, Meyerbeer's Italian operas illustrate the different possibilities of the time. In his operas we can see and hear the cross-currents of the time.

In these early works for Italy, we can see how important Meyerbeer is for understanding this period in opera as he highlights treble voices in the multiple roles for women. All six of his operas feature at least two leading roles for female singers, and three of the first five operas use travesti heroes (Scitalce in *Semiramide riconosciuta*, Edemondo in *Emma di Resburgo*, and Almanzor in *L'esule di Granata*); hence, the second woman—the female character—is paired with a woman's voice in a similar timbre.

Disguise is an integral feature in the roles for the second woman's voice. Meyerbeer always associates this voice type with disguise or a female en travesti: the second woman, at some point in the plots of all the operas, is called upon to dress in men's clothing and pretend to be a male character. The conceit of disguise and travesti constructions is the association of the second woman's voice with some element of masculinity. My point is not to pretend that these women were ever confused with, or could pass as, "real" men (as the eighteenth-century castrati could pass as women or men), but that the sound of the second woman's voice type was at home as both a female or male character. Audiences were comfortable hearing this type of voice portray either a female or male character, or both simultaneously—a female character who could also pretend to be a man. Moreover, Meyerbeer never allowed this voice, in a large role, to exclusively sing a female character; the travesti connection was always brought to the foreground. This lower female voice always juxtaposed visual and aural codes of masculinity and femininity. At some point in each of these operas, for at least some amount of time, the second women would dress and sing as men. Consequently, the preponderance of women's voices that are associated with male roles during these years is striking. These voices could portray male characters either en travesti or through the use of disguise even when their operatic character is female.

Meyerbeer's last Italian opera, *Il crociato in Egitto*, stages an aural drama in a trio of heroic voices: the castrato (Armando), the tenor (Adriano), and the second woman's voice in a pseudo heroic travesti role (Felicia). Through treble timbres he demonstrates that the fluidity in the representation of gender as it was characterized by the eighteenth-century aesthetic for flexible treble timbres is still active on the primo ottocento stage. However, the pattern where the second woman is ultimately paired with the hero changes in his last opera for Italy: the second woman— Felicia—starts out paired with the hero, but ends up alone by the opera's conclusion. Such a fate for the second woman prefigures what became the general tendency after 1830. After the popularity of the female travesti heroes waned, the second woman was frequently given a secondary status, and the prima donna's role emphasized the highest soprano range.

Such is the history that is most familiar today: the high soprano gets the tenor

at the end. Before 1830 she survives the end of the opera; after this date, she suc-
cumbs to the tragic finale that dictates her death. By recovering Meyerbeer's operas
for Italy, we see conventions that challenge this master narrative. We hear how another woman's voice, that of the second woman, presents a parallel set of situations
where she locates the point in time when a woman's voice on the opera stage could
sound as either male or female or, through a cross-gendered disguise, both male
and female simultaneously.

Interlude:
Queens, Hybridity, and the Diva

The changing aesthetics at the beginning of the nineteenth century presented a conflict. Though the *sound* of the castrato voice was desired, the *sight* of the castrato on the opera stage had fallen out of vogue. However, this situation was not difficult to remedy. Throughout the eighteenth century, women and castrati had been singing heroic roles interchangeably; when the first choice of a castrato had not been available, a female singer would be substituted. As women's voices continued to portray female characters, the popularity for their voices in heroic travesti roles was fueled by the nostalgia for the castrato voice. The preference for flexible treble timbres in heroic roles increased the demand for women's voices in opera. Hence, at the beginning of the nineteenth century women's voices ended up being the sound par excellence for both the hero and the heroine.

But gradually the nineteenth century also developed different aesthetic tastes regarding vocal timbre and operatic character. As the castrato voice became increasingly foreign and less audible to nineteenth-century audiences and performers, the voices of the hero and heroine began to move in different directions. Though first replaced by women singing en travesti, the role of the hero gradually migrated to the tenor. The tenor came to embody the "Romantic" epoch's reconstruction of what was considered to be the ideal heroic sound. Hence, the first decades of the nineteenth century in Italy witnessed several concurrent operatic practices regarding the characterization associations elicited by treble timbres produced by women's and men's voices. The rise of the tenor reconstituted the relationships among timbre, heroism, and sound. These shifting ideals had direct repercussions on the connections between a woman's voice and the type of role she sang.

In the previous two chapters I examined the nostalgia for the castrato voice in the heroic travesti roles and the use of cross-gendered disguise by the second woman in Meyerbeer's early Italian operas—notably in his final opera, *Il crociato in Egitto*. These two chapters covered the persistence of eighteenth-century bel canto conventions into the beginning of the nineteenth century. Though certainly these castrato-influenced practices were modified in the new century, they referenced an older way of doing things. In the next two chapters, I will focus on two other situations for women's voices in the primo ottocento that look ahead to the full flowering of nineteenth-century Romanticism in Italian opera. Chapter 4 explores the continuation, transformation, and reconfiguration of the travesti roles from the hero into the pageboy. Chapter 5 examines the dual representations of women in operas with two leading female characters who remain as female characters. Unlike Meyerbeer's Italian operas, which all had cases of cross-gender disguise, the operas discussed in chapter 5 do not utilize heroic travesti roles, nor do they have female characters who cross-dress within the course of the opera. Though there are pageboy travesti roles and second woman roles, the operas in chapters 4 and 5 show the path that points forward to secondo ottocento opera, where the focus of the plot is on the leading romantic soprano-tenor couple.

Changing Sounds:
From Idealized Heroism to Midcentury Realism

The move from having a woman's voice singing en travesti as the hero to having the hero voiced by the tenor affected the sonic timbral relationship between the two voices of the leading couple. In the eighteenth century the hero and heroine had similar vocal timbres: both came from the treble voices of castrati and women. Within these singers the vocal types could be combined in any of a number of ways. A soprano castrato could be romantically paired with a mezzo-soprano woman, a mezzo-soprano castrato could end up with a soprano heroine, or two sopranos—or mezzo-sopranos—could be coupled.[1] Thus, the conceit of the well-matched couple was metaphorically borne out in the intertwining of their voices: their compatibility brought together their voices and technical ability to merge into one united sound with complementing timbres. In some pairings, when blended together, the two voices became almost indistinguishable. This resultant merging of the two voices into one epitomized the unity the couple had achieved at the opera's conclusion and represented their idealized love.

In the nineteenth century the pairing of voices that coupled a higher and a lower timbre became more stabilized. Whereas the eighteenth century enjoyed the similarity in timbre for the hero and the heroine, the emerging "Romantic" ideals of the nineteenth century reflected different conventions. The model of "separate spheres," regarding a juxtaposition between men and women, as a description of nineteenth-century gender relations has been criticized and made more complex by recent scholarship. Nonetheless, an emphasis on gender complementarity and sexual difference was a strong theme in nineteenth-century European history.[2]

In nineteenth-century opera, the new aesthetics led to a stronger differentiation between the two lovers' voices: the higher voice sang the heroine, and the lower voice sang the hero. While this might seem obvious regarding the soprano-tenor pairings, this practice was also adapted when both roles in the romantic couple were sung by women. Hence, the division between the highest soprano as the heroine and the lower soprano (a mezzo-soprano or contralto) as the heroic travesti parts began to codify the nineteenth-century divisions between vocal types and character types that became dominant later in the century. Instead of the earlier premium put on the intertwining of the two heroic voices, the sonic distinction between the hero and the heroine was given a new priority. The differences between the voices of the romantic couple were articulated through higher and lower sonic realms. The high soprano heroine was paired with the lower-timbred hero—the mezzo-soprano/contralto (en travesti) or, what would later become the norm, the tenor. As the Romantic heroine evolved, her vocal register soared higher and higher. Her ability to sustain the top notes in her range was paired with the stamina needed to sing florid passages and generate enough power to have her voice heard over increasingly larger orchestrations.

The Queen Operas

To illustrate the reconfiguration of women's travesti roles from the hero to the pageboy and to outline the predecessor of the Romantic heroine as a combination of the first woman and second woman, in chapters 4 and 5 I will draw from a subgenre group of works I call "Queen" operas.[3] The operas in this group were written between 1813 and 1834, a time period that spans from before the point when the tragic ending became the convention to the early years when this was becoming the norm. All four operas feature two leading female characters (a first and second woman) and a tenor as the primary hero:

1. 1813   Giovanni Simone Mayr   *Medea in Corinto*
2. 1830   Gaetano Donizetti   *Anna Bolena*
3. 1831   Vincenzo Bellini   *Norma*
4. 1834   Gaetano Donizetti   *Rosmonda d'Inghilterra*

Each opera contains one woman who is a queen or a mythical ruler and another woman who does not have, or does not take advantage of, her access to social and political power. Two operas treat themes from British history (the popularity of English themes in Italy will be discussed momentarily). One is based in the Tudor era and concerns Henry VIII and Anne Boleyn, and the other invokes an earlier British queen from the Angevin era in the twelfth century with Henry II; his French wife, Eleanor of Aquitaine; and the legends surrounding his mistress, Rosamond Clifford (*Rosmonda d'Inghilterra*).

The other two operas, (*Medea in Corinto* and *Norma*) do not involve British queens, but rather mythical female leaders who, in a similar way to the British queens, are vested with external authority and power. In Greek mythology Medea, daughter of the Asian King of Colchis, is also the niece of the sorceress Circe; in addition to her status as a princess, she has magical powers. Norma, daughter of the High Priest Oroveso, is both the Druid High Priestess and their intercessor with the Druid goddess; she has the power to determine when and how her people can rise up against their Roman oppressors.

My choice of "Queen" operas reflects a popular theme in the first half of the nineteenth century, when many Italian operas took their subject from British history.[4] The enthusiasm for British topics in early nineteenth century Italy coincided with several factors in the years leading up to Queen Victoria's ascension to the throne (1837) and the following years of growth under her reign when the British Empire expanded its colonial interests, England became the major world power, whose influence began to be felt more strongly abroad. Lord Byron, John Keats, and Sir Walter Scott became internationally known literary figures during their lifetimes, and while their texts were translated into the European languages of the continent, Shakespeare's works were also appearing in Italian for the first time. In Italy, as the national movement for a united nation (the *Risorgimento*) became a central focus, it is likely that the perceived stability of the centuries-old British monarchy became a romanticized topos for Italians seeking an established central government. With the figures of Elizabeth I, Anne Boleyn, and Mary Stuart in several operas from this time, the emphasis on sixteenth-century England is strong. The metaphor of Tudor England becoming a world power and discovering itself as a nation under Elizabeth I provided a fitting model for the goals of the newly emerging Italian Risorgimento.[5]

Hybridity

Borrowing from the natural sciences, I find the hybrid, a cross-pollination of two different plant species to form a new one, to be a helpful image for beginning to think about how to hear two characters in a single role.[6] In chapter 4 I present two travesti roles, Smeton (in Donizetti's *Anna Bolena,* 1830) and Arturo (in Donizetti's *Rosmonda d'Inghilterra,* 1834), who function in their respective plot as the court pageboy. Within the underlying principles of midcentury realism a woman's voice was heard as appropriate for the treble timbre of an adolescent page, so these two roles look forward to the norms of Romanticism. However, Donizetti has imbued each with the added feature of valor by giving them heroic situations. Both Smeton and Arturo are infatuated with the first woman title character they each attend. When Donizetti provides them with an opportunity to become a viable romantic partner to each woman, the "period ears" of their first audiences allowed them to hear the hero in the pageboy. Hence, they both can be thought of as *hybrid travesti roles* that allow the combination of the hero within the pageboy.

The development of the early Romantic heroine interacts with two more types of hybridity. As I will show in chapter 5, the hybrid provides a model for understanding the multiple voices in the early articulations of the Romantic heroine. Like certain pageboy roles, such as Donizetti's Smeton and Arturo, the singular Romantic heroine is a role that also echoed two character types. Whereas Smeton and Arturo bring together the travesti hero and the pageboy, the Romantic heroine brings together the first and second women from operas that had two leading roles for female characters. However, the Romantic heroine goes a step further than the pageboy in terms of hybridzation. Not only does the Romantic heroine grow out of two character types, she also brings together two voices: the voices of the first woman and the second woman, the latter of whom also sang the heroic travesti roles.

Before moving onto the examples from the primo ottocento repertory of these hybrid constructions, I want to clarify the specific way I am thinking about hybridity. Though the biological science model used for different crossbred species provides a good starting point, I am using the theme of hybridity more broadly to open up the in-between spaces where binary oppositions break down. I have found Bakhtin's model of hybridization from his essay "Discourse in the Novel" to be especially relevant. In his discussion, Bakhtin presents the aural image of a single utterance that contains two messages simultaneously:[7]

> What is a hybridization? It is a mixture of two social languages within the limits of a single utterance, an encounter, within the arena of an utterance, between two different linguistic consciousnesses, separated from one another by an epoch, by social differentiation or by some other factor. . . . We may even say that language and languages change historically primarily by means of hybridization.[8]

Though Bakhtin is referring to a written language, specifically the prose in novels, it is not difficult to extend his argument to include the sonic resonance of music as a language and a vocalization, as the "utterance" of an operatic character's sounding voice. As a "social language" opera carries meaning. In line with my construction of the "period ear," Bakhtin's "linguistic consciousness" implies that contemporary audiences know how to interpret what they hear and make sense of what happens aurally. The Bakhtinian hybrid provides a way to conceptualize how early-nineteenth-century Italian opera audiences could hear two characterizations simultaneously; for example, *both* the pageboy *and* hero or *both* the first woman *and* the second woman, in the same voice.

Bahktin's discussion of hybridity that allows one articulation to produce more than one meaning is quite helpful for exploring how the "period ear" interpreted the voices of individual singers during an era when the idealized preferences of the time were changing. Alongside the last vestiges of the older eighteenth-century customs (e.g., heroism in the high flexible treble timbres of castrati and women), audiences also heard the newer Romantic innovations that became standard after 1830 (e.g., the rise of the heroic tenor and the demise of the soprano heroine). With these different practices coexisting, the 1820s–40s need to be understood as a particularly rich period aurally for the hybridization of women's vocal and character types. My construction of the "period ear," along with Bahktin's theorization of hybridity, provides a context for understanding the overlapping sonic codes of the era. In other words, going back to the examples of Smeton and Arturo, the opera audience's ability to see and hear the pageboy and hero resonating simultaneously can be explained as the "period ear" hearing these characters as hybrid travesti roles.

While the hybrid travesti roles look back in time and reconcile the eighteenth-century castrato-influenced legacy within the nineteenth-century formulation of the female travesti pageboys, the hybrid female role and the hybrid voice look forward to the Romantic heroine of the 1830s and beyond. The midcentury convergence of the first and second woman from the first half of the century involved the sound and the characterization of both earlier models. Rather than an adaptation of one over the other, the new secondo ottocento heroine is a hybrid of the first and second women. She is beloved by the tenor and dies at the end of the opera (like the first woman); however, she is not passive and knows how to act and get things done (like the second woman).

The hybrid voice constructs an imagined hearing of the original creators of the

Romantic heroine repertory by placing these performances within the critical reception of their time. These female singers were among the leading performers of their time. They were in demand as highlight attractions for the production of newly commissioned operas by composers in the most prestigious theaters in Italy and abroad in Paris and London. Whether performing a new work or the revival of an earlier one, the most sought-after singers had a repertoire out of which several operatic characters became their signature roles. As a diva's reputation rested upon her success in her performances, her acting ability and the sound of her voice were written into a role by the composer (when creating a role for a specific singer), or a part could be adapted to fit the specific strengths of the singer. If this job were especially well done, the audience and critics would have an important part in bolstering such success. A specific role would be known as "so-and-so's" role and would become a legendary paragon for comparison.

Twentieth-Century Divas

The cult of diva worship that was perfected in the nineteenth century, after women first began to find general acceptance on the opera stage, is still a well-known practice today. It continues with the dramatic intensity of Maria Callas's voice on both of her recorded Normas, the velvety creaminess of Leontyne Price's Aidas, and the pristine beauty and grace of Renée Fleming's Countess Almaviva and Marschallin.[9] Though Maria Callas died in 1976, Leontyne Price is in retirement, and Renée Fleming is still singing, the voices of all three women are alive in the memory of the audiences who experienced their live performances, the recordings they made, and the laudatory writing of their admirers.

It is not hard to bring these two phenomena of the hybrid voice and the rise of the superstar singer together into the present. As an avid opera fan, I illustrate this point further with an example from my own experience. The late diva Tatiana Troyanos (or "T.T." as she was affectionately referred to by her fans) gave me—and many others—the great pleasure of watching and listening to her elegant and dignified performances of operatic heroes and heroines.[10] I cherish my memories of her as Richard Strauss's Octavian (*Rosenkavalier*) and Composer (*Ariadne auf Naxos*) and Johann Strauss Jr.'s Count Orlafsky (*Die Fledermaus*) at the Metropolitan Opera in New York from the mid-1980s through the early 1990s. From this same time, I also treasure her portrayals of Verdi's Eboli (*Don Carlos*), Berg's Countess Geschwitz (*Lulu*), and Wagner's Kundry (*Parsifal*). Her sound was supple and extraordinary; for me, and perhaps some others, her voice gave these characters life. Her voice was the first live performance I heard of them, and I still listen for her, at least at first, when I hear performances of these operas today.

Troyanos sang across the gender line and was, arguably, equally well known for both her travesti roles and female heroines. In the audience I heard her voice portray both women and men. She crossed gender boundaries, and I accepted it. I heard her voice as a hybridized voice; it was a voice that contained the possibility of both genders.

My experience of such a hybrid voice is not a recent or new phenomenon. In the last third of the twentieth century such a phenomenon was heard in Marilyn Horne's voice as she sang Handel's and Rossini's travesti heroes as well as Carmen, Delilah, and Rossini's Rosina. Additionally, Frederica von Stade (known to her fans as "Flicka") steals the stage as either Cherubino or Charlotte (in Massenet's *Werther*). Her travesti roles have included Mozart's Sesto (*Clemenza di Tito*) and Idamante (*Idomeneo*), Humperdinck's Hänsel, Strauss's Composer, and Offenbach's Nicklausse. Yet she also excels as Mélisande, Cenerentola, and—more recently—the title character in Lehar's *The Merry Widow*.

Such female singers of today and recent memory find their direct lineage in these early nineteenth-century cases of cross-gender vocal hybridity. Unlike the eighteenth-century Baroque's delight in the interchangeability of the flexible treble timbres of castrati and women's voices, the nineteenth-century Romantic aesthetic drew a sharper distinction between the voice of male and female characters. As the heroic tenor emerged, fewer and fewer heroic female travesti were written. The leading role for a woman no longer moved between being either the hero or the heroine, but, after around 1830, the only norm was to be the heroine.

Moreover, once a diva reached a point of comfort in her career, singers in the early nineteenth century—like today—performed the roles they liked best. Most singers tend to specialize in a particular type of role. Take, for example, the career of Cecilia Bartoli. No one would disagree that she has a voice that could soar in the same type of Rossini heroic travesti roles that Marilyn Horne excelled in or in the Mozart travesti roles such as Cherubino, Idamante (originally written for soprano castrato Vincenzo dal Prato, *Idomeneo*, 1781), or Sesto (originally written for soprano castrato Domenico Bedini, *La clemenza di Tito*, 1791). However, with the exception of Cherubino, Bartoli is best known not for singing across gender, but for her performances of female characters: Rossini's Rosina and Angelina (*La Cenerentola*) and Mozart's Susanna and Despina, among others. I suspect this is because Cecilia Bartoli is such a model of vivacious Italian feminine beauty.

Cecilia Bartoli's travesti repertory is best displayed on her compact disc recordings (rather than in the opera house or in videos), where the listener hears her voice but does not physically see her on stage cross-dressed. The presentation of gender in the marketing of her career today presents a striking juxtaposition to what was considered aurally acceptable for women in the primo ottocento. Since the late 1990s Bartoli has recorded several arias by male characters drawn from lesser-known works. On *The Vivaldi Album* (1999) she sings arias for female characters as well as several heroic numbers that Vivaldi wrote for castrato voices, for example, Farnace's "Gelido in ogni vena" (*Farnace*, RV 711, 1727) and Ottone's "Dopo un'orrida procella" (*Griselda*, RV 718, 1735). On her *Dreams & Fables—Gluck Italian Arias* (2001) she used a similar formula with a combination of arias, this time composed by Gluck, written for treble timbres including two castrato numbers: Ircano's "Ciascun siegua il suo stile . . . Maggior follia non v'è" (*La Semiramide riconosciuta*, 1748) and Sesto's "Se mai senti spirarti sul volto" (*La clemenza di Tito*, 1752).

Yet Bartoli's integration of male characters into her recording repertory was long in coming. One notable exception is her performance of the entrance cavatina for

Rossini's Tancredi, including the famous cabaletta "Di tanti palpiti," on one of her first recordings released at the beginning of her career (*Rossini Arias*, August 1989). Very closely following this compact disc were three other Rossini recordings that deliberately linked Bartoli's voice to an unambiguously female characterization. First was a complete recording of *Il barbiere di Siviglia* (released in December 1989) with Bartoli as Rosina, Leo Nucci as Figaro, and conducted by Giuseppe Patané. The second was *Rossini Recital—Giovanna d'Arco/19 Songs* (released in December 1990), whose title prominently drew one's attention to the little-known solo vocal cantata as well as to link her voice (and gorgeous cover picture) with Joan of Arc, the warrior heroine who was torn between her love for God and country as well as romantic desire. Her third all-Rossini recording completely rehabilitated her voice from any potentially false reputation she might have had as an artist who was known for singing across gender roles: Bartoli became the Rossinian mezzo-soprano who embodied the feminine. With another beautiful cover picture (that arranged her thick dark hair into a soft bun with loose tendrils framing her face), *Rossini Heroines* (released in January 1992) easily erased any memory of Bartoli as hero singing to his beloved. Now Bartoli had been fully transformed into our beloved—as the listener we fell head over heels in love with her voice and picture.[11]

Primo Ottocento Divas

Like many singers in the present, a large number of nineteenth-century singers showed a preference for performing similar types of roles. Marietta Alboni, Carolina Bassi, Brigida Lorenzani, Rosa Morandi, and Rosmunda Pisaroni all specialized in heroic travesti roles. Though they each performed female characters occasionally, they were known for their portrayals of *musico* roles. All of these singers had strong high notes, but excelled in their lower register. They were the primary interpreters of several primo ottocento heroic travesti roles including Rossini's Tancredi, Malcolm (*La donna del lago*), and Arsace (*Semiramide*).

On the other hand, Jenny Lind, Henriette Sontag, and Fanny Tacchinardi-Persiani were all praised for their high, light sound, and brilliant coloratura. These women excelled in first woman roles where they played the beloved heroine. They were best known for being the voices behind the hapless type of Romantic heroine who loves unwisely and is ultimately sacrificed for her innocence. These signature roles included: Rossini's Desdemona and the title roles in Donizetti's *Lucia di Lammermoor* and *Linda di Chamounix*.

Though most of the female singers performing in the primo ottocento sang across gender at least occasionally, there were a few singers who specialized in both female and male roles. One of the most well-known performers to do so was Maria Malibran (1808–36), a bright star in the exceedingly musical García family.[12] Malibran's career was tragically cut short when she died at the age of only twenty-eight from complications following a horseback riding accident; however, her eleven-year career had already garnered her legendary musical fame and attention. As a specialist in Rossini's operas, her roles included both his leading prima donnas as well as the musico heroes. The ambidexterity in her ability to successfully portray

Maria Malibran as Leonore cross-dressed as Fidelio in the prison scene of Beethoven's *Fidelio.* London, October 10, 1836. *The Harvard Theatre Collection, The Houghton Library.*

Portrait of Maria Malibran. Lithograph by Villain, Paris. *The Harvard Theatre Collection, The Houghton Library.*

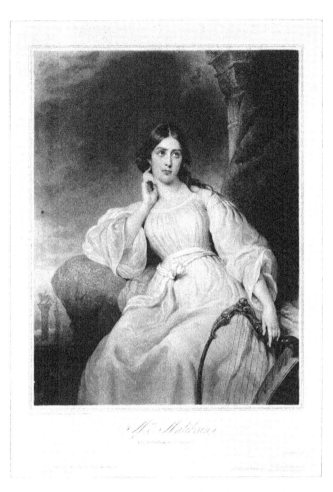

Maria Malibran as Desdemona in Rossini's *Otello*. Note the harp, a common image for Desdemona. *The Harvard Theatre Collection, The Houghton Library.*

both male and female characters is especially well illustrated in Rossini's opera *Semiramide;* Malibran had the two leading roles (Semiramide and Arsace) in her repertory, and she sang both throughout her career.[13] Beyond Rossini, Malibran was also well known in her portrayal of Bellini's Romeo (in *I Capuletti e i Montecchi*). Like the typical travesti singer, Malibran also sang "second woman" roles that engaged cross-gender disguise; she was well known as Beethoven's Leonore (in *Fidelio*), and she sang the first Felicia in the London performances of Meyerbeer's *Il crociato in Egitto* (1825).

In this context with so many travesti roles, it is important to remember that Malibran was also celebrated as a prima donna in female roles. She was comfortable both in comic and serious operas and regularly performed Rossini's Rosina and

Maria Malibran in the title role of Balfe's *The Maid of Artois,* a
role she premiered at the Drury Lane Theatre in London in
May 1836, just a few months before her tragic early death in
September of that year. Engraving, London, J. Fairburn (1836).
The Harvard Theatre Collection, The Houghton Library.

Angelina (*Cenerentola*). Her best-known roles included Semiramide, Desdemona,
Ninetta (*La gazza ladra*), as well as Amina in Bellini's *La sonnambula.* Had she not
died so young, it is quite probable that she would have had more opportunities to
collaborate with the leading composers in the 1830s and 1840s (Bellini, Donizetti,
Mercadante, Pacini, and Verdi). She was the first Maria Stuarda in Donizetti's opera, and Bellini adapted the role of Elvira in *I puritani* for her to sing in Naples;
unfortunately, this last collaboration never came about.[14]

Rossini's operas form a core canon not only for understanding how primo ottocento operas were put together, but also for getting a picture of what was popular.[15]
His operas were performed all over Italy, and by the 1820s "Rossini fever" quickly
spread to Vienna, London, and Paris. Among his most successful operas were several he wrote for Isabella Colbran (1785–1845), the reigning diva at the Teatro San
Carlo in Naples from 1811 to 1822, who later became Rossini's wife. Colbran
was the leading female voice in Rossini's nine Neapolitan operas and also created

Portrait of Isabella Colbran, whose voice was behind the leading roles of Rossini's Neapolitan operas. Colbran later became Rossini's wife. Lithograph. *The Harvard Theatre Collection, The Houghton Library.*

the title role in his last Italian opera, *Semiramide* (1823), written for La Fenice in Venice.

Though not all of Rossini's Neapolitan operas became hugely popular, his affiliation with the San Carlo from 1816 to 1822 spanned a critical point in his career. With its artistic director Domenico Barbaja, the San Carlo was one of the wealthiest opera houses in Europe. Given the strong court support and preference for serious operas (rather than comic operas), Rossini had the ideal venue to write what would become the centerpieces of his mature operatic style. As the San Carlo's leading prima donna, Colbran became the primary voice behind the Rossinian serious heroine.

Isabella Colbran, of Spanish descent, spent her career in Naples, the Italian mainland home to the Spanish Bourbon "Kingdom of the two Sicilies." The French were never great supporters of the castrati or musico roles, and after the French occupation of Naples by Napoleon's forces in the first years of the century, Colbran sang at the San Carlo at a point when the travesti tradition there was out of style. In fact, Naples became one of the avant garde locations for nurturing the rise of the tenor hero; Giovanni Davide, Manuel García I, and Andrea Nozzari were all in residence during this time. As a result, given these local preferences, Colbran specialized in singing the female leading heroine. In a similar situation to Cecilia Bartoli today, Colbran's voice certainly could have sung travesti roles; in any case, and perhaps for some of the same reasons as with Bartoli today, Colbran's public was only interested in hearing her perform female characters.

A young Giuditta Pasta in the heroic travesti title role of Rossini's *Tancredi*. Tancredi was a signature role Pasta sang throughout her career. Lithograph by Villain, Paris. *The Harvard Theatre Collection, The Houghton Library.*

MADAME J. PASTA

A young Giuditta Pasta as Rossini's Desdemona (*Otello*) when she sang this role in Paris in the early 1820s. David Pradier, artist. Lithograph by Villain, Paris. *The Harvard Theatre Collection, The Houghton Library.*

Given the growing popularity of Rossini's operas, several of Colbran's roles became the ideal repertory for showcasing rising singers in the 1820s. As was seen above with Malibran in the late 1820s, Rossini's heroines and musico roles in particular helped Malibran establish herself as a leading prima donna before she became well known in other repertory. Yet even rivaling the popularity of Malibran and Colbran (in their respective times) was Giuditta Pasta (1797–1865), a singer whose legendary reputation for her dramatic presence and powerfully affective voice can only be compared to the status that Maria Callas has held in contemporary times.[16]

Though Rossini wrote only one new role for Pasta (Corinna in *Il viaggio a Reims*, 1825), she was the primary voice who interpreted Rossini's operas in the 1820s (until she shared this position with Malibran, who made her debut at the Théâtre Italien in 1828). When Rossini and his wife resettled in Paris in 1824, Colbran's career was nearly over. It was Pasta, not Colbran, who was the reigning Rossini interpreter at the Théâtre Italien by that time, and she sang several of Colbran's former roles. More than anyone else, it was Pasta's voice that first popularized Rossini's heroines in Paris. At the Théâtre Italien Pasta sang Colbran's Neapolitan roles—Elisabetta, Dedesmona, Zelmira, Elcia (*Mosè in Egitto*)—as well as Colbran's farewell to Italy, the title role in *Semiramide*.[17] Unlike Colbran, and to an even greater extent than Malibran, Pasta sang across gender in musico roles written by Rossini, Zingarelli, Mayr, Cimarosa, and others. Her Rossini travesti roles were from operas that had been commissioned by northern theaters in Venice: the title role in *Tancredi* and Arsace from *Aureliano in Palmira* (both had premiered in 1813 at La Fenice) and Eduardo from *Eduardo e Cristina* (first performed in 1819 at the San Benedetto). Hence, during the composer's first years in Paris, Pasta's voice was the leading Rossini voice in Paris.

Chapter 5 expands on this exploration of early nineteenth-century divas and their role in voicing the character of the prototypical singular opera heroine. In tracing the development of the Romantic heroine, I follow a path that wends its way through interwoven topics. Divided into two large sections, the first part of the chapter focuses on the Romantic heroine and continues the discussion of the career and voice of Giuditta Pasta. The second part brings together the interconnections between the first and second women within all four of the "Queen" operas.

4 Taming Women's Voices: From Hero to Pageboy

Even with the rise of the tenor, the practice of the travesti tradition persevered and evolved: in the first half of the nineteenth century, women's voices continued to straddle the aural and visual representation of male and female characters. Women continued to cross-dress and sing as men quite commonly up through the middle of the century. In the same sonic world where the hero's voice needed to more closely match the new conceptions of the "virility" and "masculinity" of his behavior, women's voices needed to be heard as more "feminine." The pageboy travesti roles became the perfect compromise. Rather than an "idealized" sound for the hero, the cross-dressed female voice was heard as appropriate, even "realistic," for the adolescent boy who had not yet undergone the voice changes of puberty. Given his young age and the presence of the tenor, these roles for women as boy travesti roles could be important roles, but they were not characters that had the maturity and valor needed to be the primary contender for the hand of the soprano heroine. Going back to Cherubino, Mozart's famous page from *Le nozze di Figaro*, such roles were not new. However, their position in the nineteenth century took on special meaning as they became the preferred new standard for women's cross-dressed voices.

Romantic opera involves the intersection of these coexisting early-nineteenth-century phenomena: the move from the survival of the heroine to her ultimate death, the ascendance of the tenor, and the evolution of travesti roles (including the ultimate disintegration of the heroic travesti tradition). With all three practices in place, the types of opportunities for women in opera underwent a period of reconfiguration. As the travesti tradition was transformed, so were the meanings ascribed to women's voices. No longer the hero, and relegated to the secondary status of the pageboy travesti role, women's voices gradually lost access to their former characterization as men with power. Instead of having the leading couple written for two women's voices (the female heroic travesti role and the female heroine), by midcentury the romantic couple invariably came to mean the tenor and the soprano. Concurrently, as the sound of the hero changed (from a woman's voice to a man's tenor voice), the voice and characterization of a role became critical for defining the emergent new "masculine" hero and "feminine" Romantic heroine.

Transformation of the Travesti Roles: Rossini in the North and South

People interested in nineteenth-century Italy are accustomed to thinking of it as a country with many political and ethnic entities. Besides the regional difference between geographical divisions (e.g., the growing cities and industry in the north and the farm-based agriculture in the south), the foreign occupation by other countries (primarily the French, Austrian, and Spanish) throughout Italy added another layer of difference along the peninsula. Given the political and ethnic diversity among the many regions of Italy, it is not surprising that the musical tastes varied also. Moreover, the interaction between these different foreign cultural preferences and regional operatic practices affected the transition from the female travesti hero to the new Romantic tenor.

The use of travesti roles differed in northern and southern Italy. As outlined in chapter 3, Meyerbeer's Italian operas, all written for opera houses in northern Italy (Padua, Turin, Milan, and Venice), illustrate the enduring preference for the heroic travesti tradition in the north. The case of the Spanish and French presence in the southern part of Italy, specifically Naples, in the first decades of the nineteenth century provides an important contrasting situation to that of the north. With the French expansion during Napoleon's campaign, the Spanish Bourbon stronghold on the Kingdom of the Two Sicilies was compromised. While the Spanish continued to hold their ground in Sicily, the French took control of their areas on the Italian mainland and occupied Naples. Though Naples had been one of the leading centers of the castrato bel canto tradition with its premier conservatories in the seventeenth and eighteenth centuries, the ten years of French rule, first under Joseph Bonaparte (1806–1808) and then Joachim Murat (1808–15), reflected a shift to French tastes. The French had never favored the castrato/travesti tradition, and they supported alternatives to the heroic travesti tradition. Through their strongly subsidized court opera (enhanced by money brought in from the lucrative gambling tables allowed in Neapolitan theaters), the San Carlo opera became a major center for the rise of the tenor: the new Romantic heroic voice. The Bourbon restoration in 1815 continued many of the French developments and enjoyed the legacy of the tenor tradition. It is within this context that, in 1815, Rossini signed a contract with Domenico Barbaja, who had been the impresario and director of the Neapolitan royal theaters from 1809 and continued their management (with only minor interruptions) until 1840.

In Rossini's first opera for Naples, *Elisabetta, regina d'Inghilterra* (1815), he brought the travesti tradition he was so accustomed to using in his serious (non-comic) operas from the north. Yet he adapted his use of the travesti role in that Enrico was not the heroic lead, but rather a small secondary role in the tradition of the young adolescent boy (he is the younger brother to Matilde, one of the two primary female characters). In his ten operas for Naples, Rossini wrote only three travesti roles.[1] In addition to the small role of Enrico in *Elisabetta,* he wrote two larger travesti roles in the heroic tradition: Malcolm Graeme in *La donna del lago* (1819) and Calbo in *Maometto II* (1820).

Neither *La donna del lago* nor *Maometto II* were among Rossini's most popular operas in Naples. Given the importance of Malcolm and Calbo and the Neapolitan audience's resistance to large heroic travesti roles, it seems possible that these roles might have contributed to the cool reception of these two operas. However, the situation is more complicated; after its opening night, *La donna del lago* became more successful, whereas *Maometto II* never gained in popularity. Despite its strong cast and Charles Osborne's endorsement that it is "one of the most immediately attractive of Rossini's serious operas, its orchestration is rich and varied, its structure sound and imposing, and its dramatic impact striking," the opera was received with "indifference."[2]

Evidence suggests that Rossini also felt that *Maometto II* was a strong opera. After a few revisions, it was well received in other houses when it was revived in northern Italy at La Fenice in Venice (1822) and Milan (1824) and internationally in Vienna (1823) and Lisbon (1826). Additionally, it was one of the two Italian operas that Rossini chose to adapt and rework for the Paris Opéra where it became *Le siège de Corinthe* in 1826.[3] Not inconsequentially, given French preferences, the travesti part of Calbo was transformed to the tenor role of Néoclès and premiered by noted French Rossini singer Adolphe Nourrit.

Osborne raises a good point about the indifference Naples gave *Maometto II*, especially when contrasted with the eventual popularity of *La donna del lago*.[4] Both operas had excellent casts that included the foremost Rossini singers of the time. *La donna del lago* starred Isabella Colbran, the resident prima donna of the Teatro San Carlo and future wife of Rossini, and, in prominent roles the San Carlo's leading tenors, Giovanni David and Andrea Nozzari, both of whom had already premiered several Rossini roles.[5] *Maometto II* had a similar cast with Colbran, Nozzari, and the noted bass Filippo Galli, who had premiered Mustafà (in Rossini's *L'italiana in Algeri*, 1813) and would go on to create Assur (in Rossini's *Semiramide*, 1823). If both *Maometto II* and *La donna del lago* were strong operas and had heroic travesti roles, why was one eventually favored and the other dismissed?

If we focus on the heroic travesti roles in each opera, a plausible answer emerges. Malcolm was premiered by the well-known, and well-liked, Rosmonda Pisaroni. She had arrived in Naples in 1818 to work with Rossini and had created two earlier Rossini heroines at the San Carlo (Zomira in *Ricciardo e Zoraide*, 1818, and Andromache in *Ermione*, 1819) before Malcolm, her third principal role at the San Carlo. Even given the Neapolitan resistance to heroic travesti roles, Pisaroni's fame and warm reception in Naples most likely aided her success in the role.[6] On the other hand, Adelaide Comelli, the first Calbo in *Maometto II*, was a relatively unknown singer and a newcomer to the San Carlo. At the beginning of her career, she was singing her first Rossini role. Though she later went on to become a better-known performer, it seems likely that her burgeoning career and the general Neapolitan hesitation regarding travesti roles were enough to dampen the success of *Maometto II* in Naples.[7]

The difficulty *La donna del lago* and *Maometto II* initially faced in Naples and the success they both enjoyed in northern Italian and other European theaters suggest that the tastes of the Neapolitan audience regarding heroic travesti roles were not a minimal factor.[8] As these two operas illustrate, the aesthetics of vocal sound representing the gender of a role was a mutable element in opera characterization; the interaction of preference and practice worked hand in hand. Moreover, specific singers could influence the popularity of a work; it seems likely that Pisaroni's presence in *La donna del lago* helped make the heroic travesti part of Malcolm more palpable than the less-experienced Comelli as Calbo in *Maometto II*.

Table 4.1. Rossini's Operas Written between *Elisabetta* (His First Neapolitan Opera) and
Semiramide (His Last Opera for Italy)

boldface = operas at the San Carlo in Naples

Opera	Theater	Year	Travesti
Elisabetta	**San Carlo, Naples**	**1815**	**Pageboy**
Torvaldo e Dorliska	Valle, Rome	1815	
Barbiere di Siviglia	Argentina, Rome	1816	
La gazzetta	Fiorentini, Naples	1816	
Otello	Fondo, Naples	1816	
Cenerentola	Valle, Rome	1817	
Gazza ladra	La Scala, Milan	1817	Travesti
Armida	**San Carlo, Naples**	**1817**	
Adelaide di Borgona	Argentina, Rome	1817	Heroic travesti
Mosè in Egitto	**San Carlo, Naples**	**1818**	
Adina	São Carlos, Lisbon	[1818] 1826	
Ricciardo e Zoraide	**San Carlo, Naples**	**1818**	
Ermione	**San Carlo, Naples**	**1819**	
Eduardo e Christina	Benedetto, Venice	1819	Heroic travesti
Donna del lago	**San Carlo, Naples**	**1819**	**Heroic travesti**
Bianca e Falliero	La Scala, Milan	1819	Heroic travesti
Maometto II	**San Carlo, Naples**	**1820**	**Heroic travesti**
Matilde di Shabran	Apollo, Rome	1821	Heroic travesti
Zelmira	**San Carlo, Naples**	**1822**	
Semiramide	La Fenice, Venice	1823	Heroic travessti

The travesti roles in *La donna del lago* and *Maometto II* fit into a larger context. Having learned his lesson well with these two operas, Rossini's last Neapolitan opera, *Zelmira* (1822), did not include a travesti role. Nonetheless, his fondness for the heroic travesti roles was not stifled, and he continued to write such roles for his northern commissions. In fact, out of his last seven operas for Italy, *Zelmira* was the only one without such a role (see table 4.1).

In his opera immediately preceding *La donna del lago* he wrote the heroic travesti role of Eduardo in *Eduardo e Cristina* for Carolina Cortesi, premiered at the Teatro San Benedetto in Venice (1819). After *La donna del lago,* he wrote the heroic travesti role of Falliero for Carolina Bassi in *Bianca e Falliero* at La Scala in Milan (1819). Between *Maometto II* and *Zelmira,* his last two operas for Naples, he wrote *Matilde di Shabran* with the heroic role of Eduardo written for Annetta Parlamagni. *Matilde* was premiered at the Teatro Apollo in Rome on February 24, 1821.

Perhaps the greatest testament to Rossini's continued interest in the heroic travesti tradition in the latter part of his Italian career is, arguably, his greatest role in this genre for his final opera for Italy—Arsace—in *Semiramide* written for La Fenice in Venice and premiered on February 3, 1823. The cast was strong and included singers who had worked with Rossini at the San Carlo. Rosa Mariani, as Arsace, was joined by Rossini's wife, Isabella Colbran, in the title role and fellow San Carlo colleague Filippo Galli as Assur. These operas show how Rossini continued to write heroic travesti roles throughout his career in Italy, all the while being sensitive to the regional tastes of the time. If Naples was "ahead" of its time in its preference for the heroic tenor voice, then it seems clear from the number of operas he wrote for other houses that Rossini certainly did not mind writing in the "older" style of the heroic travesti roles for the north.

Such regional differences in aesthetic preferences regarding the pairing of operatic voice and character reveal a complicated picture of Italian operatic practice in the first decades of the nineteenth century and offer clues as to how opera characters and vocal types developed. Rather than a strict chronological shift, changes evolved according to specific areas that were either more welcoming of, or hesitant to, different practices. The year 1830 provides a good general date for when most of the peninsula was open to the heroic tenor; however, the heroic travesti practice was supported for the longest time in northern Italian opera houses.

Rossini was both remarkable and pragmatic in his ability to gauge the geographical differences in attitudes toward heroic travesti roles in the late 1810s and early 1820s. Since he was writing for both northern and southern houses, his use and modification of the travesti roles present compelling evidence for the regional differences. Rossini's slightly younger colleague, Gaetano Donizetti (1797–1848), had a slower start in his success as an opera composer, yet emerged as one of the leading composers of the 1830s and 1840s. His two operas, *Anna Bolena*, commissioned by the Teatro Carcano in Milan (1830), and *Rosmonda d'Inghiltera*, written for the Teatro Pergola in Florence (1834), were both for northern houses and illustrate ways the travesti tradition was transformed in the north. Both of these operas have young adolescent male characters that demonstrate the different blendings of the newer travesti pageboys with the older heroic travesti tradition.

The Hero within the Pageboy

Considered Donizetti's breakthrough work in establishing him as one of the leading opera composers of his time, *Anna Bolena* illustrates a combination of older and newer aesthetics in use at the time. Written to a libretto by Felice Romani in 1830 for the Teatro Carcano in Milan, the opera contains a large cast of principals. As Romantic operas were honing the number of main characters down to two, the tenor and the soprano, and maybe a third (e.g., bass-baritone) as an antagonist, *Anna Bolena* has five leading roles. Almost all of the available types of characters and vocal roles for men and women of the time were incorporated into this opera. Three substantial parts were written for women's voices and two leading characters, a tenor and bass/baritone, for male voices. The ways in which the male and female voices are paired romantically reflect the amalgamation of old and new plot situations.

Set in the 1536 British court of Henry VIII (Enrico) and his second wife, Anne Boleyn (Anna Bolena), the opera dramatizes, with broad historical license, the events

Example 4.1. Measures 1–5 of Cherubino's "Non so più," act 1, *Le nozze di Figaro*.

that led up to her execution. The two leading men's roles, Enrico (bass/baritone) and Lord Riccardo Percy (tenor), are supplemented by the two comprimario roles of Lord Rochefort (bass, Anna's brother) and Sir Hervey (tenor, an official of the King). The three roles for women's voices contain two female characters—Anna Bolena and Jane (Giovanna) Seymour—and one travesti role—Smeton.

Smeton is a special travesti role that falls in between the cracks of eighteenth- and nineteenth-century traditions. In accordance with the Romantic "realism" that replaced the female travesti hero with the tenor, Smeton is a page role, and his treble timbre reflects his youth. However, he is in love with Anna, and it is the treatment of this love that reveals the in-between-ness of his character. On the one hand, the page travesti, adolescent youth, not fully mature status of his character works against his being a serious contender for the leading soprano. This is further emphasized by the presence of Percy, the tenor, who loves Anna and is loved by her in return. However, on the other hand, Smeton's Cherubino-like infatuation goes beyond a mere dalliance of the plot. His feelings are given more weight in the way in which they are presented.

Mozart's amorous page from *Le nozze di Figaro* provides a not-so-distant cousin to the type of travesti role Donizetti writes in Smeton. Though both characters sing about love early on in the first act, Cherubino's two short numbers reflect the childlike charm of his youth. His first outburst ("Non so più cosa son, cosa faccio" [I no longer know who I am or what to do]) reveals a breathless anxiety about his awakening to new sexual urges.

In an Allegro vivace cut-time tempo, his first lines can barely be contained as he rushes in on the off-beat and stuffs as many syllables as he can into each phrase. His melodic lines contain deliberately awkward jumps that emphasize his uncertainty and mimic the effect of a pubescent boy's voice cracking when he gets excited. In the second measure he leaps the interval of a major sixth upward between an E♭ and C, two points in a woman's voice that approach the register change from the chest voice to the head voice. Depending upon the individual singer's voice (the shifting between the two registers, called the "break" or "bridge," can be slightly different), this leap needs to be negotiated carefully so that the smooth blending of the voice through this interval can be sustained. Nonetheless, even the best singers need to use caution so as not to give in to a gulping effect given the placement of this leap in the very first phrase of the aria before having had the chance to fully warm up the voice in the role.[9]

In the next phrase, the fourth measure, this leap is expanded to an octave between the two F's on the bottom and top of the treble clef. While the first major sixth jump hovered between the head and chest voices, the octave of the second leap is most certainly produced by two different sound mechanisms (where in the body—the areas around the cheeks, eyes, and forehead—the sound resonates).[10] The unavoidable result at this point is for the lower F to sound a little disconnected from the higher F. Mozart cleverly exaggerates the juxtaposition between these notes by setting them across one word, "sono" (I am). The result is that the singer cannot sneak a breath in between and has no choice but to try and minimize the difference between these two parts in her voice.

As for Cherubino, the aria illustrates the tug and pull he experiences between his "two voices." His first four phrases all proceed downward, yet the contour is not smooth: each line jumps up at an unpredictable point. In this opening section, it is as though he is trying to tame his voice and push it down to a lower tessitura, yet it keeps popping up to a higher range, almost beyond his control.[11] The treacherous octave leap in measure 4 could serve as a manifesto for his character as this point. Split between his higher and lower voices, his "I am" encompasses the two simultaneous aspects of the childlike boy and the budding adult male personalities he embodies.

Cherubino's second (and last) aria at the beginning of the second act ("Voi, che sapete") is placed fairly closely to his first number and reveals similar themes: the confusion (and tantalizing pleasure) he feels in his new desires and emotions. He even cites some of the very same feelings in the two numbers—the icy chills immediately followed by his burning ardor.[12] Yet the presentation of this second number is strikingly different. Performed by Cherubino as an intentional "song" to Susanna and the Countess, he addresses the ladies with deference and poise. In a more moderate tempo, andante con moto, this aria includes Susanna's "accompanying him" on the guitar.[13] The opening of the aria is constructed in measured phrases that take their time to unfold. After an eight-bar introduction, Cherubino's vocal part divides itself into regular groupings of six two-measure phrases, for a standard period of twelve measures, which modulate from the tonic key of B♭ major, predictably, to the dominant triad on F major. Though not without its irregularities in phrase structure (especially in the contrasting middle section later in the aria), compared to his first number, "Non so più," "Voi, che sapete" is much more predictable rhythmically and in the contour of the melodic line. Rather than the irregular jumps and odd word scansion in his first act aria, in his second act number his vocal line undulates gracefully as his voice is carried smoothly between his higher and lower registers.

The opening lines of each aria provide another point of comparison. Taking love as their central theme, both employ a form of the verb "sapere" (to know): "Non so più" and "Voi, che sapete." Cherubino's first number focuses on unknowing—his own confusion—while his second aria emphasizes knowledge—that of Susanna and the Countess—about the true ways of love. In the second act Cherubino im-

Example 4.2. Measures 1–16 of Cherubino's "Voi, che sapete," act 2, *Le nozze di Figaro.*
Susanna mimes accompanying Cherubino on the guitar.

plores the two women to look inside his heart and tell him if what he is experiencing is real love. Coming soon after the Countess's "Porgi amor" that opens the second act, Cherubino's inquisitiveness about the nature of love provides a compelling contrast to the dignified entrance of the Countess, suffering nobly through her husband's infidelities. Cherubino is on the brink of discovering a more mature adult love, while the Countess and Susanna already know the pleasure, perils, and fragility of such passion. Within the larger context of the opera, the three characters illustrate different stages of love: Cherubino in his adolescent pondering, Susanna in the full flush of romantic love, and the Countess in a marriage that has lost its spark and needs revitalizing.

If, in his exploits, Cherubino tries to seduce the Countess or Susanna, it comes off more like a pleasant diversion than as a serious threat. The two women greet his attention with playfulness for its ability to distract them from the more serious matters they are facing with their "real" partners (the Count and Figaro, respectively). Ironically, it is Count Almaviva (whose name implies that his heart, or amorous side, is alive and vivacious) who is the only one who treats Cherubino's behavior with any severity. The Count continually suspects Cherubino of having multiple romantic adventures with women in his castle including, possibly, his own wife. Yet the audience recognizes this for what it is—a manifestation of the Count's own guilty conscience, for Almaviva is actively pursuing his own exploits with Susanna. By the end of Mozart's opera Cherubino finally finds an appropriate partner; he is paired with Barbarina, a village girl who is well matched to his social position and age.

Like Cherubino, Donizetti's Smeton is also given two solo numbers in the opera, both in the first half of the opera. Near the beginning of act 1 Smeton's first song,

110   *Voicing Gender*

"Deh! Non voler costringere," is requested by Anna as a diversion to cheer her up while the court waits for Enrico. Crafted with a subtle message, Smeton presents his own hidden love for Anna in a stylized manner—the strophic romance—a form more popular in France than in Italy.[14] Accompanying himself on the harp, he ornaments his melody with grace notes, dotted rhythms, and cascading sixteenth notes. Yet despite his earnest efforts, his sentiments miss their mark when Anna cuts his song off abruptly. Rather than igniting her passion for him, Smeton's song agitates Anna as she is reminded of her still-ardent first love for Percy.

Unlike Cherubino's awkwardness, Smeton performs an eloquent expression of his love for Anna and is in full control of his voice. Like Cherubino's second aria, Smeton's first aria is a song—a sung moment in the drama. While Cherubino is accompanied by Susanna on the guitar, Smeton accompanies himself on the harp.[15] Written in the same key (E♭ major) as Cherubino's first aria, both numbers share the same highest note, G (at the top of the treble clef). However, the two young men each incorporate this high note, near the top of their respective ranges, into their melodies quite differently. Smeton sings this note only twice, both times quickly (a sixteenth note) as a passing note in a repeated arpeggiated cadential figure, near the end of the second stanza, just a few measures before Anna interrupts him. Each time the high G adds a brilliant effect as it is tossed off quickly and, seemingly, effortlessly while the voice is immediately carried down into a more comfortable range.

For Cherubino this high G is given emphasis in duration (lasting up to a half note) and frequency (it appears four times) throughout his song. Like a nagging reminder, this note seems to metaphorically illustrate what is just beyond his comfortable grasp. All four separate occurrences underscore text that refers to things he is not yet able to attain: "donna" (woman) (example 4.3a); "desio" (desire) (example 4.3b); "donna," again in the repeated opening section; and his great longings that are carried off in the wind, never reaching their intended audience ("che il suon de' vani accenti, portano via con sé") (example 4.3c). In this last case near the end, the high G prolongs its poignancy receiving its longest note value (a half note, half a measure) on the final word ("sé"). Given the sustained duration and high placement in the voice, it almost certainly provokes anxiety for the singer as she is left desperately trying not to run out of breath and not have her voice crack on the note.

In a contrasting manner, Smeton is able to more deftly navigate his amorous emotions and steer his voice into its comfortable range. Instead of having his melodic line continually spike upward toward awkwardly placed high notes, he smoothly carries his voice down to his lower range. Starting out with a melody that begins on the same note as Cherubino's "Non so più," Smeton's melody gently swoops downwards an octave to the B♭ below the treble staff in its first phrase. Three of his opening four phrases conclude on this low B♭, a note that has a sweet mellow resonance and strong dark timbre from its low placement in the female singer's throat. In Cherubino's first aria, his lowest note is an E♭, a perfect fourth above the lowest note in Smeton's opening phrase and the interval of a perfect fifth above Smeton's lowest note in the aria (the A♭ below middle C). The wider vocal

4.3a

4.3b

4.3c

Example 4.3a–c. Cherubino's high Gs in "Non so più," act 1, *Le nozze di Figaro.*

4.4a

4.4b

* Highest note - G - worked into vocal line without much emphasis

Example 4.4a–b. Excerpts from Smeton's first aria, act 1, *Anna Bolena*. In Smeton's first stanza (4.4a), Anna Bolena sits, surrounded by her ladies-in-waiting; Smeton mimes accompanying himself with the harp. Smeton's second stanza (4.4b) includes Donizetti's written ornamentation (equivalent to first stanza, mm. 60–68).

range Smeton sings presents a fitting metaphor for the vaster sonic regions Smeton is allowed to explore. However, the primary aural difference is that Smeton's voice gets to sing in a deeper range than Cherubino's and resonate as a lower, more mature, timbre overall.

Though Smeton is not successful in wooing Anna for himself, his music partially accomplishes its intended goal in the feelings it elicits from the queen. Unfortunately for Smeton, he is not the one for whom Anna pines. In an aside, Anna dismisses any possibility of her seeing Smeton as a potential lover. As she listens to his song about first love, she thinks of her original love for Percy. While her memories overtake her, she can hardly keep her composure and interrupts the song after the first line of its third strophe. In an aside, she first comments on Smeton's young age and her own lost love:

Anna's Asides to Smeton's First Aria, *Anna Bolena*

(*fra sé*)	(*an aside to herself*)
Come, innocente giovane, come m'hai scosso il core!	How, innocent youth, how you have shaken my heart!
Son calde ancor le ceneri del mio primiero amore!	The ashes from my first love are still warm!
Ah! Non avessi il petto aperto ad altro affetto,	Had I not opened my heart to another love,
Io non sarei sì misera, nel vano mio splendor.	I should not now be so miserable in the vanity of my splendor.

Deep in her reverie, she does not complete his song by singing the rest of what would have been his third stanza, but begins a new melody that commences her own formal aria with a cavatina and cabaletta.

With its curvaceous contour and duskily hued timbre, Smeton's song takes on the character of a seductive serenade. His music is so effective that it conjures up Anna's most hidden thoughts of love; his voice sends her into a reverie about Percy. Though Smeton's voice can remind Anna of love, she does not hear it as the voice of love itself. Instead, in 1830, Smeton's voice, the travesti voice, is a conduit through which love can flow, but might not reach its destination. It is not inconsequential that Percy is a tenor. As Anna hears the new hero in the voice of Percy, Smeton's voice reminds her of love but cannot fulfill her dreams. The travesti voice is relegated to that of a proxy where it can stand in for the tenor when he is not there, but can no longer embody the character of the hero.

It is in Smeton's second appearance when his romantic feelings for Anna permeate the plot most thoroughly. Like Cherubino, his second number is more formal in structure regarding the conventions of the time. Rather than his earlier interrupted serenade, Smeton's second act number follows the conventions of la solita forma which encompass the aria form. His opening scena finds him alone in Anna's private apartments. In his recitative he explains how he had stolen a small portrait of Anna to admire. Reluctant to return the miniature, he gazes upon it, kisses it, and tells how he has kept it close to his heart. In his cantabile ("Un bacio, un bacio

Example 4.5. Excerpt from the cabaletta of Smeton's second aria, act 1, *Anna Bolena*.

ancora") and cabaletta ("Ah! parea che per incanto") he describes how he has nurtured a private love for Anna that has filled him with hope and desire. With no one
around to hear him, Smeton lets his voice soar. Through triplets, sixteenth notes,
and dotted rhythms he sings expansive phrases that encompass scalar descents that
span as much as an octave plus a major sixth in one breath. With an embellished
vocal line, Smeton's music attains the sophistication of the other principals in the
opera. As his scene takes its time to unfold, his hesitations have delayed him too
long; before he can safely put the picture back, he hears someone coming. Stuffing
the picture back into his doublet, he hides behind a curtain just before Anna and
her brother, Rochefort, enter the room.

Both Cherubino and Smeton are given moments in their respective plots when
they find themselves hiding in places where they should not be. In fact, with Cherubino we see this twice, one time with Susanna and the Countess (and we hear about
a third time with Barbarina).[16] All three incidents provoke the increasing ire of the
Count, yet ultimately result in harmless consequences. In the first act Cherubino
comes across as a naughty boy, caught and then punished by the Count, who sends
him off to the military to grow up and become a man. In the second act, Cherubino
evades the military and ends up hiding in the Countess's closet. Though the Countess's reputation is on the line, everything works out when Susanna intervenes at
the last moment and saves the situation.[17] With Cherubino there is a spirit of playfulness in his popping up unexpectedly rather than the real danger of something
seriously going wrong. With Smeton, however, the stakes are higher and the conclusion different: he bears the blame. Cherubino gets away with his shenanigans
because, ultimately, he is still a boy. Smeton, on the other hand, is held responsible
as a man.

In the scenes which lead into the first act finale Smeton quietly witnesses Rochefort compel his sister to see Percy and the subsequent meeting between Anna and her former lover. Though the lovers do not know that Smeton is watching them, we, in the audience, know that he has been there the whole time. Hidden in the shadows the travesti pageboy, in love with the heroine, is reduced to silence as he watches the tenor woo the soprano. In the preceding moments when he was alone, Smeton's declaration of love was directed to the stolen miniature of Anna. He can sing of love, and, as in his first act serenade, his voice can even evoke her feelings of love; however, he can never directly engage her voice about love. As he watches Anna and Percy from behind the curtain, he is cut off from any interaction with her as a potential lover. When he sees Percy draw his sword to dramatically emphasize that he would rather die than live without Anna, the only thing Smeton can do is try to protect her when he fears for her safety.

Yet his well-intentioned action comes to disastrous ends. Shocked to discover that Smeton has overheard their conversation, Anna and Percy's ensuing confusion attract the attention of the court. When Enrico arrives, Smeton heroically rushes to Anna's aid, defending her innocence.[18] As Smeton offers himself to be killed if the King finds anything wrong, Smeton dramatically opens his doublet to underscore his fervor. With this ill-timed gesture, the hidden portrait of Anna slips out and falls to the ground. The stolen picture gives Enrico enough evidence to accuse Anna of adultery. Later at the court tribunal, the King tricks Smeton into thinking that the only way he can help Anna is to admit that they are guilty. Thus it is Smeton who, inadvertently, seals Anna's fate.

Smeton's position in the drama partially fulfills a couple of different functions. Reading on a surface level, he is a page role who is there to provide a pleasant diversion in his harp-accompanied song while the Anna and the court await the King's arrival. The opening chorus had already set up a tense atmosphere; the men and women of the court have noted that Enrico's attentions might have drifted to someone else:

Opening Chorus of Act 1, *Anna Bolena*

Cavalieri	*Gentlemen*
Né venne il Re?	Is the King not here yet?
Silenzio. Ancor non venne.	Silence! He is still not here.
Ed ella?	And she [the Queen]?
Ne geme in cor, ma simula.	She is heartsick, but conceals it.
Tramonta omai sua stella.	Her star is setting.
D'Enrico eil cor volubile arde d'un altro amor.	Henry's volatile heart burns with another love.
Fors'è serbata, ahi misera! A duol maggior,	Ah, the wretched soul! Perhaps a greater woe is in store for her.
Fors'è serbata, ahi misera! Oh ciel! Ad onta e duol maggior!	Oh, heaven, the wretched soul! Perhaps greater shame and woe is reserved for her!

The scene presents what turns out to be a futile vigil because Enrico never shows up. It is within this context that Anna requests that Smeton enliven her court with music. Rejected by her husband, Smeton's attention and flattery in his music is welcome. Yet his entertainment heads off in the wrong direction when his song about first love (his own veiled love for the Queen) does not calm her agitation, but rather provokes her anxiety as she dreams of her first love for Percy.

On another level, Smeton is a travesti figure in love. Such heroic roles were still being written, albeit in limited numbers, when *Anna Bolena* was composed; Smeton's behavior in his second number is closer to this model.[19] His extended solo scene in the Queen's apartments, complete with a twenty-measure orchestral introduction and full aria, give him the opportunity to explicate his love for Anna. His words are compelling and more directly express the depth of his emotions than in his earlier song. With heightened language he reveals the "palpitations of his heart" and the "desire, courage, and voracious passion" he harbors for Anna. He kisses her picture twice and refers to the enchanted "spell" (incanto) that he feels has bound them together. Later in the scene when Percy unexpectedly draws his sword, it is Smeton's sense of valor that propels him from the safety of his hiding place to heroically save her life. Eager to prove his devotion to protecting her honor, it is his dramatic gesture when he undoes his doublet offering himself to Enrico that sabotages his intentions when the incriminating stolen picture of Anna falls to the ground.

Though Enrico, and for that matter the rest of the court, might see Smeton as a mischievous young boy (à la Cherubino) and not really believe that Anna has had a liaison with him, the situation deserves further scrutiny. As a travesti role who has just been given the opportunity to sing, center stage, about his beloved in a florid style and then demonstrate his bravery by risking his life for her, Smeton cannot easily be dismissed as a lovesick boy. Nevertheless, his heroism goes awry at the end when it turns out to that it is his testimony, albeit manipulated and misguided by the King, which ends up convicting Anna.

Smeton's love is neither exclusively a categorical adolescent infatuation nor a heroic conceit. With the presence of the "grown-up" vocal contenders in the tenor and baritone (Percy and Enrico), Smeton ends up being an only marginally viable rival for Anna's attentions. Though Anna never gives any indication that she notices, let alone returns, his amorous glances, the rhetoric surrounding the presentation of his second number reveals the seriousness of his feelings and importance of his character. Tangled in a web of love intrigues that involve Anna, Percy, Giovanna, and the King, Donizetti weaves together two different dramatic directions and associations within Smeton's voice. As the amorous page, his adolescent youth implies the child not-yet-full adult hero. In his early oblique song about love for the Queen, his intentions are kept veiled, and the depth of his character is not fully revealed. Yet once his true feelings are brought to light in his second number, his role takes on a different function. Though he hides and tries to keep this new persona hidden, the inevitable happens, and he is thrust in the middle of the central conflict as one of Anna's illicit relationships. This metamorphosis from pageboy to rival suitor is possible because his voice and male attire simultaneously signal parallel sets of expectations when given the proper stimulus. In such cases the voice, as well as the character, are both cross-dressed. The double interpretation of Smeton drawing from the page and heroic travesti traditions enrich the layered meanings of his role in the vocal and visual drama.

Donizetti extended the function of the page travesti in a similar way again four years later in the role of Arturo in *Rosmonda d'Inghilterra* (premiered in Florence at the Teatro della Pergola in 1834). Based on a libretto Romani had adapted from his earlier collaboration with Carlo Coccia in 1829 (*Rosmonda*, La Fenice, Venice), Donizetti was the third composer to set this subject with this libretto (the second was Luigi Majocchi, whose *Rosmonda* was performed in Milan, 1831). Though Donizetti decreased the size of Arturo, his character still retains elements of the page and the heroic travesti.[20]

In a similar assortment of voices to *Anna Bolena*, two principal male roles (tenor and bass-baritone) and three substantial parts for women's voices, *Rosmonda* re-aligns the relationships between the characters. Like Anna, the title character in *Rosmonda* is involved in an illicit love with the tenor, this time King Henry II (Enrico). Clifford, the bass-baritone and Rosamond's (Rosmonda's) father, is the other leading role for a man's voice. The three roles for women's voices are Rosmonda, Eleanor of Aquitaine (Queen Leonora of Guyenne), and Arturo, the travesti page.

Unlike Smeton, Arturo has interactions with all of the other principals. In *Anna Bolena*, Smeton's dual character resides primarily in his connection to Anna: he is her page, and, if he could have his way, he would also be her lover. In *Rosmonda* we learn more about Arturo's history. We find out in his first scene, immediately following the opening chorus, that Queen Leonora found him as an orphan and took him under her protection as a page. While the King is away fighting in Ireland, he uses Arturo to keep watch over Rosmonda, Enrico's new love interest, whom he has hidden in a tower. By the middle of act 1, Arturo meets Clifford, the final principal, when the bass-baritone is brought to meet the King's mistress and is horrified to find out she is his own daughter. Arturo and Clifford sing together for a slightly more extended period later in the second act.

In the beginning of the opera, Leonora has wrested the secret from Arturo that the King's mistress is ensconced in the tower; Leonora has also astutely figured out that Arturo has fallen in love with his charge. From this first appearance, Arturo is presented as the young travesti page whose love seems to be an infatuation. However, the text and music in his first scene with Rosmonda suggest otherwise. As with Smeton's concealed love song to Anna, Arturo's text declares his love, and Rosmonda reinterprets his words to refer to her beloved tenor.

Yet the "veiled" nature of Arturo's first scene with Rosmonda is achieved quite differently than Smeton's entertainment for Anna's court. The formal structure of Smeton's love song is strophic in two parallel stanzas with eight lines each. Both verses employ the same music, and when Anna interrupts him after the first line of his next verse, the opening melody of the now-familiar music lets us know that this would have been the third stanza. Arturo's music with Rosmonda follows a much different plan. Unlike Smeton, Arturo has the opportunity to express his feelings in a type of mini-duet that he sings with Rosmonda. Though their music together is not written as a conventional duet—it takes place within the larger context of Rosmonda's entrance aria—they sing a considerable portion of the cantabile section as if they were singing in a traditional duet form.[21] As Arturo approaches the tower, he hears Rosmonda singing and responds to her music while he is still off-stage:

The Quasi-duet between Rosmonda and Arturo within the Framework of Rosmonda's Entrance Aria, *Rosmonda d'Inghilterra*

CANTABILE

Rosamonda

Perchè non ho del vento	Why do I not have the indefatigable
L'infaticabil volo?	Flight of the wind?
Lunge in estraneo suolo,	Far upon foreign soil
Ti seguirei, mio ben.	I would follow you, my love.
Dove tu sei . . . sen volino	Wherever you are . . . at least
I miei sopsiri almen	Let my sighs fly to you.

Rosmonda listens to the off-stage repetition of the last two lines of her melody by Arturo and comments:

Tenero Arturo! Ei sol m'ascolta, ei	Tender Arturo! He alone hears me.
solo in queste a'miei martir mura	Within these walls that are deaf to my
tacenti mi compiange, e risponde a	sufferings he alone pities me and re-
miei lamenti.	sponds to my laments.

Arturo (sings from offstage)

Perchè non ho del sole	Why do I not have the all-seeing
Gli onniveggenti rai?	Rays of the sun?
Sempre dovunque vai	Wherever you go
Io ti vedrei, mio ben.	I would always see you, my love.
Ah! Ove tu sei—ti veggano	Ah! Wherever you are—at least
I miei sospiri almen.	Let my sighs be with you.

Rosmonda and Arturo

Invan da te mi parte	In vain the course of adverse fate
Di rio destin tenore:	Parts me from you:
Varca ogni spazio amore,	Love crosses over all space
Teco son io, mio ben.	So that I am with you, my love.
Lontane ancor s'incontrino	Though still far apart, at least
L'anime nostre almen.	Let our souls be together.

The scene opens with a lengthy orchestral introduction that features a languid oboe melody as Rosmonda is seen alone in her tower. After an extended recitative, she sings the first six line stanza of her cantabile, "Perchè non ho del vento." Following her cadenza, Arturo makes his vocal entrance and repeats her two last lines from offstage. Rosmonda's response to hearing Arturo's voice is one of pleasure; besides Enrico, he is the only one who knows she is in the tower, and she welcomes his company. From offstage Arturo continues with his own stanza that follows the same basic melody (without all of the extended melismas) that Rosmonda sang and picks up on the same textual theme—the wistful longing to be with the beloved. Rather than repeating Rosmonda's text about having the energy of the wind to fly to the beloved, Arturo's stanza provides a complementary image of the all-seeing rays of the sun that could follow the loved one and be with her forever. Arturo sings the first four lines alone and then is joined by Rosmonda for the final two verses—"at least let my sighs be with you wherever you are." In the third stanza Rosmonda leads, and Arturo sings with her at the end of each line. In the repetition of the last two verses, "though still far apart, let our souls be together," the two voices sing intertwined together in a cadenza, typical of most duets at this point in the form—the end of the cantabile section.[22] The "duet" ends here and the next two sections, the tempo di mezzo and cabaletta, are sung alone by Rosmonda, thus ultimately fulfilling the expectations for the solo aria promised at the beginning of this scene.

The intimacy created by the interaction of the two voices in the cantabile section of this aria is juxtaposed to the theme of the distance between two lovers. Rosmonda sings of her physical distance from "Edegardo," the name her beloved told her is his, whom she has not seen in three months. The distance for Arturo lies not only in the spatial geography between the offstage hall in the tower outside of Rosmonda's suite and her onstage chamber, but also in the difference between his status as the page and that of his rival. While Arturo longs for Rosmonda to be his, she sees him only as her temporary protector as she awaits Edegardo's return.

Edegardo is the identity Enrico took on to woo Rosmonda. The King, who is married to Leonora, realizes that if he were to try to seduce Rosmonda with his true identity, her innocent and virtuous nature would never allow her to return his love. Hence, the king created the persona of Edegardo to initially win her over, and, once he had her devotion, he figured that he would be free to reveal his real name. Rosmonda naively believes Edegardo to be unmarried and devoted to her alone; she has no idea who he really is. As she sings from her tower, her beloved Edegardo is an idealized hero who has won her heart.

Though Rosmonda sings to Edegardo, it is Arturo who responds. Arturo hears the song from outside of her room and replies. His wish to be the "all-seeing rays of the sun" seem appropriate given his role as her sentinel; however, within the layers of their quasi duet, he ends up being the voice that is heard and not seen. The visual and sonic elements come together to emphasize the dual resonance of these two women's voices: aurally they invoke the vocal pairing of the heroic travesti role-soprano couple, yet visually they reinforce, or at least support, the tenor-soprano pair that Rosmonda laments. As Rosmonda hears Arturo (from offstage) she thinks of her love for Edegardo. Though Rosmonda and Arturo are far apart in terms of their individual intentions, their voices are united in harmony, as if the only way they can share such a time together is through sound.

Noticeably missing from the opera is the expected love duet in which the tenor and soprano, despite all the odds against them, confess their love to each other. We almost get this situation near the end of the opera when Enrico reiterates his love for Rosmonda and reminds her of her love for him. Nonetheless, Rosmonda is quick to point out that her love was for Edegardo, and that she is not able to love the King, whose love should be with his Queen. In both of her scenes with Enrico,

Rosmonda's resolve is strong. We do not see the young woman seduced who is wavering between duty and love; instead, we see her pain and shame of having loved unwisely. Whatever love she had felt for Enrico, the man, has been transferred to her idealized memory of Edegardo.

The love duet that does not happen between Rosmonda and the King takes place, to a certain extent, between Rosmonda and Arturo. With Arturo's voice emanating from offstage in her first act aria, their ensuing duet centers on each one's expression of love. The feelings Arturo's voice conjures up in Rosmonda for Edegardo provide the most intimate vocal coupling in the opera, both in the text and in the interaction, between the two voices. The love between the high soprano and her beloved is transferred from Edegardo to Rosmonda's hearing Arturo's voice. Though at this point in the opera she has not yet had her first scene with Enrico, we can see in retrospect that her music with Arturo is the only point in the opera where male and female characters have sung with hope to each other about love. While it is clear from Rosmonda's text in between the first and second stanzas of the cantabile and in her tempo di mezzo that she recognizes Arturo's voice and her love is specifically directed to Edegardo, it is Arturo who shares her music and participates in this dialogue.

When Rosmonda first learns exactly who Edegardo is from her father (Clifford), she is heartsick and decides to have nothing more to do with Edegardo/Enrico. Even in the two points in the opera when Rosmonda and Enrico sing together (both after she finds out his real identity), she is adamant in refusing him. Rosmonda's first scene in the opera with Enrico takes place near the end of act 1, just moments after she has learned that he is the King. As Enrico approaches, his voice is heard before he is seen. At the sound of his voice Rosmonda denounces him as her betrayer and falls into a swoon. When she regains consciousness a few moments later, she denounces him again and reveals that she now knows who he is and that he is married to Leonora:

Enrico
Ah! Sentimi!   Ah! Hear me!

Clifford
È vano!   It is in vain!

Enrico
Ascoltami almen, Rosmonda, tu!   Rosmonda, at least listen to me!

Rosmonda
Io ti ascoltai . . .   I listened to you [already] . . .

The King's tactic in the duet is strategic: Enrico implores Rosmonda to hear him. When Clifford tells him there is no use, Enrico tries again: "*Listen to me*, at least, Rosmonda." Letting him know that, though it worked before, even this—his voice—will not help now, she responds, "I have already *listened* to you."

Near the end of the opera Rosmonda has her second, and final, scene with Enrico. She has just agreed to her father's wish that she leave England, but Enrico inopportunely appears shortly before she is to depart. Once again, they speak specifically about the sound of his voice:

Enrico-Rosmonda Duet Excerpt, Act 2, *Rosmonda d'Inghilterra*[23]

EXCERPT FROM OPENING SCENA

Enrico
Rosmonda!   Rosmonda!

Rosmonda
(*Oh fatal voce!*)   (*Oh fatal voice!*)

Enrico
Edegardo non odi?   *Do you not hear your Edegardo?*

TEMPO D'ATTACCO

Rosmonda
Ah! *Mai non fossi stato Edegardo tu! Mai non t'avessi nel mio ritiro udito! A che mai vieni? Il mio pianto a mirar? Onta mi fora, barbaro innanzi a te versarne ancora.*

Ah! *Would you had never been Edegardo! Would that in my retreat I had never heard you!* Why ever do you come? To see my tears? Barbarous man, in your presence it would be shameful of me to shed more.

Enrico
Più non ne verserai, mai più, Rosmonda. *Già d'Enrico sposa t'acclamano i primate, e d'Inghilterra universal desio, ti chiama al trono . . .*

You will shed no more, Rosmonda. No more. *Already the primates acclaim you as the bride of Henry, and the wishes of all England call you to the throne . . .*

Rosmonda
Al pianto, al pianto condannata io sono. Tu stesso al padre or rendimi . . . consola il veglio afflitto . . . minori il tuo delitto quest'atto di pietà.

To weep, to weep I am condemned. Do you yourself restore me to my father . . . Bring comfort to the afflicted old man . . . Let this act of compassion mitigate your crime.

Enrico
Te vuol rapirmi il barbaro te sposa altrui destina; quando sarai Regina grazia, e favore avrà.

The barbarous man wishes to tear you from me. He intends to make you the wife of another. When you are Queen he will find grace and favor.

Rosmonda
Regina! Io? . . . Nol credere; mai nol sarò.

Queen! I? Do not believe it; never will I be Queen.

Enrico
Già il sei.

You already are.

Rosmonda
Ah! *Sol di te son vittima . . . Ah! Fuggi dagli occhi miei. Ch'io più non t'oda . . .*

Ah! *I am only your victim . . . Ah! Flee from my sight. Let me no longer hear you.*

Enrico	
Ingrata! Tanto sei tu cambiata! Sì ria mercè tu dai all'amor mio fedel?	Thankless girl! How you have changed! Do you give such evil thanks in exchange for my fidelity?

Rosmonda	
Il deggio . . . io lo giurai.	I must . . . I have sworn it.

Enrico	
A chi?	To whom?

Rosmonda	
Lo giurai all'onore, al Ciel.	I have sworn it to honor, to Heaven.

CANTABILE

Enrico	
Giurasti un dì . . .	There was a day when you swore . . .
rammentalo . . .	remember it . . .
D'amarmi ognor giurasti;	When you swore to love me forever.
Presente il Ciel medesimo	You called upon Heaven itself
Ai giuri tuoi chiamsti:	to witness your oaths:
Speranze, onor, ventura,	Hopes, honor, future, fortune,
Ah! Tutto ponevi in me . . .	Ah! All you placed in me . . .
Ah! Non sarai spergiura	Ah! You will not go back on your word,
Non mancherai di fè.	You will not prove faithless.

Rosmonda	
Non io, non io dimentica	You know that it is not I, not I
Son di que' giuri, il sai:	Who forgets these oaths:
Quell' Edgardo rendimi	*Give me back that Edegardo*
Cui l'onor mio fidai . . .	To whom I entrusted my honor . . .
Quell'alma onesta e pura,	That honest and pure soul,
Ah! Quell nobil cor dov'è?	Ah! Where is that noble heart?
Oh! Eterna mia sventura!	Oh! My eternal misfortune!
Qui non vegg'io che il Re.	Here I see but the King.

When Enrico calls out her name, she replies: "Oh *fatal voice!*" In a move to recapture her heart he asks her, "Do you not *hear* your Edegardo?" Rosmonda's response is a bit curious. Not only does she say that she wishes that he, the King, had never been Edegardo, but she adds that she wishes that she had never *heard* him. Instead of saying that she "would have rather never *seen*" or "*met* him" (e.g., "Mai non ti avessi nel mio ritiro *visto*" [or *ti encontrato*]), two more typical statements, she highlights his voice and its implied irresistible—as well as destructive—charms. Enrico continues to try and keep the illusion going a little longer by referring to her as the Queen. She responds by calling herself a "victim" (a victim of his voice) and then appeals to him again, even more fervently, to "flee from my sight, that I might no longer *hear* you."

Rosmonda can, and certainly does, hear the difference between the travesti voice and the tenor voice. In their first scenes with her, she is given the opportunity to hear both Arturo and Enrico from offstage, and she instantly recognizes each one.

She also responds to each voice differently. Her reactions show us that Henry's voice sounds dangerous; it makes her swoon into unconsciousness, and she refers it as that "fatal voice." It is a voice that victimizes her and one from which she tries to escape. Arturo, by contrast, has a voice that sounds safe and sympathetic. Between the first two stanzas of her first act cantabile where she reflects upon his offstage voice, she calls him "tender Arturo" and mentions how he is the only one who *hears* her and is sympathetic to her suffering. In the tempo di mezzo, she again turns her attentions to "gentle Arturo" and comments on how young he is, as was she, to have learned of such longing and grief:

Excerpt from Rosmonda's Tempo di Mezzo, Act 1, *Rosmonda d'Inghilterra*

Rosmonda

Oh come tosto,	Oh, how quickly
Il giovine gentil la mesta apprese	The gentle youth has learned
Canzone del dolor! Anch'io l'appresi	The song of grief! I, too, learned it
Dell'età sull'aurora.	In the first dawn of youth.

In Arturo's solo number in the second act, we get to hear another version of the wishful love song directed to the distant beloved, this time, one that is entirely his own when he allows himself to dream about the possibility of having his feelings for Rosmonda returned. Ever aware of the power of the King, his rival, the central theme in the cantabile section of his aria is the genuine love he can offer Rosmonda—a gift, he promises, that is far more valuable than the material glory and glitter of the throne. His cabaletta celebrates the "audacious hope" that he might one day experience happiness with her:

Excerpt from Arturo's Act 2 Aria, *Rosmonda d'Inghilterra*

Cantabile

Arturo

Io non ti posso offrir	I cannot offer you
Nè Gloria nè splendor:	Glory or splendor:
Ah! Cara, non ho che amor,	Ah! My dear, I have only love.
Non ho che un core.	I have only one heart.
Ma questo cor morir	But this heart would not hesitate
Non sdegnerà per te;	To die for you.
Ma lo splendor d'un rè	*Even the splendor of a king*
Non vale amor.	Is not as valuable as love.

Cabaletta

Ritorna a spledere	Come back to shine within me
Audace speme;	*Audacious hope;*
Possente all'anima	Speak strongly once more
Favella ancor.	Within my soul.
E contro i palpiti	And to the palpitations
D'un cor che geme,	Of a heart that groans

Opponi i fervidi	Oppose the fervent
Desir d'amor.	Desires of love.

Just like the actions immediately following Smeton's solo scene four years earlier in *Anna Bolena,* Arturo plays a critical role in setting the final denouement in motion. Both opera plots are constructed in such a way that the travesti role has the opportunity to "save" the heroine. Unlike Smeton, Arturo has a practical plan to do so. In *Anna Bolena,* Smeton believes that he can save Anna by denouncing her (because the King has cunningly misled him). If Smeton had not fallen prey to the King's deception, and instead had told the truth, it is likely that the tribunal would not have condemned her. In *Rosmonda* the travesti role is given a more viable opportunity. Clifford has proposed a plan to have Rosmonda and Arturo leave England together and get married. This would allow Rosmonda to "save face" for her own reputation, as well as for her father's, and it fulfills Arturo's dreams of finally winning his beloved. Although the plan is foiled, and Leonora ends up killing her rival, for a short period of time, Arturo is the legitimate betrothed to Rosmonda.

With this development, the romantic tension underlying the Arturo-Rosmonda "duet" in their first scene together is highlighted and given its proper release. Arturo is no longer the infatuated page, but rather the plausible match—the deus ex machina device—for the title heroine. For the original audiences, such a conclusion would not have been such an aural stretch. With the heroic travesti tradition still in practice (though certainly on the wane), cross-dressed male characters had multiple options for their position in the plot. Arturo's part could easily be reheard as heroic, given his quasi love duet with Rosmonda in the first act and the noble sincerity of his love song for her in the second act. But the presence of Enrico as the tenor and primary contender for Rosmonda's hand should discourage any serious consideration of Arturo as suitor; how could the old-fashioned travesti practice compete with the new innovations in tenor singing?

The rhetoric of the heroic voice is complicated in this opera through the different male characters that court Rosmonda. Rather than Enrico and Arturo, it is Edegardo's voice that has won the love of Rosmonda: she has fallen in love with "Edegardo's voice." Yet Enrico's flawed character (in his deception and seducing her into an adulterous relationship) makes his voice sound dangerous to Rosmonda, and she steadfastly refuses him despite his promises of fame and wealth in their two scenes together. She treats him as an antihero and rejects both his philandering character and his seductive voice. However, even before she finds out about him, she allows herself to enter into a love duet style of singing with Arturo's disembodied voice while he is offstage. She can still be true to Enrico because her words are directed to him (as Edegardo) and, one could argue, she is not singing to Arturo as a character—he is not physically in the room with her—only his voice. She sings with Arturo because his voice sounds familiar, she knows it and feels comfortable with it.

Arturo's voice is familiar—both to Rosmonda (because he has been watching over her for three months) and to the audience who is accustomed to women singing en travesti. To both Rosmonda onstage and the audience in the theater, Arturo's treble-timbred voice sounds safe because it is reminiscent of the heroic travesti singers. Rosmonda and Arturo's voices are powerfully drawn together through this history; their combined sound evokes nostalgia for the earlier tradition of singing. Being so comfortably matched vocally, their voices engage in a deeper relationship, one more intimate than their quite-different intentions. When Clifford suggests leaving England and marrying Arturo to Rosmonda as an eleventh-hour solution, the audience is able to accept this "fatherly advice" as a plausible option because we have already been set up to think of them together when we heard their voices coupled earlier. Their failure to escape from England comments less on Arturo's effectiveness as the hero than on the competing need for the newer conceit of the dying heroine and a tragic ending. Had the opera been written ten years earlier, the chance would be greater that the love between Rosmonda and Arturo could have been further developed in the plot, and they would have escaped together successfully and happily. Since Enrico has been revealed as a negative character, Arturo could have very easily stepped in as the new hero.

The fact that Arturo has been positioned in such a way between the pageboy and heroic travesti traditions reveals the sophistication in the way his voice could be heard both onstage by the other characters and offstage by the audience. As the page, Arturo should be a secondary role who assists and/or meddles in the affairs of others. Cherubino and Smeton are elevated in the importance they are each given, with solo numbers and tight connections to the unfolding of the plot; they can hardly be thought of as smaller comprimario roles. However, Cherubino and Smeton's romantic aspirations for the main women in the drama can hardly be taken seriously because each woman has a more viable match (Countess-Count, Susanna-Figaro; Anna-Percy/King, Giovanna-King). In *Rosmonda* it seems as though both Queen Leonora and Rosmonda contend for the same man. Yet things are not fully what they seem because Rosmonda really pines for Edegardo, a feigned identity. It is clear that Rosmonda did not fall in love with the character—the attributes and personality—of the King, for when she finds out who he really is, she shuns him. It was the voice that had initially seduced her. When that voice is paired with the character of the King, she regards it as "dangerous" and "fatal" and feels she is its "victim." Rosmonda only admits to having loved Edegardo. Even when the King tries to invoke Edegardo, she cannot pretend and hears only the King's voice.

At different points in the opera Arturo gets to assume the identity of Edegardo. When we are first introduced to him, he appears to be the simple travesti pageboy role as we see him attend Queen Leonora. However, his character is transformed with Rosmonda. From his first appearance with her, his voice gets to stand in for the distant beloved. As he sings from offstage, he responds from afar as the sonic embodiment of the absent Edegardo. With this voice, Rosmonda is temporarily appeased, because she carries on the illusion of a love duet with Edegardo. Though it was Enrico's tenor voice that had initially seduced her before the opera began, we (the audience) get to hear the female travesti voice behind Arturo as the voice that carries out the deed. Unlike Cherubino and Smeton, Arturo is given the chance to step in for the hero when he and Rosmonda plan to leave England and get married. At this point, the transformation is complete, and Arturo is given the opportunity to become Edegardo: what Rosmonda has dreamed of having happen with Edegardo, Arturo is able to now fulfill.

The phantom voice of Edegardo acts as a proxy lover for both Enrico and Arturo. The problem is that Rosmonda has fallen in love with her understanding of who Edegardo is, which is in fact neither man's true identity and, consequently, turns out not to exist as a real person. In 1834 Enrico, the tenor, is her "correct" match vocally. Ironically, it is Enrico's flawed character that seduces and deceives that is expressed through his innovative Romantic tenor voice. Arturo better fulfills Rosmonda's vision of her ideal beloved. Arturo is devoted to her, available (unmarried), and most probably closer to her age than the King is. Arturo's noble intentions and heroic character present his old-fashioned treble travesti voice. In their first scene together, the presence of Arturo's offstage voice singing interwoven with Rosmonda's invokes the love scenes between the heroic travest roles and the soprano.[24]

At different points in the plot, both Enrico and Arturo conjure up Edegardo's voice to elicit Rosmonda's love. Almost unknowingly, Arturo evokes Rosmonda's feelings for Edegardo by responding to her aria from offstage and providing the missing voice for the absent Edegardo. Though Arturo sings of his own love for Rosmonda, he inadvertently stumbles upon her reverie for Edegardo, and becomes his vocal stand-in for Rosmonda's wistful longing.

Though we do not get to see the King's seduction of Rosmonda, as it occurs in the prehistory to the opera, we see his successful results with Rosmonda's willingness to be installed in a tower indefinitely to await his return.[25] First performed by renowned French tenor Gilbert-Louis Duprez (1806–96), Enrico was sung by the leading pioneer of the chest voice high C (the do di petto) and the new style of Romantic tenor singing with heft in the top register of the voice. Not only was Duprez one of the first *tenore di forza* (tenor of force), he also represented a break with the earlier style of Rossini singing, the so-called *tenore di grazia* (graceful tenor), that looked back to the eighteenth-century bel canto model.[26]

The voice that first seduced Rosmonda was a newcomer in opera, the new Romantic tenor. The added commentary in the vocal drama is that this new hero is dangerous to the older aesthetics heard in the travesti hero. As Donizetti's *Rosmonda* presents the new Romantic tenor hero along with hints of the older tradition, Rosmonda is alternately paired with Enrico and Arturo. While Arturo's offstage voice becomes a plausible substitute for Edegardo's voice, Arturo's functions as a faux-heroic travesti voice. Within this context, the ghostly presence of Edegardo provides the perfect metaphor for the 1830s heroic role. Her ideal lover is her new memory of the heroic tenor encompassed within the trustworthy sound of the female travesti voice.

When Cherubino and Smeton find themselves in places they should not be, they each hide. Cherubino emerges unscathed, yet Smeton has to pay the price for being accused of what he only dreams (being Anna's lover). Cherubino has a much less active role in the second half of Mozart's opera. In the conclusion of *Figaro*, Cherubino ends up paired with Barbarina, a compromise between the maturity of settling down and youthfulness—he is associated with a young girl rather than the more experienced and mature figures of Susanna and the Countess. In 1830 Smeton enters as a dream-struck pageboy infatuated with his Queen and is transformed into one of Anna's suitors, complete with assumed adulterous experience. As a victim of circumstance, he gets caught in a situation beyond his control when he confronts Anna's real love interests: Percy and, albeit for a short time, Enrico.

Arturo is not given the explicit direction to hide; however, his voice precedes his physical entrance in his first scene with Rosmonda during their "mini-duet" within her cavatina. As the image of "disguise" was prominent in Meyerbeer's second woman, the veiled voice emerges as a primary aural conceit for Smeton and Arturo. Though they sing *to* the beloved, they cannot sing *with* her in her presence. As Semeton tries to sing a love song to Anna in his first number, she misses his meaning. Smeton's voice agitates her as it reminds her of her first, and still true, love with Percy, the tenor. Meanwhile, Smeton silently witnesses the real love duet between Percy and Anna from behind the curtain, when his own declaration of love to her was made to her portrait as he sang alone in her empty chamber. When Arturo's voice gets to stand in for the real beloved (Enrico, the tenor), Rosamonda can hear him, but not see him. He is hidden from her view, but the sound of his voice is able to remind her of the man she loves. It is as if the female voice were allowed to cross-dress aurally while it said two things simultaneously. Arturo's voice can be heard projecting the sound of the page as well as the hero for all of those who know how to listen to the heroic travesti tradition: Rosamonda, the original audiences, and opera lovers today.

In their respective operas Smeton and Arturo, two early pageboy travesti roles of the nineteenth century, contend with the new tenor hero. As they assume the position of the page, their relationship to the first woman shows vestiges of their past as heroic roles. Though they are not beloved in a romantic sense by the heroine, this does not discourage their feelings. They daydream and sing about their love for her with genuine sincerity in both their emotion and their stylized music. While today we might be tempted to look back at these two pageboys as naïve youths in love, perhaps a less serious love subplot, there is nothing to suggest that they were written as parody or satire: they straddle the line between the hero and the pageboy. While they still maintain enough of their "masculinity" to be plausibly paired with the title-role first woman, they are tamed so as not to be "virile" enough to win the heart of this heroine. Smeton and Arturo fit in between the hero and the pageboy, revealing aspects of both character types over the course of the opera. They signal a multivocal role: a hybridized type of voice.

5 Women's Voices in Motion: Voices behind the Romantic Heroine

The Death of the Heroine

Between the hero and female leading characters, the voice of the Romantic heroine was born. She is ultimately a hybridized voice who found inspiration from both the eighteenth-century bel canto singing technique of the castrati and the interests of nineteenth-century composers and singers that led to a new articulation of realism for their own time. While the bel canto legacy provided a foundation for the new aesthetic, the Romantic heroine inherited several voices that were subsumed into one female character.

Both of the women's voices in the travesti operas (the heroine and the female travesti role) fed into the Romantic heroine, for both kinds of female singers were accustomed to singing primary roles. Leading up to the Romantic heroine, the types of roles for women in opera varied considerably; the female voice that rang triumphant at the conclusion one night could be silenced in a tragic outcome the next. Around 1830, as it became more fashionable for women to consistently sing as female characters, a generation of travesti singers was pressured to move into the Romantic heroine roles. Some of them continued to specialize in the travesti roles, some retired, and some took up the challenge to compete with the singers who had performed consistently as the first woman.

For my purposes here, what I am calling the classic formation of the "Romantic heroine" involves the simultaneous occurrence of three primary factors. (This is not meant to be an inclusive list of all characteristics of every heroine in Romantic opera, but rather a working set of criteria that most clearly illustrates what led into the secondo ottocento.) My discussion of the Romantic heroine refers to (1) operas with one leading role for a woman's voice that (2) portrays a female character who (3) dies by the conclusion.

Of course, there are precedents before 1830 with operas that have one leading woman (e.g., Rossini's Armida, 1817) as well as, though much less frequently, operas where this leading female character dies at the end (e.g., Rossini's Desdemona in Otello, 1816).[1] Moreover, in the 1830s through the 1840s, it was still not uncommon for operas to retain two leading roles for women. In these years, for operas with two prima donnas, women's voices depicted either two female characters (which was quite common) or a female character and heroic travesti hero (much less common after 1830 with the rise of the heroic tenor). The 1840s saw a decade where it was popular to write operas with two leading female characters (a first and second woman). Yet around the midpoint of the century, in Italy, the norm becomes operas with one, singular principal woman: the full-fledged Romantic heroine.

The difference is that the Romantic heroine is a new type of leading woman in opera. Starting around 1830, with increasing frequency, she becomes a standard character in Italian opera so that by 1850 it is uncommon to have an opera with two principal roles for women's voices. The Romantic heroine loves the tenor hero (not a travesti hero), and she dies at the end. The 1820s through the 1830s were transitional years where some leading singers sang travesti heroes, second women, and first women heroines interchangeably. What these voices, such as Maria Malibran's and Giuditta Pasta's, so compellingly demonstrate is that the Romantic heroine is not a continuation of either the second woman or the beloved first woman; instead she is a *combination* of both kinds of roles for women. Hence, the Romantic heroine is a hybrid female role; she combines the characterizations of both types of early primo ottocento female characters. As the singular heroine, she is the object of the tenor's affection, and she returns his love.

As the Romantic heroine faces the inevitable barrier to the man she loves, she has more options in the plot than the first woman who preceded her. After 1830 it becomes standard for the beloved heroine to die, whether she is the first woman (in an opera with two leading women) or the singular Romantic heroine. Yet these two types of female characters have different deaths. Unlike first women such as Creusa (in Mayr's *Medea in Corinto*), who is unwittingly poisoned by Medea's bewitched robe, or Rosmonda (in Donizetti's *Rosmonda d'Inghilterra*), who is brutally stabbed by Leonora, the singular Romantic heroine does not helplessly suffer at the hand of a jealous rival or spurned lover. The Romantic heroine stands up to her situation and, frequently, tries to change it. Therefore, though the Romantic heroine is doomed to die, her death follows a confrontation with injustice; she dies for what she believes in.

My use of the term "Romantic heroine" overlaps with the characterizations of operatic women in recent opera scholarship. Though there are many compelling responses to Catherine Clément's now classic construction of the weak and suffering heroine, one must also concede that for most of the nineteenth century the heroine in Italian opera does, indeed, meet her untimely demise. Yet the Romantic heroine à la Clément, who loves too much and then dies, seems to have little in common with the behavior seen in other types of roles for women's voices. How could she be related to the noble valor of the heroic travesti tradition or the fearless and successful second women in Meyerbeer's Italian operas who undergo cross-dressed disguises to prove their devotion? How could she have the ruthless actions of Medea, who murders all who get in her way (including her own children), and Donizetti's Leonora, who stabs Rosmonda in cold blood? The so-called undone and hapless victims of the Romantic era have been seen as though they come from a completely different stock than the second women who not only survive the opera's conclusion but also are frequently left alone, outside of any romantic coupling, at the end.[2]

The Romantic heroine has the second woman in her ancestry and utilizes this resourcefulness and energy to stand up to her fate. While Donizetti's Lucia certainly does not present a twenty-first-century modern woman, her death reveals a greater agency than many of her first woman colleagues that compels her to do something instead of passively await her fate.[3] Since the first performance of Donizetti's *Lucia di Lammermoor* in 1835 audiences have loved Lucia despite, or perhaps because of, her descent into madness that allows her to fight the system that binds her to marry against her heart. Within the veil of madness Lucia is forgivable for murdering her new husband, and the audience laments along with Edegardo when her death is announced from offstage.

Even a heroine who seems to embody the quintessential victim, like Gilda in Verdi's *Rigoletto* (1851 [written sixteen years after Donizetti's *Lucia*]), takes an active role in deciding to do what she believes in. Though Gilda is under the oppressive watch of her overprotective father, abducted to become a conquest of the libertine Duke, and then forced to witness his infidelity (in the act 3 quartet), she remains steadfast in her love for him. In the third act outside of the inn Gilda makes a decision that shows her first independent action in the opera. Rather than following her father's orders to leave Mantua and head to Verona (where he would join her later), she returns to the inn and decides to sacrifice herself for the Duke when she overhears the conversation between Maddalena and Sparafucile in the trio that follows the more famous quartet.

As with Donizetti's Lucia before her, it is easy to look back and agree that Gilda made the "wrong" decision when she chose to sacrifice herself for the Duke. Yet my point is not whether or not the Romanic heroine is a modern "liberated woman" by today's standards. Instead, I am interested in tracing the development in how women's behavior in opera changed over time. Like everyone in opera—both male and female characters—Lucia and Gilda are given situations that are far from ideal. Within the narrow range of options that were available to women on the nineteenth-century opera stage (alternatives that resonated with the norms of the real-life limited opportunities for women at the time), Lucia and Gilda do something different from the earlier model of the first woman. As Romantic heroines, Lucia and Gilda take action and respond to what fate has handed them.

How did we get from the multiple possibilities women's voices could achieve before 1830 to the more strictly enforced rules that govern female characters afterward? Where do the slippery aesthetics that allow for an eleventh-hour solution in one case and the sacrifice of the innocent in another intersect? My entrée into interrogating these changing characterizations of women in opera is to reconstruct some of what nineteenth-century audiences could have experienced. Such an endeavor considers the coexisting practices that allowed the same singer to be heard as a valiant hero, a vengeful scorned lover, and a lovesick heroine who is driven to the end of her capabilities.

The Career of Giuditta Pasta

Giuditta Pasta (1797–1865), one of the foremost singers of the primo ottocento, possessed a voice that captured the broad aesthetics of her time. Endowed with a wide vocal range and a stupendous dramatic presence onstage, her voice opens up the aural world of the principal roles of Rossini, Bellini, Donizetti, and many of the other leading composers writing from the 1810s through the mid-1830s. Additionally, she was a persistent supporter of the heroic travesti tradition through her frequent performance of such roles throughout her career. Pasta's hybrid voice encompassed both the sound of the hero and the heroine.

Looking back today, one way Pasta outshines other nineteenth-century female singers is in the number of her collaborations, where she created and premiered principal roles, with the leading composers of her time whose operas have remained important up through the present. In the primo ottocento repertory, Pasta was nearly impossible to rival. Of all the singers in her time, Giuditta Pasta is uniquely positioned as the singer who came to embody the voice and characterizations of the largest number of principal roles by the three most important composers of the era: Rossini, Bellini, and Donizetti. She created Rossini's Corinna in *Il viaggio a Reims;* Donizetti's *Anna Bolena* (title role) and Bianca in *Ugo, conte di Parigi;* and the title roles in Bellini's *La sonnambula, Norma,* and *Beatrice di Tenda.* Throughout her career she became associated with other leading works; her signature roles included heroic travesti (Rossini's Tancredi and Zingarelli's Romeo, in *Giulietta e Romeo*) as well as leading female characters (Mayr's Medea and Rossini's Desdemona and Semiramide). Additionally, Pasta was a leading interpreter of roles by other prominent composers of the time: Giovanni Pacini, Saverio Mercadante, Simone Mayr, Domenico Cimarosa, Giuseppe Nicolini, and Giuseppe Farinelli.[4] In the variety of roles she performed, her legendary success onstage, and her extensive work with practically all of the leading—and many of the lesser-known—composers of the primo ottocento, she embodied one of the central hybrid voices of the time. In operas written by a broad spectrum of contemporary composers, she mastered all of the possibilities a woman's voice on the opera stage could articulate. Pasta's was the voice of the era.

Today, writing about a specific voice from this early-nineteenth-century period could seem futile. Written descriptions of a voice vary and, at best, can give only an impression of what the original sounded like. Since there are no recordings of Pasta's voice (needless to say, her career predates recording technology), we cannot listen and hear her for ourselves. However, through a combined approach of examining Pasta's repertory, the characterizations of her signature roles, and discussions of her voice from contemporaries who knew it well, we can begin to get a multiple-layered image of her voice. Her reputation and position in this time period make her a critical link to understanding the singing voice in this era. Pasta's stage career outlines a telling story of how a voice, her voice, produced simultaneous meanings to both her audience and the composers writing for her.

Giuditta Pasta's career did not, at first, get off to an auspicious beginning. In an early debut at two major theaters (1816 at the Théâtre Italien in Paris and 1817 at the King's Theatre in London) Pasta did not garner special notice. She then took a few years to hone her skills and sang at smaller houses that were primarily based near her home in northern Italy.[5] It was her return to the Théâtre Italien in the summer of 1821 in the roles of Desdemona (in Rossini's *Otello*) and the castrato/travesti role of Romeo (in Zingarelli's *Giulietta e Romeo,* first created by Girolamo

Crescentini in 1796) that marked a turning point in Pasta's career.[6] She soon became the leading singer of Italian opera in Italy, London, and Paris from the mid-1820s through the early 1830s.

In addition to her portrayals of Rossini's heroines and heroic travesti roles, Pasta was also a central voice in Bellini's career and was closely associated with five, out of his eight, successful operas.[7] In April 1830 Pasta added her first Bellini role to her repertory when she sang Imogene in *Il pirata* at the Theater am Kärntnertor in Vienna. She then went on to premiere his next three operas in Italy: she created the first interpretations of Amina in *La sonnambula* (March 1831, Teatro Carcano, Milan) and the title roles in *Norma* (December 1831, La Scala, Milan) and *Beatrice di Tenda* (March 1833, La Fenice, Venice). Later in 1833, Pasta added his Romeo (*I Capuletti e i Montecchi*) when she sang in London. With the exception of Henriette Méric-Lalande, who had premiered four of his earlier operatic heroines, no other singer was as closely connected to Bellini's repertoire during his lifetime.[8] Certainly no one else at the time was as central to his mature works, as a creator and leading interpreter of so many roles.

Pasta was also a key figure in Donizetti's career. She was the voice behind the title role in his breakthrough opera *Anna Bolena,* which opened the Carnival season on December 26, 1830, at the Teatro Carcano in Milan and finally established him as a major Italian opera composer (he had been writing operas since the late 1810s).[9]

At this point in her career, Pasta's input in the shaping of the roles she was to premiere went beyond the usual primo ottocento concern to fit a role to the specific singer's voice. As with Bellini during his composition of *Norma* in 1831, Donizetti stayed at Pasta's Villa Roda on Lake Como the month before to work on the opera and flesh out the title character with her. Pasta premiered one other role by Donizetti shortly after *Anna Bolena*. In 1832 Donizetti wrote Bianca for Pasta in his *Ugo, conte di Parigi* (Hugh [Capet], Count of Paris) for La Scala, an opera that opened later the same season at the same opera house as Bellini's *Norma*. Like *Norma, Ugo* used the same cast with Giulia Grisi as the second woman (Adalgisa and Adelia), Domenico Donzelli as the tenor (Pollione and Ugo), and Vincenzo Negrini as the bass (Oroveso and Folco di Angiò).

Pasta's collaboration with Donizetti, Bellini, and the other composers whose operas she performed needs to be contextualized within the conventions of the primo ottocento. The interaction between the composer and the leading singers was one that presented a mutually beneficial arrangement. The success of an opera was largely due to the strength of its performance. In tandem, the reputation of a singer was heavily dependent upon the power of his or her performance in a role. When an opera went well the singer benefited, and vice versa.

The stakes were even higher when the opera was brand new and in its premiere season. At the beginning of the nineteenth century, the concept of "repertory operas" was new in practice.[10] Up until that point, operas were largely occasional pieces that were performed, sometimes revived within a few years, but were usually out of circulation long before the next decade. An early foreshadowing of the new practice can be found in the performance of Mozart's operas after his death in

Giuditta Pasta as Donizetti's first Anna Bolena (1830s). *The Harvard Theatre Collection, The Houghton Library.*

1791. Within the first decades of the nineteenth century, Mozart's operas were performed abroad in London, Italy, and Paris. Pasta's early career in 1816–19 included several performances of Mozart's operas in Paris at the Théâtre Italien, in London at the King's Theatre, and in northern Italian theaters. Her Mozart repertory included all three women in *Don Giovanni* (at various points in her career), Cherubino (*Le nozze di Figaro*), and Sevilia (*La clemenza di Tito*).[11]

As was still common during the 1810s through the 1830s, singers continued the seventeenth- and eighteenth-century practice of carrying around their *arie di baulo* (suitcase arias), their favorite arias that showcased the best features of their voice and dramatic capabilities.[12] As a practitioner of the tradition, Pasta had no trouble inserting an aria of her own choosing from her collection of suitcase arias to enhance an operatic situation. She did this most frequently in operas that either did not make a strong impression on the audience or in order to use arias from another opera with which she had a special affinity and wanted to highlight in her signature roles. Though such a practice might seem unusual, or perhaps even

Giuditta Pasta as Enrico, the travesti hero of Mayr's *La rosa bianca e la rosa rossa*. *The Harvard Theatre Collection, The Houghton Library.*

offensive today, composers in the primo ottocento seem to have had a different opinion.

With a singer of Pasta's influence and status, the substitutions sometimes seemed like a collaborative effort. An example can be seen with an aria specifically tailored to Pasta's voice by Meyerbeer as he specially adapted Armando's entrance aria for her when she took on the castrato role for the Parisian premiere of *Il crociato in Egitto* in 1825. This aria became one of Pasta's favorites, and she frequently interpolated it into Rossini's *Otello* when she performed Desdemona.[13] In a revival of Mayr's *La rosa bianca e la rosa rossa* for Paris in 1823 Pasta introduced Rossini's "Dolci d'amor parole" as Enrico's (the heroic travesti role) entrance aria.[14] In Pasta's performance of *Tancredi*, one of her signature roles, she regularly interpolated Giuseppe Nicolini's "Il braccio mio conquise" as Tancredi's final number. As in Meyerbeer's adaptation of Armando's aria from his *Il crociato*, Nicolini's aria was

Table 5.1. List of Giuditta Pasta's Roles in Her Early Career: 1816–20

* Travesti role   ** Premiere   Bracketed roles are repeated and not new repertory.

Role	Composer	Opera	Place	Date
Donna Elvira	Mozart	*Don Giovanni*	Paris, Italien	Aug. 1816
Giulietta	Zingarelli	*Giulietta e Romeo*	Paris, Italien	Sept. 1816
Telemaco*	Cimarosa	*Penelope*	London, King's	Jan. 1817
Cherubino*	Mozart	*Nozze di Figaro*	London, King's	Feb. 1817
Despina	Mozart	*Così fan tutte*	London, King's	June 1817
Servilia	Mozart	*Clemenza di Tito*	London, King's	July 1817
Adelaide	Pacini	*Adelaide e Comingio*	Venice, Benedetto	Sept. 1818
Angelina	Rossini	*Cenerentola*	Padua, Nuovo	Oct. 1818
Linceo*	Mayr	*Danao***	Rome, Argentina	Dec. 1818
Clodomiro*	Nicolini	*Giulio Cesare in Gallie*	Rome, Argentina	Jan. 1819
Arsace*	Rossini	*Aureliano in Palmira*	Rome, Argentina	Feb. 1819
Marc'Antonio*	Nasolini	*Morte di Cleopatra*	Brescia, Grande	July 1819
Curiazio*	Cimarosa	*Oriazi e i Curiazi*	Brescia, Grande	Aug. 1819
[Angelina	Rossini	*Cenerentola*	Trieste, Comunale	Jan. 1820]
Diana	G. Farinelli	*Festa patria*	Trieste, Nuovo	Feb. 1820
Ippolito*	Orlandi	*Fedra*	Padua, Nuovo	June 1820
Matilde	Pacini	*Sposa fedele*	Turin, Carignano	Sept. 1820
Zora	Pacini	*Schiava in Bagdad*	Turin, Carignano	Oct. 1820
Gonzalvo*	Nicolini	*Conquista di Granata*	Venice, La Fenice	Dec. 1820
Arminio*	Pavesi	*Arminio*	Venice, La Fenice	Mar. 1820
Agnese	Paër	*Agnese*	Trieste, Nuovo	Feb. 1820
[Curiazio*	Cimarosa	*Oriazi e i Curiazi*	Padua, Nuovo	June 1820]

also originally written for the castrato Velluti (in Nicolini's 1820 opera, *Il conte di Lenosse*). To add a further twist, Rossini wrote two sets of embellishments to Nicolini's aria for Pasta's performances of Tancredi in Paris and Brussels.[15]

From the beginning of her career, Pasta sang female and male characters. In the twenty roles she sang early in her career, between August 1816 and June 1820, there is an equal division between the travesti roles and female characters: ten of each (see table 5.1).[16] As her early career in Paris and London reveals, most of the characters in the beginning are not the leading roles in their respective operas.[17]

The turning point in Pasta's career came in June 1821 when she reappeared at the Théâtre Italien in Paris in leading roles. She sang three new roles, two of which were in operas in which she previously had sung a smaller role during her first season at the Italien six years before. In her first season at the Italien in 1816, she had sung Mozart's Donna Elvira (*Don Giovanni*) and Zingarelli's Giulietta (*Giulietta e Romeo*). Now, five years later, she sang Donna Anna and the travesti role of Romeo (two roles that were considered larger in their respective operas than her earlier roles). Additionally, she added Rossini's Desdemona (*Otello*). From this point on,

Giuditta Pasta as Romeo, the travesti hero of Zingarelli's *Giulietta e Romeo*. Zingarelli's Romeo was originally written for the castrato Girolamo Crescentini in 1796. Lithograph by C. Motte. *The Harvard Theatre Collection, The Houghton Library.*

Pasta's reputation as a leading prima donna was set. Pasta continued her career in Paris for the next few years except for a short season in Turin at the Teatro Regio in December 1821–January 1822. In Turin Pasta sang two travesti roles that were new to her, but evidently did not please her enough to keep them in her repertory: Rossini's Eduardo (*Eduardo e Cristina*) and the Macedonian King Clearco in Giuseppe Farinelli's *I riti d'Efeso*.

In March 1822 Pasta returned to Paris and stayed there until April 1824, performing at the Théâtre Italien. Besides repeating Zingarelli's Romeo, Cimarosa's Curiazio, Paër's Agnese, and Rossini's Desdemona, she learned eight new roles, three of which were in the Paris premieres of the operas (see table 5.2).[18] For her return, Pasta's repertory had a strong focus on Rossini's operas. Desdemona was a big success the year before, and three, of the eight, new operas were by Rossini. Pasta was the first to introduce the title role in *Tancredi* and Elcia (from *Mosè*) to Paris and enjoyed great success in both roles. At this point in Paris, Pasta was the ideal Rossinian voice and continued to lead in this area for several years. Writing about this time period, Henry Sutherland Edwards comments that "All Madame Rossini-Colbran's characters suited Pasta to perfection"[19]

True to her earlier pattern in the beginning of her career, in 1822–24 Pasta kept a mixed diet of female characters and travesti roles. As Zingarelli's Romeo and

Table 5.2. Giuditta Pasta's Return to the Paris Théâtre Italien: 1821–24

* Travesti role   ** Paris premiere

Role	Composer	Opera	Date	Notes
Desdemona	Rossini	*Otello*	June 1821	
Ninetta	Rossini	*Gazza ladra*	1821	New role
Eduardo*	Rossini	*Eduardo e Cristina*	Dec. 1821	Turin, Regio
Clearco*	G. Farinelli	*Riti d'Efeso*	Jan. 1822	Turin, Regio
Romeo*	Zingarelli	*Giulietta e Romeo*	Mar. 1822	
Tancredi*	Rossini	*Tancredi*	Apr. 1822**	New role
Elisabetta	Rossini	*Elisabetta*	Sept. 1822	New role
Elcia	Rossini	*Mosè in Egitto*	Oct. 1822**	New role
Desdemona	Rossini	*Otello*	Jan. 1823	
Medea	Mayr	*Medea in Corinto*	Jan. 1823**	New role
Enrico*	Mayr	*Rosa bianca*	May 1823	New role
Curiazio*	Cimarosa	*Oriazi e i Curiazi*	Aug. 1823	
Elisa	Mercadante	*Elisa e Claudio*	Nov. 1823	New role
Nina	Paisiello	*Nina, pazza per amore*	Nov. 1823	New role
Agnese	Paër	*Agnese*	Jan. 1824	

Rossini's Tancredi were quickly becoming staples in her repertoire, she continued with Cimarosa's Curiazio and added the travesti role of Enrico from Mayr's *La rosa bianca e la rosa rossa*. In 1823, ten years after it was written, Pasta gave the Paris premiere of Mayr's *Medea in Corinto* (yet another role originally written for Colbran during her Neapolitan years at the San Carlo); Medea became one of Pasta's greatest interpretations.

Pasta's career spans a period in Italian opera when the aesthetics regarding plot, characterization, and vocal type were shifting to reflect the newer themes of Romanticism. Yet with the beginning of the practice of repertory operas, it was also important for the top singers to be able to prove themselves in the starring roles of their predecessors and help sustain the popularity of the leading composers. Pasta's relationship with Rossini's operas allowed her to accomplish both goals: she was able to excel in the roles of her immediate predecessor, Isabella Colbran, and was a critical figure in popularizing Rossini's operas in Paris and London.

In terms of the opera narrative, most of Rossini's serious operas reflect the older trend of having plots based on ancient and mythological subjects with large numbers of principal characters (e.g., *Semiramide, Tancredi, Armide, Mosè in Egitto,* and many others). Increasingly, Romantic opera featured plots drawn from modern sources. Beginning in the 1810s, and becoming the norm around 1830, libretto sources were more frequently drawn from contemporary literature. Adaptations of novels and plays by current authors such as Sir Walter Scott, Lord Byron, Alexandre Soumet, and Victor Hugo as well as recent translations of Schiller and Shakespeare provided new and rich material. As the middle of the nineteenth century approached, operas focused on fewer principal roles that had more intimate interactions than those employed in the late eighteenth century and first decades of the nineteenth century. This new emphasis allowed the drama to center on one principal romantic couple and the overwhelming obstacles that prevent their final union.

Pasta's collaborations with Donizetti and Bellini reflect many of these newer Romantic aesthetics for the plot. Both Donizetti operas she premiered were based on early modern history. Felice Romani's 1830 libretto for *Anna Bolena* is an adaptation of sixteenth-century English history; when Henry VIII decides to marry Jane Seymour, his second wife, Anne Boleyn, is unjustly accused of adultery and executed. Two years later, Romani's libretto for *Ugo, Conte di Parigi* treated the tenth-century history of Blanche of Aquitaine, King Louis V (the last of the Carolingian rulers of France), and Hugh Capet (the first of the Capetian Kings of France, whose dynasty continued until the French Revolution, crowned in 987).

Anna Bolena and *Ugo, Conte di Parigi* each embraces older and newer practices. The principal romantic couple concerns a soprano (Pasta) and a tenor (Rubini as Percy, Donzelli as Ugo). Both operas also make use of a travesti role. As discussed earlier, Smeton is a hybrid travesti role in that he is a court pageboy, but is also given a strong romantic connection to Anna. In *Ugo*, Donizetti once again uses a hybrid travesti role for the young Luigi V (first performed by Clorinda Corradi-Pantanelli). Though Luigi is young, he is also betrothed to Bianca (Blanche, Pasta's role) and is put in the double position of being an adolescent court figure, yet also the leading soprano's "official" romantic pair (similar to Smeton's position as a hybrid pageboy/heroic role). Finally, these two operas fit the new Romantic plot device that the soprano must die at the end. Bianca dies of the poison she has taken when she is not able to stop Ugo from marrying her sister. Anna is even further "Romanticized" when she is given a mad scene before her execution.[20]

Bellini's third opera, *Il pirata*, became his breakthrough work and his first international success. The success of his first student opera *Adelson e Salvini* (1825) earned him a commission at the Teatro San Carlo, where his *Bianca e Gernando* was performed a year later.[21] After studying at the Naples Conservatory and writing his first two operas, *Il pirata* was his first opera written for a non-Neapolitan theater and saw a successful premiere at La Scala on October 27, 1827. Giuditta Pasta's first Bellini role was that of Imogene (*Il pirata*) in April 1830 at the Theater am Kärntnertor in Vienna.[22] Within a year of her first encounter with his music, she became his new prima donna voice and premiered three of his last four operas: Amina in *La sonnambula* (1830) and the title roles in *Norma* (1831) and *Beatrice di Tenda* (1833).

Giuditta Pasta's collaborations with Donizetti and Bellini position her as one of the defining voices of the Romantic heroine. Yet Pasta happened to some of age as a prima donna in a time when a woman's voice could sing in many types of roles. Hence, such a critical voice in developing the ultra-feminine Romantic heroine also happened to be a voice well known for singing heroic travesti roles. Just a few years before her first encounter with Bellini's Imogene, Pasta signed a contract with John Ebers in 1826 for London's King's Theatre as *Prima Donna Assoluta* and *Musico Assoluta*, which guaranteed that she would only sing leading roles, both male and female characters.[23] Her contract that season stipulated that her repertoire be drawn from the following roles and operas: Mayr's *Medea* (Medea) and *La rosa bianca e la rosa rossa* (Enrico); Paisiello's *Nina* (Nina); Rossini's *Otello* (Desdemona), *Semiramide* (Semiramide), and *Tancredi* (Tancredi); and Zingarelli's *Giulietta e Romeo* (Romeo).[24]

Pasta sang heroic *travesti* roles throughout her career. As late as the 1829–30 carnival season in Verona, Pasta sang the title role in the newly commissioned opera *Malek Adel* by Nicolini and took the opera with her to Milan and London.[25] In Vienna in 1830, the same season that Pasta first sang Bellini's Imogene, she also sang Desdemona, Nina, and Semiramide, as well as Tancredi and Zingarelli's Romeo.[26]

In fact, Pasta's reputation for singing male and female characters was so well established by 1830 that Bellini originally intended that his first part for her would be a *travesti* role. Having just come off the success of *I Capuleti e i Montecchi* (Venice, La Fenice, March 1830) where Romeo is a late triumph in the musico repertoire, Bellini was interested in another cross-dressed hero. In 1831 Bellini and Romani wanted to compose an opera based on Victor Hugo's *Hernani* with Pasta in the leading role; however, due to problems with the censors in Milan, they ended up writing Amina in *La sonnambula* as their first role for her.[27] Though they ended up writing two other prima donna Romantic heroines for Pasta, she eventually added their Romeo to her repertory as well. In her engagement at the King's Theatre from May through August 1833, Pasta introduced her interpretations of three Bellini operas: Imogene (*Il pirata*), the title role in *Norma*, and Romeo (*I Capuleti e i Montecchi*). During this season she continued to sing across gender and performed Anna Bolena, Medea, Tancredi, and Semiramide.[28]

The roles that Pasta sang in the late 1820s and early 1830s illustrate the critical turning point in the new evolving genre of Romanticism in opera. As the Romantic heroine developed out of the new aesthetics of Romanticism, Pasta's voice articulated an important part of the sound of this character type around 1830; the roles that Donizetti and Bellini wrote helped to construct the new profile. As the leading interpreter of Italian opera during this time Pasta (rivaled only, perhaps, by Maria Malibran) literally embodied the voice of these seminal characters as they led to the midcentury archetype of the Romantic heroine.

Recapturing the Voice

Reviews of Giuditta Pasta's voice from throughout her career emphasize the dramatic power she conveyed across the stage was achieved through the way she was able to act out a character through her voice. In 1827 Pasta sang the title role in Mercadante's *Didone* at the King's Theatre in London. Though the opera did not stay in her repertory, Pasta drew strong reviews. The critic for the *New Times* wrote, "The concluding address to the Furies, 'Furie terribili,' was given as though she [Pasta] already felt possessed by the avenging Deities—the words were heaved from her breast hot and burning, as if emitted from a *human volcano*."[29]

The ability to infuse such drama into her roles was fostered by a strong technique. The comments about Pasta's voice from throughout her career all mention an instrument that was schooled in the bel canto method. Like the castrati before her, her messa di voce—the ability to start a note very softly, crescendo, and then decrescendo so that the sound is almost imperceptible—is continually praised, as is her ability and taste in executing ornamental embellishments.[30] Another, somewhat surprising, element that comes through is the specific character of Pasta's voice. In the *Life of Rossini* Stendhal wrote,

> Madame Pasta's incredible mastery of technique is revealed in the amazing facility with which she alternates head-notes with chest-notes; she possesses to a superlative degree the art of producing an immense variety of charming and thrilling effects from the use of *both* voices.[31]

A little further on, he continues,

> But think how much pure artistry, and how much discipline and training has been necessary before this enthralling singer learned to harness the restive secrets of weaving such divine enchantments out of *two different and utterly contrasting voices.*[32]

Stendhal was an astute listener and his comments are informed by the "period ear" of his time. His *Life of Rossini* is not only a tribute to Rossini, but also includes an expansive discussion of opera in Paris through the early 1820s. Out of the forty-six chapters on Rossini's operas and various topics relating to the operatic scene in Paris, only two chapters are devoted to individual singers. Chapter 21 is concerned with the Giambattista Velluti, the last of the great castrato voices of the eighteenth-century bel canto, and chapter 35 presents the first diva of Romantic opera, Pasta, indicating her critical importance to these new developments in the genre.

Stendhal was able to witness the best years of Pasta's career; writing in 1824, he reports on the early part of her rise to fame in Paris that led directly into her prime singing years. Her career reached its apex in the late 1820s through the early 1830s, which included her most memorable collaborations with the leading composers of the time. Her operas with Bellini and Donizetti reflect her ability to inspire the leading contemporary composers to write roles that capture the new aesthetics of Romanticism.

Other descriptions of Pasta's voice discuss the difficulties she had and the amount of work it took to achieve the dramatic sound for which she became so famous. Henry Chorley, whose *Thirty Years' Musical Recollections* provide a view into the operatic musical scene in London between 1830 and 1860, presents Pasta's voice from another vantage point. In 1833, a few years before Pasta went into semiretirement, Chorley writes about hearing Pasta's voice:

> The glory of Madame Pasta already showed signs of waning: she steadily began her evening's task half a tone too flat. Her acting was more powerful and striking than ever, if that could be. This, however, was her last season of being the presiding divinity of the opera.[33]

In Chorley's chapter devoted to Pasta, he outlines the process by which she worked on her vocal technique between her first appearance in 1816 and then her return in 1821:

She subjected herself to a course of severe and incessant vocal study, to subdue and to utilize her voice. To equalize it was impossible. There was a portion of the scale which differed from the rest in quality and remained to the last "under a veil," to use the Italian term. There were notes always more or less out of tune, especially at the commencement of her performances. Out of these uncouth materials she had to compose her instrument, and then to give it a flexibility. Her studies to acquire execution must have been tremendous; but the volubility and brilliancy, when acquired, gained a character of their own from the resisting peculiarities of the organ.[34]

Here we have a quick outline of Pasta's voice in the decade between the early 1820s and the 1830s. She was the leading singer of her time, but her fame was not due to the dazzling perfection in the beauty of her voice. In fact, Chorley's comments indicate that she tended to sing out of tune. There was an unruly nature to her voice, and she exerted effort to tame and control the sound. He states that it was impossible to "equalize it" and that portions of her voice remained "under a veil." Even during her heyday in the early 1820s, her staunch admirer Stendhal talks about her "two voices" as being "different" and "utterly contrasting."

The "double voiced" quality in Pasta's singing continued through the end of her career and is mentioned by a critic for the *Morning Herald* in a review from a concert she gave in London at the Drury Lane Theatre on May 17, 1837. Though her voice was still able to thrill the audience, the reviewer mentions the "soprano" and "contralto" portions of her voice having different qualities:

No artiste ever coped with the difficulty of concert singing so successfully as Pasta, because acting with her is not an art, but her very nature; and if there was any very perceptible result from the absence of progressive excitement, it was, perhaps, an occasional little imperfection in those abrupt transitions from low to high of which Madame Pasta is fond, and which, in the torrent of her passion on the stage, she dashes off with the boldest and finest effect. Her voice is still what it was, delicious in the sweetness of its soprano, most touching the slight huskiness of its contr'alto, in both having a separate and peculiar quality of which seems essentially the grand—the epic. We never heard her sing more delightfully than she did occasionally last night, or execute with a more delicate trill some of the prolonged shakes which always formed so special a feature in her style.[35]

For many who heard Pasta's voice it was the epitome of dramatic and powerful singing. The "contrasting," "veiled," and "separate qualities," so provocatively mentioned by Stendhal, Chorley, and the 1837 reviewer for the *Morning Herald,* all came out of the same throat and complicate the way we think about the understood codes—varied meanings—such a voice could engender for its audiences. Audiences could hear simultaneous voicings, of her other roles, within each operatic character Pasta performed. Her voice represents the fusion of multiple characters from the ethereal voice of the castrati (in the roles she sang originally written for the castrato voice) and the "male" voice in the heroic travesti roles. Her voice also encompassed all of the different configurations of operatic female characters from the beloved "first woman" to the scorned "second woman" and eventually created the first Romantic heroines who combined elements from all of her previous roles.

As a leading singer whose dramatic presence and voice were both recognized and beloved on the opera stage, Pasta had a hybrid voice that evoked the history of her wide range of roles through the sound of her voice. Her interpretations of the titular heroines in Mayr's *Medea in Corinto* and Bellini's *Norma* present especially rich examples of the ancestry of the second woman (Medea) being audible in the first woman (Norma). The relationship between the two principal women in each opera illustrates a critical focal point for understanding how the singular Romantic heroine ends up replacing both of them. As a way to mediate between the two-women to one-woman models, two of Donizetti's operas from the 1830s, *Anna Bolena* and *Rosmonda d'Inghilterra*, provide helpful links. More than the connection between student and teacher, in the case of Mayr and Donizetti, or the competitive rivalry between two contemporary composers, Bellini and Donizetti, all four operas have a common factor: the same architect built each plot. Each one was a collaboration between the composer and the leading librettist of the time, Felice Romani.

In the fall of 1830 Donizetti, Pasta, and Bellini were all in Milan. The Teatro Carcano had commissioned Donizetti and Bellini each to write operas with Pasta leading the cast. Opening the Carnival season on December 26, 1830, Donizetti's *Anna Bolena* met with great success. Not without some degree of difficulty, Bellini and Romani finally settled on *La sonnambula,* an opera semiseria, as his debut opera both for the Carcano and for Pasta.[36] According to Romani's widow, Bellini was further motivated by not wanting to risk a competitive comparison with another opera seria immediately following *Anna Bolena.*[37] Whatever the reasons for the change in the original plan, *La sonnambula* premiered on March 6, 1831, and was a strong success in its own right.

Bellini's next opera was his La Scala commission for the following Carnival season in 1831 with Pasta again heading the cast. Having witnessed her success in *Anna Bolena* at the other leading opera house in Milan (the Teatro Carcano), Bellini's *Norma* bears the mark of his keen observation. Like *Anna Bolena, Norma, ou L'infanticide,* the Alexandre Soumet play on which the libretto is based, ends with a mad scene for the title character (a scene that was eventually left out of the opera). Another similarity between the two operas is the interaction between the two leading female characters (which will be discussed below). Bellini's opera opened a year to the day after Donizetti's *Anna Bolena:* December 26, 1831.

Pasta's Voice in Character on Stage: *Medea in Corinto*

Although Mayr's *Medea in Corinto* (1813) was written when happy endings were the norm (where no principals die and the conflict is resolved peacefully); this opera ends unhappily. By the final curtain Creusa (Giasone's [Jason's] new intended bride) is dead, Giasone and Medea's two children are dead, and the distraught Giasone has to be restrained from killing himself out of his grief. Even the title character, Medea, has a less than happy ending. Though she lives and has a spectacular exit in a dragon-pulled chariot, a striking device used by Rossini four years later at the end of *Armida* (both operas were written for the San Carlo in Naples), she does not get what she really wants in the end: reconciliation with her husband.[38]

In the prehistory to the opera she had done terrible things in helping him obtain the Golden Fleece, including deceiving her family so that her father and brother end up dying. With all she had done for Giasone, she is anguished that he can so easily discard her, plan to marry another, and agree to her banishment.

Medea's character moves from one of scorned love to revenge. When she is not successful in getting Giasone to love her, she is able to exercise her powers for reprisal. In a dramatic *scongiuro* (invocation) scene (reminiscent of the incantation scenes in eighteenth-century opera) she summons up the furies from the underworld to cast a spell on her bejeweled robe—which becomes the fatal wedding gift she gives to Giasone's intended bride, Creusa. The poisoned gown achieves its effect, and Creusa's death is a direct result of Medea's vengeance.

Our sympathies are pulled in a couple of different directions regarding the plight of the two women, Medea and Creusa. It is impossible not to feel the betrayal and unfair treatment Medea receives in this opera. In act 1 we learn that the peace King Creonte of Corinth has negotiated with Acasto, his enemy, is for Medea's exile. Corinth gets peace, and Creonte gets to see his daughter (Creusa) marry the man she loves (Giasone) without any obstacle. Yet Creusa has not intentionally tried to deceive Medea. Like most first women, Creusa loves innocently and finds herself in the center of a bad situation.

Unlike the others in the opera, in addition to her duets with different characters, Medea has solos (two or three, depending on the version of the opera) that address and engage the gods of the otherworld.[39] Her entrance aria, "Sommi Dei"; the *scongiuro* scene (including her aria "Ogni piacer è spento"); and the penultimate scene in the opera, "Miseri pargoletti"; present three dramatic highpoints that underscore Medea's "unnatural" and dangerous powers. In "Sommi Dei" Medea implores the gods of love and vengeance to help her in her suffering. The *scongiuro,* one of the central climactic scenes in the opera, presents Medea the sorceress invoking the dark powers of the underworld. At the end of the opera in Medea's last aria ("Miseri pargoletti"), she refers to herself as "una madre snaturata" (an unnatural mother) as she contemplates murdering her own children.[40]

The turning point in the opera occurs in her first act duet with Giasone. This extended duet, which follows her entrance aria, "Sommi Dei," continues the sentiments in the aria: Medea admits that, despite Giasone's betrayal, she still loves him, and she implores him to come back to her:

Tempo d'attacco of the Giasone-Medea Act 1 Duet, *Medea in Corinto*

Giasone

Cedi al destin, Medea;	Submit to destiny, Medea; you are
Contro il destin non basti	Not strong enough to contend against destiny.
Pugnar con lui tentasti,	You tried to do battle with fate,
E te perdesti, e mi.	And you destroyed both yourself and me.

Medea

Era Medea, lo sai,	Medea, as you know,
Del suo destin maggiore,	Was stronger than her destiny;

Barbaro, oh dio! Minor	O God! Barbarous man, it was only
Si fece sol per te.	For you that I belittled myself.

Giasone

Vinci te stessa, e questo	Conquer yourself, and this
Sarà maggior, tuo vanto.	Will be your greatest claim.

Medea

Ah! Erba o virtù d'incanto	Ah! There is no herb or magic spell
Che sani amor no v'è.	That is capable of curing love.

Following a lengthy accompanied recitative, the first lyrical section of the duet begins with Giasone's urging Medea to submit to her destiny ("Cedi al destin, Medea"). After an eight-measure introduction, Giasone sings his melodious opening lines in an asymmetrical phrase structure: 5 + 8 measures that make his opening statement an unusual thirteen measures (see example 5.1a). Harmonically these opening phrases are more normative and move from the tonic (B♭ major) to the dominant (F major). The rest of his opening stanza is more regular in phrasing and ends in the home key where it began, B♭ major. When Medea enters, she follows his opening thirteen-measure statement closely and sings an only slightly altered repetition of his melody (see example 5.1b).

After following his half cadence in F major at the end of this opening statement, Medea's music takes a turn of its own and begins to incorporate G♭, D♭, and E♮, chromatic accidentals foreign to the B♭ harmony, which moves the harmony to F minor. Additionally, Medea's vocal line begins to show signs of a different style of singing. As she reminds Giasone that it was only for him that she conceded to use her sorcery to commit heinous deeds for his benefit, her voice extends down to a lower range than her opening statement. In her initial statement she sang within the staff (her range was the octave F–F), in her second statement, she extends her melody down to D♭ (to cover the range of a major tenth). Moreover, her vocal line is more disjunct. Her part has more leaps and no longer utilizes the primarily conjunct stepwise motion of her first thirteen measures. The contour of her line is steeper with more leaps in the same direction, hence covering a wider range. The most pronounced example of this leaping style is found in the first iteration of "fece sol per te" (I only did it for you). As she quickly covers over an octave, from a high E♭ to a low D♭, the sustained notes in her melody emphasize the dissonant intervals of a minor seventh (E♭ down to F) and the outer interval of the major ninth (see example 5.2).

All in all, the sum effect of this second vocal style is one of singing more emphatically with less significance given to lyrical legato lines and more prominence given to stronger accents and a heavier weight. While the character of the tempo d'attacco movement in la solita forma is frequently more disjunct than the lyrical adagio movement, in this duet (and, as will be shown, in her other numbers) Mayr's writing for Medea strategically employs disjunct and conjunct singing styles to dramatically emphasize her text and mental state.

The next section of the duet, the lyrical cantabile movement in a Largo tempo,

Example 5.1a. Giasone's opening phrase from the tempo d'attacco of Giasone-Medea duet, act 1, *Medea in Corinto*.

Example 5.1b. Medea's opening phrase from the tempo d'attacco of Giasone-Medea duet, act 1, *Medea in Corinto*.

Example 5.2. Medea's emphatic voice (wide range and frequent leaps). Excerpt from the tempo d'attacco of Giasone-Medea duet, act 1, *Medea in Corinto*.

is set in the subdominant key of the opening (E♭ major), a related, yet new, key signature to designate a separate harmonic sphere (see example 5.3).

Cantabile Movement of the Medea-Giasone Act 1 Duet, *Medea in Corinto*
Set as parenthetical asides

Medea
(O mia virtude antica   (O my ancient powers,
Dove n'andasti mai!   whatever has become of you!
L'empio, che tanto amai,   The wretch I loved so much
Tutto scordar me fè.)   Has made me forget you all.)

Giasone
(O prima fiamma antica   (O my ancient flame,
Non ti svegliar giammai.   may you never revive.
Pensa, o mio cor, che assai   Think, my heart, that it has already
Colpevole ti fè.)   Made you guilty enough.)

With the full text of the cantabile movement set as parenthetical asides (so that they each do not "hear" what the other is saying), this slow section involves a good bit of simultaneous singing in thirds and sixths (see example 5.3). The melodious ornamented lines they sing together present a harmonious sonic space. This lyrical section of the duet presents a double message. If the audience were to believe their ears, they would think that the couple were going to end up happily together. However, their texts reveal the contrasting message that they are trying to resist the love they once felt for each other. At this point in the opera, their two voices are blended and intertwined as a romantic couple should be: Medea sounds like the first woman who is beloved by the tenor. Yet this section is short lived, and the intervening tempo di mezzo returns to a dialogue style where Medea finally understands that

Example 5.3. Simultaneous, cantabile duet singing. Excerpt from the cantabile of Giasone-Medea duet, act 1, *Medea in Corinto.*

Giasone will not return to her; when asked, he says that it is "la fatal necesità" (the fatal necessity) the prevents him from loving her.

In the concluding section, back in the home key of B♭ major, we are brought into the reality of the situation. As was seen in the cantabile, Giasone and Medea sing together in a duet style; however, instead of the lyrical undulating contour where the melody gracefully moved stepwise and used leaps sporadically, Medea is back to the emphatic singing she let come through in the tempo d'attacco. Now, in the cabaletta section, her text and vocal character are synchronized:

Cabaletta of the Giasone-Medea Act 1 Duet, *Medea in Corinto*
Set as parenthetical asides

Medea
(Sgombri amor: da me s'asconda,	(Let love be swept away: let it hide itself from me,
Si confonda un empio core,	May his evil heart be confounded;
Si respiri omai furore,	Henceforth let me breathe fury,
E vendetta e crudeltà.)	Violence and revenge.)

Giasone
(Sgombri amor: da me s'asconda,	(Let love be swept away: let it hide itself from me,
Si confonda un empio core,	May her evil heart be confounded;
Ah! Respira vendetta	Ah! She pants for revenge,
Furore e crudeltà.)	Breathes fury and revenge.)

As she sends Giasone away and cries for vengeance, Medea's music is spiked with sharp angles that outline the jagged nature of her vocal lines. Leaps that span large intervals and several leaps in the same direction illustrate the extremes in her range and mood. Her extended range again outlines the top and bottom of the treble clef; her vocal line reaches up to high G as well as down to middle C, adding heft to her sentiments. This, her voice of vengeance and betrayal, perfectly resonates the anger Medea as a second woman feels and is antithetical to the melodious lyricism she

Example 5.4. Excerpt from the cabaletta of Giasone-Medea duet, act 1, *Medea in Corinto*.

sang in the Largo section when her voice was momentarily transformed into appearing as if she were the first woman in love, singing as though it were an abbreviated love duet with the tenor.

While Medea's voice in her first act duet with Giasone is able to masquerade as the first woman for a short period of time, the *scongiuro* is almost entirely written for her as a second woman. The scene is divided into two main sections. The first ("Dove mi guidi?") includes Ismene, Medea's confidant; the second ("Ogni piacer è spento") is a solo scene for Medea with an offstage chorus of subterranean voices. After a lengthy sixteen-measure Adagio orchestral introduction that sets the dark scene with prominent low woodwinds and brass, the first section has Ismene and Medea singing an accompanied recitative dialogue with sectional tempo changes (Adagio-Moderato-Adagio).

After Ismene leaves, Medea's scena continues with the accompanied recitative and then moves into the aria proper. The aria invokes

Tartaro profondo	Deep Tartarus,
Ecate spaventosa, ombre dolenti	Fearful Hecate, grieving shades,
O furie, voi che del perduto mondo	And the Furies who guard
Siete alle porte, armate di serpenti.	The gates of the lost world with serpents.

With a dramatic vocal setting that moves in a deliberate Adagio tempo, Medea's vocal line is filled with wide descending leaps, dotted rhythms, and a deep range that emphasizes the bottom of her register (with low notes hovering around D–C♯–B♭ around middle C). Her excitement grows when she hears the spirits gathering, and her vocal line extends up to the medium part of her range, while continuing to stay rooted in the low notes, and alternates sustained heavy singing with faster dotted rhythms. When the offstage furies enter, they immediately let Medea know that it was the sound of her voice that penetrated their subterranean regions and compelled them to appear ("penetrò la tua voce sotterra" [your voice reached us underground]).

The voice that Medea uses to call the dark spirits in her *scongiuro* scene is a different voice than that which she used in the Largo section of her duet with Giasone. In the Largo section, her voice blended with Giasone's harmonically (they sang in thirds and sixths) and melodically (they sang lyrical phrases together homorhythmically). Though no such indication is explicitly noted in the score, Medea's vocal

Example 5.5. Medea's wide descending leaps, dotted rhythms, and emphasis on the low range (B♭–C♯). Excerpt from Medea's invocation scene, act 2, *Medea in Corinto*.

style changes radically in relation to her emotional state and position in the drama. When needed, she can sing lyrically as the first woman in love. Yet when Giasone rejects her, she sings in another voice, one that she later uses to call on the subterranean furies and cast the spell on her robe that poisons and kills Creusa. The rugged contour of steep angles formed by multiple leaps, and the measured emphasis given to these wide intervals through dotted rhythms and sustained note values, characterize a different side of Medea's vocal identity. With this other voice, she sings as the second woman.

In her final solo, "Miseri pargoletti," Medea combines both vocal styles that serve as a fitting way to musically set her fragmented mind. In this harrowing scene where she first contemplates and then decides to kill her children, she suffers a crisis of identity. At the beginning of her opening scena in recitative with Ismene she refers to herself as "una madre snaturata" (an unnatural mother) and then states "io son fuori di me" (literally, "I am outside of myself"). Later, once the aria begins, she continues the disassociative pattern and denies her former identities as a wife and a mother. To her children nearby she sings, "Più sposa non son io/Io non vi son più madre" (I am no longer a wife, I am no longer your mother).

What makes this point in the opera so eerie is the effect of listening to the graceful florid melodies and long flowing legato lines (see example 5.6). Though the aria is in a sectional form with contrasting key areas, throughout the number the grisly meaning of her text is uncannily aestheticized by the musical setting. The first section of the aria is preceded and accompanied by an obbligato English horn.[41] As Medea reflects on the innocence of her two small children, the gentle undulating rise and fall of the vocal and English horn melodies soothe the listener, and perhaps also her children onstage, into a false sense of security.

The character changes suddenly with an Agitato section ("Ah! no fuggite") when the key moves from F major into the related key of D minor. Though the tempo is

Giuditta Pasta as Mayr's Medea as she is about to kill her children. Drawn on stone by John Haytner (London, late 1820s). *The Harvard Theatre Collection, The Houghton Library.*

faster, the English horn disappears, and the vocal line is more chromatic, but the melody continues its primarily stepwise motion and legato phrasing. When the final section ("Deggio svenarli?") modulates to the dominant major (A major), the tempo continues its anxious character. As Medea decides to murder her children, her vocal line continues its conjunct contour and melismatic legato motion. Even the musical style of the orchestra and intermittent offstage chorus of Corinthians calling for Medea's punishment (for causing Creusa's death) do not expose the gory nature of the reality of the situation. Instead, their parts add to the vitality and intensity of this dramatic moment. The meaning of the disaster, however, is never explicitly revealed in the sound.

What do the music and, more specifically, Medea's voice tell us about the end of the opera? Her duet with Giasone and her solo numbers illustrate that she can rise to the occasion and sing with different "voices" depending on the different situation. Her final aria sounds like she is triumphant. Having killed Creusa, Medea is able to co-opt the style of the first woman's conjunct melodies, smooth legato phrasing, and florid coloratura writing to achieve her own ends. Yet the connection between the music and her actions presents a dissonance for the audience. Though Medea can imitate the vocal style, her behavior does not fit the character of the first woman.

Creusa is as far from Medea in behavior and character as possible. The opening

Example 5.6. Medea's final aria, with English horn obligato. Excerpt from "Miseri pargoletti," act 2, *Medea in Corinto*.

chorus of Corinthian handmaidens sings Creusa's praises. While they refer to the "excesses" in character that have obscured Medea's beauty, Creusa is cherished by all of Greece for both her physical attractiveness and her inner refinement from her "innocence of life" that makes her all the more appealing. The opera opens with a chorus of Creusa's handmaidens:

Opening Chorus of *Medea in Corinto*

Creusa's handmaidens

Perchè temi? A te l'amante	Why are you afraid? Medea cannot
Involare non può Medea.	Steal your lover from you.
Tanti eccessi, ond'ella è rea,	The many excesses she is guilty of
Ecclissar la sua beltà.	Have cast their shadow over her beauty.
Ama in te la Grecia intera	All Greece cherishes in you
Del sembiante a' vezzi unita	Not only the beauty of your features,
L'innocenza della vita	But that innocence of life
Che più amabile il fa.	Which makes you all the more loveable.

From this opening chorus, the terms for beauty and goodness in women are defined. The juxtaposition of these two dispositions—Medea's use of her power and experience contrasted to Creusa's innocence—is what is really at stake here. Creusa is absolved from any wrongdoing, despite the fact that she has fallen in love with a married man who has a wife and two children. Because Medea has been ordered into exile (for the deeds she committed in the prehistory of the opera when she helped Giasone obtain the Golden Fleece), Creusa's love is exonerated from any negative association, and her character remains pure. Medea, perhaps rightly so, is seen as a tainted woman for having done all that she did for Giasone—her "excesses." Creusa is beloved by the people; hence her love is "innocent." The energy of the opera is focused on the love between Creusa and Giasone; it is approved by the Corinthian people (the Greek chorus) and her father (King Creonte of Corinth), and, by extension, we in the audience are asked to do the same.

Rosmonda d'Inghilterra and Medea in Corinto

Though there is no record of Giuditta Pasta ever singing in Donizetti's opera Rosmonda d'Inghilterra (1834), a similar pattern emerges between the two women in Donizetti's opera and in Mayr's Medea in Corinto (1813). However, in the twenty-one years between their premieres there is a progression in the depiction of each leading woman that reveals a subtle evolution between the two operas. In Donizetti's opera the title character, the first woman young ingénue, is Rosmonda; in Mayr's opera, Medea is the second woman.

In both operas the first woman has fallen in love with the tenor but does not realize that he has a commitment to another woman. Also, in the plots of the two operas the second woman is to be exiled so that the tenor is free to marry the first woman. In Mayr's opera, Giasone and King Creonte have annulled Giasone's marriage with Medea as a consequence of her intended exile; hence, Creusa and Giasone's love is celebrated in the opera. Donizetti's opera presents the seemingly humble and modest "Edegardo," an effective disguise that the King, Enrico, uses as he seduces the lovely and naive Rosmonda. When she finds out that he is really the King of England and is married to Queen Leonora (the second woman), Rosmonda is filled with guilt and remorse and refuses to continue the affair. Nevertheless, the pattern seen in Medea is fulfilled when the second woman cannot regain the love of her husband and, out of vengeance, decides to kill the first woman: Medea poisons the robe she gives to Creusa, Leonora finds Rosmonda and fatally stabs her. In death the two first women's helplessness is magnified.

The second woman is treated differently in each opera. In Donizetti's opera, Leonora's negative character is given more weight than Rosmonda's responsibility for having had an adulterous relationship with the King. In the beginning of act 2 the King's councilors agree to approve the annulment of his marriage to Leonora.

Excerpt from the Opening of Act 1, Rosmonda d'Inghilterra

Udimmo, o re: qual suddito	We hear you, oh King: what subject
Potria cangiar tua voglia?	Would he able to change your wish?
Se giarie è tanto e orribile,	If you marriage is so grievous and horrible
Il nodo tuo, si scioglia.	Let it be dissolved.

When the councilors mention that Leonora could become a potential threat (she brings and takes with her the alliance of the Aquitaine), Enrico decides to banish her from England at dawn the next day.[42]

Following this point of business with the councilors, Enrico and Leonora have a duet. Like Giasone in his duet with Medea, Enrico tries to evade Leonora's desire to talk with him and enters the duet only reluctantly.[43] Once the duet begins, we learn of Leonora's alleged transgression and why the King is allowed to dissolve his marriage. Like Medea, Leonora helped her husband gain his power. Unlike Medea, Leonora's fault was not in how she helped him obtain the throne, but what she did once he became King. Enrico accuses her of desiring too much power:

Duet between Enrico and Leonora, *Rosmonda d'Inghilterra*

E vi sedette il tuo superbo orgoglio.	And there [the English throne] set up your own overwhelming pride.
Sola regnar volevi,	You wanted to reign alone,
Tu sola, in nome mio; ferreo stendesti	You alone, in my name; you extended your iron scepter
Sulla corte il tuo scettro, e su me stesso:	Over the court, and over my very self:
Devoto, e a te sommesso	You sought a devoted husband,
Per appagare ambizion fatale,	One subservient to yourself
Sposo cercavi.	To satisfy your fatal ambition.

Like Medea, Leonora is punished for her strength. Continuing along the pattern of Medea, Leonora also declares her continuing love for Enrico; despite his infidelity she would take him back. When he refuses, betrayal turns to vengeance, and her final actions of vengeance toward Rosmonda are set in motion.

Both Medea and Leonora are scorned women who have reason to be upset. Both have used their influence and power to help their husbands, the tenor, attain his current position. Yet their husbands are involved with someone else, and each man plans to replace his wife with a naive and less self-assured younger woman. Additionally, the men have arranged for their wives to be banished from the court and exiled. Medea and Leonora are two women who go through the same ordeal and have similar reactions. Yet between these two operas, a shift occurs in whose position is emphasized. While the scorned wife does not disappear, she inhabits a different dramatic place. Medea occupies center stage, and we see the opera through her eyes. Twenty-one years later, it is Rosmonda's perspective that is highlighted and becomes the primary focus.

In 1813 Medea had the power to magically call devils to her side and fly away in a dragon-pulled chariot to escape unscathed after her most gruesome deed: murdering her own two children. Since Creusa is positioned as the innocent victim, her death is easy to mourn. Yet the challenge of Medea's role is to keep her ferocious as well as to infuse her with enough humanity so that we can see the lengths to which she has been driven. While Creusa has only two featured numbers in the opera (a duet with Giasone in act 1 and an aria with the chorus in the beginning of act 2), Medea has five spread throughout the two acts (three solo arias and two duets). Medea is given ample opportunity to reflect and express her betrayal, grief, and passion; she evolves as a character and experiences a wide range of emotions. In the beginning she is angry at her exile, devastated at Giasone's betrayal, and yet still begs him to come back to her. When he firmly refuses her in their duet and ultimately calls her "a thing of impiety/ungodliness" (un oggetto d'empietà) her grief turns to vengeance. In her incantation scene (the *scongiuro*) we see her rage and invoke all her powers when she summons the shades from the underworld. In her last aria, "Miseri pergoletti," we see her vacillate between the love she has for her children and the still unquenched desire for revenge (even after Creusa's death).

Medea shows us what it is like to be a woman pushed to the edge and then hurled over. She is an important character not only for her outrageous behavior. She is an unforgettable character because she has such incomprehensible actions. As a woman onstage, she embodies the extremes. She is driven by her love that has turned into an obsession, and we see the negative result of this force; she ends up murdering anything that she perceives as getting in her way—her family, her rival, even her children. Creusa, the foil to Medea's character, is swallowed up and obliterated. With Medea's presence, the model of womanhood that survives is a woman who cannot be tamed. Her role, emblematic of the second woman, is not repentant.

Mayr's opera presents the characters of the first woman and the second woman in sharp contradistinction. Creusa, the first woman, is beloved by all, yet she ends up dying. Creusa's defenselessness against Medea is indicative of a deeper characteristic: the first woman does not initiate action, and she usually has a tough time responding to it. She does her ineffectual best to react to the difficult situations presented before her. Though she is loved by the tenor, this love is always blocked by something she has no control over; hence, her inherent powerlessness. Her only fault is to love the tenor, who, for some reason, is not available to her. Nonetheless, the love between the first woman and the tenor is always privileged as a pure love that really should be allowed to exist, despite the obstacles.

Medea is an apotheosis of the second woman and uses her power to excess. Not only does she live through the conclusion (the second woman always survives), but she is given a grand exit in a dragon-pulled chariot. The conflict between Medea and Giasone has less to do with Creusa's luring the latter away than with his loosing faith in Medea. In the scene leading up to their tempo d'attacco of their first duet, he beseeches her:

Giasone to Medea, Leading into the Tempo d'Attacco of Their Act 1 Duet, *Medea in Corinto*

Abbi pietà di te. Deh! Volgi intorno	Have pity on yourself. Ah! Look around you.
Un sol sguardo, Medea. Fosti regina: Regina più non sei.	For a moment, Medea, you were a queen: You are a queen no more.
[beginning of the tempo d'attacco]	
Cedi al destin, Medea; Contro il destin non basti.	Submit to destiny, Medea; You are not strong enough to contend against destiny.

She responds in her beginning of the tempo d'attacco; a turning point when she realizes that he will never return to her:

Era Medea, lo sai	Medea, as you know,
Del suo destin maggiore,	Was greater than her destiny;
Barbaro, oh dio! Minore	O god! It was only for you, barbarous man,
Se fece sol per te.	That I belittled myself.

The first woman has to accept her destiny, and it is rarely pleasant. Though the second woman is not, as Medea desires, "greater than her destiny," she does help to shape it. While Medea and Donizetti's Leonora do not like the fact that their husbands will not return to them, they have the energy and determination to do something about it: they take revenge. In Italian opera of this time, virtually all women—and this includes *both* the first and second woman—love where there is an obstacle. The first woman almost never gets what she wants, and, after 1830, she usually dies because of it. The second woman always gets to make a choice about how to respond to the obstacle; this choice gives her the power to do something. The range of her behavior, including brutal deeds, further separates the two principal women in characterization. Medea makes such choices when she kills Creusa and murders her own children. Leonora's response is similar; she stabs Rosmonda.

However, the final moments of both operas reinforce the different treatments each woman receives: the difference between 1813, when women sang heroic travesti roles almost as commonly as female characters, and 1834, when a woman's voice was usually denied heroic triumph and survival. After Medea reveals what she has done and throws down the bloody knife that she used to kill their children in front of Giasone, a storm rises, and she curses him further. Right before she makes her grand exit in the dragon-pulled chariot, her final words emphasize her vengeance as an act of punishment upon Giasone:

Medea's Curse on Giasone and the Final Moments of the Opera, *Medea in Corinto*

Medea

Resta: asilo ti nieghi la terra,	Stay there: may earth deny you shelter,
Mai sereno ti splenda un sol giorno,	May never a single day shine serenely upon you,
Ah! Le furie ti vengan d'intorno,	Ah! My the furies that you see rampant
Che nel seno mi vedi regnar.	In my breast encircle and surround you.

. . . . .

Medea

Mira: non hai consorte;	Look: you no longer have a wife;
Più non ti resta un figlio;	Not a child is left you;
Ed all'ingiusto esiglio	And thus Medea departs
Parte Medea così.	Into unmerited exile.

She crosses the stage on a chariot drawn by two dragons.

Giasone

Mi sveni il ferro stesso	May the same blade slay me
Che il sen de' figli aprì.	That shed the blood of my children.

He is about to stab himself, but is restrained.

All [Chorus]

T'arresta . . . misero prence! . . .	Stop . . . wretched prince! . . .
Ah! Toglasi a tanto orrore . . .	Ah! Let us escape from all this horror . . .
Ah! Par che da' suoi cardini	Ah! The whole world seems to be
Si svegla il mondo tutto . . .	Torn from its hinges . . .
Che scena! Oh Dei! Che lutto!	Ye gods! What a scene of grief!
Che sanguinoso dì!	What a day of blood!

After having committed such crimes, Medea still has the indignation to call her exile "ingiusto" (unjust, unmerited). The Greek chorus, which has the last word, does not chastise her; instead, they comment on the grief of the entire situation. Hence, Medea's actions—at least on some level—are placed within the context of righteous retribution, even with their grisly and tragic nature. Her character is allowed to execute such deeds, and her punishment is exile, and not death.

Donizetti's second woman, Queen Leonora, experiences a different fate at the opera's conclusion.[44] In a moment of reflection immediately after she stabs Rosmonda, Leonora turns to her husband:

The Last Moments of *Rosmonda d'Inghilterra,* Right after Leonora Stabs Rosmonda

Leonora

Tu! Spergiuro, disumano,	You, perjured inhuman man,
mi spingesti al nero eccesso;	you forced me to this black excess;
Io l'acciaro, tu sei la mano	If I am the blade, you are the hand
che il delitto consumò.	that committed this crime.
Già d'entrambi ah! L'innocenza,	Ah! Already her innocence invokes
chiese al Ciel vendetta eterna;	Heaven's eternal vengeance upon us both;
Già d'entrambi la sentenza, con quel sangue Iddio segnò!	Already with that blood God has signed sentence upon both of us!

Enrico

Va, crudele! Tu m'hai spinto . . .	Be gone, cruel woman! You have pushed me too far . . .

Clifford

Sventurato genitor! Figlia mia!	Unfortunate father! My daughter!

Leonora

Tu, crudele, sei la colpa, tu solo. . . .	You, cruel man, you alone are to blame.
Tu! Spergiuro, disumano, etc.	. . . You, perjured, inhuman man, etc.

All of the Others

Misera! Quale orror!	Poor woman! What horror!
Così amor la vendicò.	Thus love has avenged her.

Rather than the airborne Medea in her magical escape, the final image in *Rosmonda* is the ever-increasing innocence of Rosmonda and the vitriolic curses of Leonora. Enrico blames Leonora for what has happened, Clifford mourns his daughter's death, and Leonora, in her last words, tries to evade the guilt by holding Enrico responsible for her actions. As in *Medea,* the final statement is given to the chorus; yet here either Leonora or Rosmonda could be the "Misera!" and/or the referent for whom love has avenged. Though their comments are applicable to both women, the opera ends with Leonora as the villain and Rosmonda elevated to the status of a martyr.

In the structure of the plot and the relationships between the two principal female characters, Donizetti's *Rosmonda d'Inghilterra* echoes patterns employed by his Bergamo teacher, Simone Mayr, in *Medea in Corinto.* In both operas the second woman kills the tenor's beloved (the first woman) in an act of vengeance motivated by betrayal. Yet the conventions surrounding how each woman is configured within the dynamics of the plot are different. In 1813 the second woman's voice was still aligned with the hero, and her voice signaled noble behavior. Within this context even brutal deeds could be presented as the righteous fury of a vindicated protagonist. After 1830, when the second woman's voice was further removed from the hero, the energy of the opera placed emphasis on the innocence of the first woman. With the tenor becoming the new Romantic voice of the hero, the associations between women's voices and noble valor became less audible. Women's voices had an expanded range of options open to them in the early 1810s, as is amply illustrated by Mayr's *Medea:* innocence and vengeance, helplessness and dynamic retribution, virtue and rage. By the 1830s, the second woman could still do outrageous things, but she had to pay the price in the negative repercussions to her reputation; she now became the villain without much sympathy.

As a singer of roles written within both sets of conventions, Giuditta Pasta's voice spanned the variety of characterizations. When she premiered roles in the 1830s (e.g., the title characters in *Anna Bolena* and *Norma* and Bianca in Donizetti's *Ugo, Conte di Parigi*) she was able to bring aspects of the second woman into the first woman heroines she sang. Because she continued to sing travesti heroes and her earlier female characters, such as Medea, throughout her career, Pasta's creations of prototypical Romantic heroines were sung side by side in her repertoire with the earlier primo ottocento heroines who got to survive.

Medea and Norma

Though other scholars have noted similarities between Mayr's *Medea* and Bellini's *Norma* (particularly in their stories and that Giuditta Pasta, the first Norma, was also well known in the title role of Mayr's opera), I would like to probe more deeply as to what some of these connections could have meant for audiences in Pasta's time as well as in ours today.[45] As mentioned above, all four of the operas discussed in some depth in this chapter (Donizetti's *Anna Bolena* and *Rosmonda,* Mayr's *Medea,* and Bellini's *Norma*) are collaborations with the leading librettist of the time, Felice Romani. In this context, it is less surprising to find similarities and subtle associations between these four operas. Yet I would like to propose that some of these interconnections go beyond the general conventions of plot design at this time (admittedly a time when formulaic patterns facilitated the speed with which new operas were written to supply the demand). I assert that many of the cross-references between the characters of Medea and Norma are amplified, and comment on the development of the Romantic heroine, when viewed in the context that Pasta was the voice most associated with the role of Mayr's Medea and the first interpreter of Bellini's Norma.

Starting early in the first act of *Norma*, after the opening scene with the Druid chorus, a veiled reference to Mayr's *Medea* is made when Pollione and his assistant Flavio sneak into the Druid woods to wait for Adalgisa. While they wait, Pollione tells Flavio of a foreboding dream he had about Norma and Adalgisa:

Pollione's Dream, Act 1, *Norma*

In rammentarlo io tremo.	In remembering it, I tremble
Meco all'altar di Venere	With me, at the altar of Venus,
Era Adalgisa in Roma,	Was Adalgisa in Rome,
Cinta di bende candide,	Swathed in white veils,
Sparsa di fior la chioma;	Her hair decked with flowers.
Udia d'Imene i cantici,	Heard the chants of Hymen,
Vedea fumar gl'incensi,	I saw the incenses smoking;
Eran rapiti i sensi	My senses were transported
Di voluttade e amore.	In pleasure and love.
Quando fra noi terribile	When between us a terrible
Viene, viene a locarsi un'ombra:	Shadow comes, comes to place itself:
L'ampio mantel druidico	The full, druidic cloak
Come un vapor l'ingombra:	Enfolds it like a mist:
Cade sull'ara il folgore,	The thunderbolt falls on the altar,
D'un vel si copre il giorno,	The day is covered by a veil,
Muto si spande intorno	A sepulchral horror
Un sepolcrale orror.	Spreads all around, silent.
Più l'adorata vergine	I no longer find the adored maiden
Io non mi trovo accanto:	At my side:
N'odo da lunge un gemito,	From afar I hear a moan of hers,
Misto de'figli al pianto!	Mingled with children's weeping!
Ed una voce orrible	And a horrible voice
Echeggia in fondo al tempio:	Reechoes in the depths of the temple:
Norma così fa scempio	Norma thus destroys
D'amante traditor!	Her faithless lover!
(Squilla il sacro bronzo).	(The sacred bronze resounds)

(Thus signaling the beginning of the rites that lead to Norma's entrance and that Pollione and Flavio need to leave.)

Like most dreams in drama, Pollione's provides an added commentary to the story (e.g., Klytämnestra's dream in Richard Strauss and Hugo von Hofmannsthal's *Elektra*). I would like to extend the metaphor of the dream for an interpretation that not only illuminates Pollione's fears for the new relationship he plans to begin with Adalgisa (he is about to leave Norma, his mistress and the mother of his two children), but also encompasses a collective understanding and allusion that is shared by the audience hearing Pasta sing *Norma*. Pollione's dream is filled with visual and aural imagery. If we "listen" to his dream through the ears of Pasta's admirers who knew her famous portrayal of Medea, the connections between the two are striking.

The altar of "love" (Venus) in Rome, a basic image for marriage (the marriage Pollione would like to have with Adalgisa when he takes her back to Rome), also works as a reference back to the intended marriage of Giasone and Creusa. As in Pollione's dream in *Norma*, at the end of act 1 in *Medea*, the chorus sings hymns to Hymen as the anticipated wedding between Giasone and Creusa is about to take place.[46] The mantle of darkness that engulfs Adalgisa invokes the enchanted robe that Medea gives to Creusa as a fatal wedding present (this is the robe that Medea had laid out on an altar, in her *scongiuro* incantation scene, when she called on demons to curse and poison it). With the sound of weeping children in the background, the horrendous infanticide Medea commits against her own children is brought to mind and signals to the audience that the two children (same number as in *Medea*) that Norma and Pollione have might later encounter danger. The last line of Pollione's dream strengthens the connections between the two operas with the themes of vengeance and wrath spelled out. Hence, at the beginning of *Norma*, before we even meet the title character, she has been allied with Medea.

The allusions to *Medea* in Pollione's dream set up an extra layer of drama for the audience at Pasta's *Norma*. With the role of Medea being one of Pasta's most famous interpretations, how could the original audiences watch Norma with her small children, agonizing over her rejection by the man she loves for someone new, and not draw the parallels between them? With this association, a key point of suspense is created in the beginning of the second act. It must have been an electrifying experience for both Pasta and her audience when Norma looks her children and says, "Dormono entrambi, Non vedran la mano che li percuote. Non pentirti, o core" (They are both asleep. They will not see the hand that strikes them. No remorse in my heart). We are back in the same situation with an opera written almost twenty years earlier, yet kept alive through Pasta's regular performances of it in the late 1820s through the 1830s: Pasta performs a betrayed woman who is quite capable of killing her own children.

While the similarities between Medea and Norma are strong, the type of woman we see in *Medea* in 1813 is given a very different characterization in 1831. Mayr's *Medea* and Bellini's *Norma* are both operas with two principal women written by two of the leading opera composers of their day. With Romani as the librettist for both operas, each libretto reflects the different aesthetics of its time.[47] Though Colbran and Pasta had different strengths, their voices and repertory corresponded closely, and (as seen earlier) Pasta was successful in several "Colbran" roles, particularly as Medea. With the overt references to *Medea* in *Norma* and the voice of Pasta behind both roles in the early 1830s, it is surprising how different the two roles really become by the end of their respective operas.

As we get to know Norma throughout the first act, she seems to have all the fire and drive of Medea. Her first appearance is dazzling, and she commands complete authority over her Druid compatriots in her entrance scene ("Sediziose voci" [Seditious voices]) with her ability to prevent them from gong to war with the Romans before she gives her permission. In her cavatina "Casta diva" (Chaste goddess) she performs the holy rites of cutting the sacred mistletoe with controlled precision as she navigates the sustained breath control and dizzying fioratura in a stratospheric tessitura that keeps climbing higher.

While maintaining the public front needed for her official duties, she also expresses conflicting emotions in her cabaletta, "Ah! bello a me ritorna del fido amor primiero" (Ah! Bring back to me the beauty of our first love). Delivered entirely as a parenthetical aside (so that the audience can "hear" the meaning of the words while the others onstage do not), we hear her public and private personas in opposition as she secretly fantasizes how wonderful it would be if Pollione—enemy and oppressor of the Druid people, forbidden love of Norma, and the father of her children—would, once again, return her love. Later in the first act when her duet with Adalgisa turns into the trio finale with Pollione's entrance, Norma can show Adalgisa forgiveness and simultaneously vent her scorn at the unfaithful Pollione. Like Medea, Norma is a complex character who commands respect, yet who lives with painful secrets, betrayal, and desperation.

At the end of the first act in their duet (before it becomes a trio when Pollione unexpectedly enters), Adalgisa tells Norma that she has broken her temple vows and has fallen in love. Norma's reaction goes beyond sympathy; given her own broken vows for her secret love, she is able to empathize with Adalgisa. During the slow section of their duet, in several parenthetical asides, Norma responds to Adalgisa's story of seduction as it rekindles memories of her own experience:

Norma's Memories during Act 1 Duet with Adalgisa, *Norma*
Norma's comments are made as parenthetical asides.

Norma

(Oh! Rimembranza!	(Oh what memories!
Io fui così rapita	I was thus enraptured
Al sol mirarlo in volto!)	When I first saw his face.)
. . . . .	. . . . .
(Io stessa arsi così. Oh rimembranza:	(I too felt that.
. . . . .	. . . . .
Oh, rimembranza!	Oh, memories!
. . . . .	. . . . .
Io fui così sedotta!)	I was also thus seduced!)
. . . . .	. . . . .
(Oh, cari accenti!	(Oh, dear words!
Così li profferia,	So my lover spoke to me—
Così trovava del mio cor la via!)	Thus opening the way to my heart!)
. . . . .	. . . . .
(L'incanto suo fu il mio!)	(Her enchantment was mine!)

As in her cabaletta to "Casta Diva," these parenthetical asides allow the audience to have a glimpse of another side of Norma: a more personal and hidden side of her as a vulnerable woman. While Adalgisa confesses her broken vows, Norma sees herself reflected back. Her last aside about having been caught in an "incanto," an enchantment or spell, lets the audience see that the two women are in the same situation, just at different stages. Adalgisa is in the first blush of love, Norma is facing a later stage of betrayal.

By releasing Adalgisa from her temple duties, in this first act duet, Norma gives Adalgisa the opportunity that she herself was never allowed; the chance to make a public life with the man she loves. In this way, Norma hopes to make it possible for Adalgisa to become the woman Norma wishes she herself could have been. Instead of running the risk of having to raise children in hiding, Norma is willing to help Adalgisa make a family for herself without the shame of secrecy.

In opera of this time period, it is not uncommon for the tenor to have seduced both women, either within the opera or in the opera's prehistory. Additionally, it is typical for both women to be in love with the tenor: hence, the love triangle. Yet it is less common that both women love the tenor *and* promise to keep their friendship in high regard. In their next duet (at the beginning of the second act), Norma and Adalgisa make this type of pledge to each other. Rather than the usual reaction of increased rivalry, their second act duet reveals their solutions: each woman is willing to cede Pollione to the other. In the tempo d'attacco of their second act duet, Norma is willing to relinquish her connections to Pollione over to Adalgisa and then kill herself. In return she requests that Adalgisa and Pollione look after the two children they have had together so they will not become slaves. Shocked at such a drastic plan, Adalgisa puts her honor and friendship with Norma before her own love of Pollione and makes a decision that will leave her alone at the end. When Adalgisa realizes that Pollione has two children with Norma, she makes a critical move. In light of his obligation to Norma, Adalgisa rescinds any claim to Polllione; she promises to talk to him and convince him to return to Norma. Not surprisingly, Norma accepts Adalgisa's plan. However, Norma questions Adalgisa about her feelings for him. Adalgisa explains how she feels and her new resolve. The culmination of Norma and Adalgisa's relationship is achieved in the cabaletta that immediately follows this section. Having worked out a plan that they both accept, the two women pledge their eternal friendship:

Norma-Adalgisa Duet, End of the Tempo di Mezzo and Cabaletta, Act 2, *Norma*

Adalgisa
L'amai. Quest'anima   I loved him. Now I feel
Sol l'amistade or sente.   Nothing but friendship.

Norma
O giovinetta! E vuoi?   Oh, child! What do you want [to do]?

Adalgisa
Renderti i dritti tuoi,   Render to you your rights,
O teco al cielo agli uomini   I swear to always hide myself,
Giuro celarmi ognor.   From God and men.

Norma
Sì. Hai vinto . . . hai vinto. Abbrac-   Yes. You have won, you have won. Em-
ciami.   brace me.
Trovo un'amica ancor.   I have found my friend again.

Norma and Adalgisa

Sì, fino all'ore estreme	Yes, up to the final hours
Compagna tua m'avrai.	You will always have me
Per ricovrarci, per ricovrarci insieme	As your friend.
Ampia è la terra assai.	The earth is big enough
Teco del fato all'onte	To shelter us both from the shame of fate.
Ferma opporrò la fronte,	To oppose the difficulties together,
Finchè il mio core a battere	As long as my heart beats,
Io senta sul tuo cor.	I will feel your heart.

Their dramatic vow of friendship is followed by a somewhat unexpected ending. In a recitative by Clotilde (Norma's *comprimaria* attendant) we find out that Adalgisa's plan was unsuccessful; Pollione will not return to Norma. Though Adalgisa returned to the temple resolved to make her final vows to chastity, Pollione pursued her into the temple, where the Druids ended up capturing him. His judgment and sentence are left up to Norma. In their ensuing scene, Norma tries to convince Pollione to renounce Adalgisa, but to no avail. In the final reference to *Medea*, Norma holds up a dagger and mentions her earlier attempt on their children's lives:

Norma-Pollione Scene near the End of the Opera, Act 2, *Norma*

Norma

Sì, sovr'essi alzai la punta.	Yes, I raised the point [of the dagger] over them.
Vedi, vedi a che son giunta!	See, see what I have become!
Non ferii, ma tosto, adesso	I did not strike—but soon—now
Consumar potrei l'eccesso.	I shall commit such excess!
Un istante, e d'esser madre	One instant, and it is possible
Mi poss'io dimenticar!	I could forget that I am a mother!

With the mention of "excess" and reference to the dangerous mother, Pasta's role as Medea bleeds through and compels the audience to remember Medea's vengeance. The reference is strategically placed; Pollione has just stated that he would rather die than give up Adalgisa. With the allusion to *Medea*, we are all reminded of what Medea did to Creusa and how Norma now holds the power of life and death over Adalgisa. As Norma discovers that sacrificing Adalgisa would make Pollione suffer more than murdering their children, she triumphantly tells him: "Adalgisa shall be punished: she will perish in the flames" (of the funeral pyre that has been built).[48]

The final denouement of the opera comes after the Druids are assembled, and Norma announces the sacrificial victim who violated her vows as a Priestess. To Adalgisa's, Pollione's, and the audience's surprise, it is not Adalgisa who is named, but Norma herself. In the fast-paced confusion that follows when Norma confesses and asks her father for forgiveness and mercy for her children, Pollione suddenly finds new respect and a rekindled love for Norma's noble dignity. As they both mount the steps to the funeral pyre, he swears his eternal love to Norma.

As a product of its time, *Norma* fits the profile of having the leading women, a "first woman" and a "second woman," who both love the tenor, Pollione. However, the romantic love triangle takes on a different nature when the alliances between the three characters keep shifting; hence, the positions of Norma and Adalgisa as the first and second woman keep seeming to flip-flop. As we have seen, in the pre-history to the opera, Norma and Pollione secretly loved each other and had two children. At the beginning of the opera, however, Pollione has grown tired of Norma and has become enamored with Adalgisa. In the first act, Norma appears to be more of a second woman, as was Medea, with the power she exerts as the Druid High Priestess and having to bear Pollione's betrayal. Adalgisa, the woman who is loved, seems to fit the model of the first woman. Yet by the end of the opera, it is Norma who ultimately recovers the love of Pollione and ends up dying as an instrument of fate (a typical first woman ending). Adalgisa, alone and without the love of the tenor, survives the opera (a typical second woman ending).

However, this is an incomplete picture of the two women's characterizations. Even up through the end of the opera, Norma is making decisions regarding whom she will name as the sacrificial victim—Adalgisa or herself. She marches to the funeral pyre having tied up all loose ends: she confesses her misdeeds, asks for her father's forgiveness, and makes sure that her children will not be raised as Roman slaves. Though she is immolated at the end, her final actions hardly appear to be those of utter defeat.

But where does that leave Adalgisa? Adalgisa disappears in the second act; her last solo vocal appearance is in the beginning of the act in her duet with Norma. After Adalgisa promises to compel Pollione to return to Norma in their duet, we find out, through Clotilde's recitative, that Adalgisa was unsuccessful in convincing him. Clotilde relates that Adalgisa has remained true to her Priestess vows and has returned to the temple; we never hear Adalgisa's voice again in the opera. Yet Adalgisa's role remains crucial for the working out of the drama. Since she had been so important throughout the first act and beginning of the second act (*Norma* is in two acts), why is she left out in the final scenes? Despite Adalgisa's absence, her character is very much felt in the ending of the opera. Norma's threat to sacrifice Adalgisa, as a way to hurt Pollione, keeps Pollione—and the audience—wondering what Norma will do to resolve the tense situation at the end.

Norma and *Anna Bolena*

Donizetti's *Anna Bolena*, created by Pasta the year before, presents a similar situation for the two female characters. Like Adalgisa, Giovanna Seymour (the second woman in *Anna Bolena*) disappears before the end of the opera; neither woman is in her opera's finale. Giovanna's last appearance is just before the opera's conclusion, in her scene with Enrico, when she pleads, to no avail, for mercy on Anna's life. The conclusion of *Anna Bolena* gives Anna a climactic mad scene where she slips in and out of delirium as she leaves her prison cell in the Tower of London and is taken to her execution. From offstage, near the end of the mad scene, sounds of cheering are heard. As Anna is roused from her delirium and inquires about the far-off sounds, Smeton, Percy, and Rochefort tell her that the commotion is celebrating Giovanna as the new queen.[49] Though Giovanna is not onstage for the finale, she still plays a role in the concluding scene as a poignant juxtaposition to Anna's sad plight.

The pivotal time for both Adalgisa and Giovanna occurs in their duets, with their respective title character, near the beginning of act 2 (both operas are in two acts). For Adalgisa, this point was critical for her realization that her new romantic relationship was at Norma's expense, and Adalgisa chooses her friendship with Norma over her love for Pollione. With this resolution Adalgisa completes her action in the plot. Like Giovanna, despite her absence in the last scene, Adalgisa retains an important function in the narrative; her presence is invoked for Pollione (and the audience) as Norma considers naming her as the sacrificial victim at the end.

In their second act duet, Giovanna finally confesses that she is the one who is Anna's rival for the throne. Leading up to the confession, Anna had cursed the woman who was her adversary, "Al par del mio, / sia straziato il vil suo cuore" (With a parity to mine, may her vile heart be tortured). After Giovanna confesses, she begs for Anna's forgiveness, which Anna finally grants. In her pardon, Anna says, "La tua grazia or chiedo a Dio, / e concessa a me sarà" (I now ask God to have mercy on you, and it will be granted to me).

This sentiment is emphasized with its repetition, and two similar meanings emerge. As she asks God to have mercy on Giovanna, Anna feels assured that God will grant her [Anna's] request. However, the wording could also mean that the mercy Anna has asked God to have for Giovanna, will also be granted to Anna. The slight differences in these translations/interpretations allow for a reflexivity between the two women; the grace that Giovanna receives will also be shown to Anna. This theme is again brought back a little later when Giovanna beseeches the King to have mercy on Anna and prevent her execution. Giovanna states, "Il suo pianto ho nel cor; di lei pietade, in un di me" (I have her pain in my heart. Show mercy to her and at the same time to me).

More than merely a catalyst for setting things in motion, Adalgisa and Giovanna are important characters whose juxtapositions with the title role enrich the drama. The two women in each opera present contrasting portrayals of women in love. Norma, the Queen figure as the Druid High Priestess, has power and authority, yet spends most of the opera (until the very last moments) as the woman betrayed and cast aside. Adalgisa, the neophyte and young temple virgin, is seduced, innocently falls in love, and then renounces Pollione when she finds out about his relationship with Norma. Anna Bolena as the Queen should have power and authority; nevertheless, she is supplanted by Giovanna (her attendant) when Enrico falls in love with Jane Seymour. The two operas differ at this point. While we might believe that Giovanna was innocently seduced, we also see that she is not without ambition; throughout the opera she is torn between her friendship and guilt toward Anna and her own desires for advancement. Unlike Adalgisa, Giovanna does not relinquish her relationship with the King, when she sees the suffering she is causing and Anna's more legitimate claim.

In *Anna Bolena*, Giovanna's torment throughout the opera involves her ability to see that what has happened to Anna could very well happen to her: the King could grow tired of her and decide to replace her with another wife. As Giovanna tries to resist his advances, she is drawn in more deeply. In their act 1 duet (the King's first entrance in the opera), Giovanna sets up an early comparison between herself and Anna:

Giovanna-Enrico Duet, Act 1, *Anna Bolena*

Giovanna

Ah! Non io, non io v'offria	Oh, but I did not offer you
Questo core a torto offeso . . .	This heart which you now so wrongly accuse . . .
Il mio Re melo rapia,	My King stole it from me;
Dal mio Re mi venga reso;	Let my King give it back.
Più infelice di Bolena,	I shall be more wretched than Anne Boleyn,
Più da piangere sarò.	More to be pitied:
Di un ripudio avrò la pena,	I shall experience the misery of a repudiation [divorce]
Né un marito offeso avrò.	Without having wronged a husband.

In this duet Giovanna's protestations to the King to break off their affair only increase his desire. She is concerned about her honor and reputation if they continue to see each other in secret and worries that he does not take her seriously. Should their relationship end, Giovanna fears that she would be in a situation that would be even worse than the one Anna is in now—at least Anna is the legitimate Queen through marriage.

The connections between Giovanna and Anna go beyond their status as women in the court whom Enrico eventually marries. Both women love unwisely: Anna had still harbored feelings for Percy when she married the King, and Giovanna loves the already-married King. Yet their positions in the drama are given deeper connections. Both women try to find mercy, and when they ask for it, they each seek it for themselves and the other. As Anna implores God's grace for Giovanna in their act 2 duet, she also looks for it for herself. When Giovanna begs Enrico to spare Anna's life (in Giovanna's last appearance onstage), she tells him how his mercy for Anna will also help her. The two women are complementary characters whose lives run in parallel directions: Anna's experiences are echoed in Giovanna's situation. With the history of Henry VIII's many wives Jane Seymour could be seen, like Anne Boleyn, as one wife in a succession of several other wives. As Anne replaced Catherine of Aragon in Henry's affections to become his second wife, she also became the best hope for producing a male heir. Catherine had borne a daughter (Mary I/Mary Tudor) but no sons. Jane Seymour followed the same course in becoming Henry's third wife. Anne had given birth to one daughter (Elizabeth I) but no sons. Like Anne, when she won the King's attention, Jane became his best hope for giving him a prince.[50] At the end of the opera, Giovanna is not needed in the finale because she will live out her own personal version of the events of the opera in the coming years.

Like Anna and Giovanna, Norma and Adalgisa become two parts of the same character. In Norma and Adalgisa's first appearance together (their first act duet), when Norma is reminded of when she first fell in love, she sees herself in Adalgisa. In fact, right before she finds out that Pollione is the object of Adalgisa's affections, Norma is ready to grant Adalgisa permission to renounce her Priestess duties. Norma's hope is that Adalgisa will be able to have the life that Norma wishes she could have led herself.[51] In their act 2 duet, after Adalgisa has found out that Norma also loves Pollione, Adalgisa makes the difficult decision to extricate herself from the situation and not to get in the way of Norma's claim to the father of her children. Rather than become bitter rivals (as in *Medea* or *Rosmonda*), the two women pledge their friendship and erase any tension between them. This is the last time we hear Adalgisa's voice in a solo capacity. Adalgisa and Norma effectively become two parts of the same shared identity—both women are Durid Priestesses, both have fallen in love with the same person, and both would like the same thing to happen: the reunion of Norma and Pollione. In this way the two women provide alternative endings for the same composite character. Adalgisa—the one who renounces love—gets to live; Norma—the one who chooses love—gets to die.

In modern times, *Norma* is infrequently performed. The vocal writing of the title role is viewed today as requiring a big voice with power, agility, and some heft. Adalgisa's role is also considered demanding, but, given its somewhat lower tessitura, it appears less daunting. The younger Druid Priestess has been an effective role for several late-twentieth-century (mezzo-)sopranos with high extensions and the ability to keep their singing light enough to sound youthful; ideally, Adalgisa's is not the heavier voice.[52] When the opera is performed today, it is nearly impossible to expect that the same two singers would comfortably be able to exchange roles.[53] Currently most people think of Norma and Adalgisa as requiring two very different voices. However, the performance of these roles was different in the nineteenth century, particularly in its early casting.

Giulia Grisi (1811–69), the first Adalgisa, was a high soprano at an early stage in her career (she was twenty years old). Following their first performances in *Norma* (premiered on December 26, 1831), Pasta and Grisi were again paired later that same season at La Scala in Donizetti's *Ugo, conte di Parigi* (premiered on March 13, 1832). Complementing the almost sisterly relationship between Norma and Adalgisa, in *Ugo* the two women played sisters and were, once again, in love with the same tenor. Still the less established singer at the point, Grisi (who was fourteen years younger than Pasta) again sang the smaller role.[54] After *Ugo*, Grisi broke her contract in Italy and left to sing abroad. She went on to have an outstanding career outside of Italy that was primarily focused in Paris and London.[55] Bellini and Pasta collaborated one last time on the title character in his next opera, *Beatrice di Tenda* (1833, La Fenice, Venice).

In Bellini's following opera, his debut in Paris, he once more worked with Grisi, this time in the leading role in *I puritani* (1835, Théâtre Italien, Paris). This opera was a huge success for both Bellini and the singers—so much so that the four principal singers, who were among the leading performers of their day (Grisi as Elvira; Giovanni Battista Rubini as Arturo, tenor; Antonio Tamburini as Riccardo, baritone; and Luigi Lablache as Giorgio, bass), became known as "the *Puritani* quartet" from the premiere and the revivals in London and Paris. Given the popularity of *I puritani* and Bellini's experiences with Giulia Grisi, it is quite likely that she would have continued to be the leading heroine in at least a few of Bellini's future operas. Unfortunately, Bellini died eight months after the premiere of *Puritani,* and it was to be his last opera.

I have briefly outlined the career of Giulia Grisi because though she was the first voice behind Adalgisa, she went on to sing other leading soprano roles. One of her most famous Bellini roles turns out to have been her interpretation of Norma; she sang it nearly every season in London (at Her Majesty's Theatre and Covent Garden) between 1837 and 1861.[56] Writing from Paris in 1844, noted French arts critic (especially in ballet, opera, and theater) Théophile Gautier praised her interpretation:

> Norma is Giulia Grisi, and never, for sure, did Irminsul have a priestess more lovely or better inspired. She surpasses the ideal. . . . *Norma* is Giulia Grisi's triumph. . . . Giulia Grisi achieves a sublimity in this [opening scene of act 2] which has never been surpassed; truly this is the tragic Muse, the Melpomene of whom Aeschylus and Phidias might have dreamed.[57]

As two roles, Norma and Adalgisa can be blended into one persona thematically (in terms of characterization) and musically. As a few modern-day divas have shown, and as was the case of Giulia Grisi, both roles can be contained within the same throat and voice. This hybridity of their characters and voices presents an innovative prototype of the Romantic heroine. As different sides of operatic woman in love, the conflation of their two roles into one reveals their deeper-level connection. Seen and heard together, they provide complementary pictures of the evolving Romantic heroine.[58]

Norma and *Anna Bolena,* two collaborations among the leading composers, librettist, and singers of the time, are pivotal works in the formation of the Romantic heroine. As both operas begin with two women, their stories are interconnected and ultimately woven into one. At the beginning of each opera, the title character has been forsaken in favor of her attendant; Enrico has lost interest in Anna and loves Giovanna; Pollione is tired of Norma and has turned his attention to Adalgisa. By the end of each opera, the principal romantic couple (the title character and the tenor) affirm their love even though they both face execution; due to the insurmountable obstacles on Earth, they are reunited only in death.[59]

In the last moments of *Norma,* right after Norma asks Oroveso (her father and the Head Druid Priest) to have mercy on her children, Oroveso replies, "Oppresso è il core. Ha vinto amor!" (My heart is heavy. Love has conquered!) In the immediate context, his response can have two meanings. First, it indicates that his fatherly love has won out over his castigation, and he will make sure that his grandchildren are cared for. The second reading is that it is his interpretation of what

Giulia Grisi (Bellini's first Adalgisa) in the title role of Bellini's
Norma in the 1830s. *The Harvard Theatre Collection, The Houghton Library.*

happened to his daughter—love conquered her—and this is what results. In the
larger picture, the second reading provides a concise and fitting statement for the
broader plight of the Romantic heroine in operas of this time: love conquers her.
Such a statement is radically different from Medea's, albeit exaggerated, declaration
to Giasone in their duet: "Era Medea, lo sai, / Del suo destin maggiore" (Medea, as
you know, was greater than her destiny). Yet it shows the distance that roles written
for female characters undertook in the first decades of the nineteenth century.
What threaded these roles together were the singers who moved across gender and
the simultaneous conventions of happy and tragic endings.

The voice of Giuditta Pasta was a vortex that brought everything together. One
night she sang as the triumphant hero in her armor with a helmet covering her hair.
A few nights later as Medea she summoned up the demons of the underworld to
kill her rival and then flew away in a dragon-pulled chariot. Later that month she
stumbled in and out of delirium for Anna Bolena's mad-scene finale. A little while
later that same season, she marched to her funeral pyre as the Druid Priestess who

stayed true to her heart, regained the love of Pollione and maintained her dignity, and became a martyr for the love she held dear to her heart. As one of the central voices of the time, her career demonstrates the simultaneity of how the voice of heroism evolved through the different representations of masculinity (the castrato, heroic travesti, and the tenor) and what a female voice was allowed to express regarding triumph, revenge, defeat, and self-sacrifice.

Coda: Looking Ahead to Risorgimento Heroism

Today we have no problem thinking of nineteenth-century Italian operas with only one leading female role. The title roles in Donizetti's *Lucia di Lammermoor* (1835), Verdi's *La Traviata* (1853), and Puccini's *Tosca* (1900) provide only a few of the most popular examples. However, these heroines do not represent the most common female character type found in the primo ottocento. While Violetta (*La Traviata*) and Tosca epitomize the unrivaled Romantic heroine, in step with their time, Lucia was less typical for the first audiences precisely because of her primary importance. This singular leading lady was not a standard phenomenon in Italian opera until the second half of the century.

Two critical factors influencing this shift were the increasing preference for the tenor voice as the hero and the changing practices of how opera plots concluded. In the first decades of the nineteenth century, the tenor was not yet the normative hero. The move into this new paradigm generated a period of transition with multiple articulations of what was heard as heroic. Much of the vocal drama underlying the shift between the travesti hero and the second woman is due to the associations that the heroic travesti voice still maintained as the treble timbred legacy of the castrati while also contending with the sound of the new tenor hero. As the tenor displaced the musico roles, these travesti singers sang as women and became the voice of the second woman.

In the second half of the nineteenth century, the era of Verdi's Violetta through Puccini's Tosca, the sound of the high soprano voice came to be equated with the suffering heroine. Though she loved the tenor hero and he loved her, there inevitably was some situation or person that prevented their ultimate union. In most operas before 1830, including plots that involved either one or two romantic couples, the conflict keeping the lovers apart was remedied at the very end. In an interaction between the heroic tenor sound and the new vogue for tragic endings, operas after 1830 employed a new ending for the heroine that required her death by the final curtain. The death of the soprano heroine (and sometimes the death of the tenor hero, as well) became a conceit to illustrate the fated hopelessness of their situation.

The production of the Romantic heroine involved a realignment of narrative plot with narrative voice. For women in opera, this had repercussions both within the plot and in the construction of the cast. Whereas the heroic travesti and their heroines survived the end of the opera, the Romantic heroine expired. Yet the Romantic heroine achieves an element of independence as she faces death. Usually suffering alone, her death is a direct result of her decision to remain true to her personal code of honor. As audiences flocked to the opera houses in the first half of the nineteenth century, the new convention of the plot resonated strongly with their contemporary situations. With period ears the Italian public was able to hear and understand the relevant message that extended past the opera stage and into the political drama they faced in their daily lives.

Nineteenth-century Italian opera scholarship has long recognized that the opera house has provided the opportunity for a staged microcosm of the contemporary political arena outside of the theater. In extremely turbid times, the great drama across the Italian political landscape was the Risorgimento, the struggle for a united national Italian identity. As a country inhabited by foreign nations divvying up political and economic control, the Austrians and French held sway across the north, the Kingdom of the Two Sicilies was under Spanish Bourbons in the south, and, among other independent regions, the Papal States around Rome and its adjacent provinces kept Italy divided into several parts. With the foreign nations charging extra tariffs on commerce, requiring documentation to travel between cities, and imposing oppressive codes of censorship (presenting a particularly tough situation for opera), Italy was fragmented. Though foreign occupation dated back before the nineteenth century, the Napoleonic era and the nationalist movements in other parts of nineteenth-century Europe led into an intensified political and economic situation that fueled the energy of the Risorgimento.

To its northern neighbors, Italy's warmer climate and artistic treasures have provided an important travel destination for, among other things, diversion and cultural enrichment during the eighteenth century and up to the present. Commenting on the effect that Italy's political situation was having on artistic expression, Germany's Heinrich Heine and France's Henri Beyle (writing under the pen name of Stendhal) wrote about the mounting frustrations of the Italians in the 1820s. Heine described the important space that music filled in occupied Italy:

> Even the use of speech is forbidden to poor enslaved Italy, and she can only express by music the feelings of her heart. All her resentment against foreign domination, her inspiration of liberty, her rage at the consciousness of weakness, her sorrow at the memories of past greatness, her faint hopes, her watching and waiting in silence, her yearning for aid—all is marked in those melodies which glide from an intense intoxication of animal life into elegiac weakness, and in those pantomimes which dart from flattering caresses into threatening rage.[1]

Stendhal echoes Heine's sentiments in his *Life of Rossini* (published in 1824). In his chapter about the Teatro San Carlo, Stendhal writes about the "numerous different factors [that] serve to intensify the Italian's natural leaning towards music."[2] After citing the difficulty Italians had to gain access to uncensored literature, Stendhal focuses on music and the Neapolitan everyman:

> Alone amid the enforced and silent solitude of booklessness, living in a land bowed low beneath the double tyranny of Church and State, in towns whose very streets are paved with spies, our poor young man knows no escape from his own depressing company save in his voice and in his crack-toned harpsichord; and further, he is driven to contemplate at length the images and impressions formed within his soul—the only *novelty* which lies within his grasp![3]

Further on, Stendhal continues with the critical work music accomplished in the creative and cultural life of the Italians:

> But in Naples, as far as I was to observe, there is precisely *one* distraction, *only* one, which the law does not forbid to those passions which the climate breeds in Neapolitan hearts, and that is *music;* and music itself, being but another expression of these same passions, thus tends only to increase their agonizing violence.[4]

Given the nineteenth-century tendency toward florid and comparatively exaggerated prose, Heine and Stendhal outline a situation in Italy where music, and opera specifically, was able to fulfill a central cultural role.

In a study on the interaction of politics and opera, Anthony Arblaster enriches this scene with his assessment of how and why opera renegotiated its relationship to politics in its history:

> Once it [opera] moved beyond its courtly beginnings, as it very soon did, it became a form of public entertainment for substantial audiences. It therefore had to address themes that would be the common property of those audiences. It was pushed in the direction of public and political themes by its own nature as a form. Opera is more like drama than it is like the novel: the stage is naturally a public arena, and opera, like drama, tends to happen in public places.[5]

In language that, as Arblaster readily admits, is indebted to Joseph Kerman's *Opera as Drama,* he articulates one of the central ideas behind the scholarship that has examined the interaction between secondo ottocento opera and Italy's struggle for nationalism, most notably, the area of Verdi studies and the Risorgimento. The central premise that such Verdian scholarship posits is that Italy's struggle for a united national identity is borne out in, sometimes thinly veiled, references in his operas. The frequent plot situation where an oppressed people persevere against the odds for their liberty and freedom reflects the heroic spirit of the time for the national struggle. This plot situation is present in many of Verdi's operas from his earliest celebrated opera *Nabucco* (1841), with the ever-popular chorus from part 3 sung by the enslaved Hebrews, "Va pensiero," up through *Aida* (1871) and Egyptian domination over the captured Ethiopians. Nonetheless, his operas most closely associated with the Risorgimento date from the 1840s, for example, the choruses from *Nabucco, I lombardi alla prima crociata* (1843), and *Macbeth* (1847). Though Verdi did not consider himself a leading member of the political struggle, his commitment was backed up by his actions; from 1861 to 1865 he served in the first Italian parliament. In fact, Verdi's association with the Risorgimento was strong enough that his name became a symbol of the movement when the slogan "Viva VERDI!" (VERDI being an acronym for "Vittorio Emanuele Re D'Italia [King of Italy]") was used as a popular chant by the people in 1859.[6]

Against this backdrop, I am suggesting that there are some broad connections between the formation of the Romantic heroine and the cultural and political situation in the beginning of the nineteenth century in Italy. With notable exceptions, writings on primo ottocento opera have tended to place less emphasis on the political context of their times than the scholarship that has examined Verdi and the Risorgimento.[7] Even less common are analyses of how an opera's plot and the voices and characterization of the leading roles are related to cultural and historical issues during the time of its composition. Nonetheless, I am going to assert that the death of the Romantic heroine prompts the interaction of opera and the contemporaneous arena of Italian politics. Her fate can—and, I argue, should—be situated within the larger social context of the Risorgimento.

Taking a broad and overly simplified view of Italian political activity, 1830 and 1849 provide two critical dates for defining new articulations in the Italian political movement for national unity. The arrest of Giuseppe Mazzini in 1830, which brought on revolutionary turmoil throughout Italy, led to increasing popular participation in the unification movement on the local level. As the political climate intensified and was taken into the streets in 1830, following in the wake of Mazzini's arrest, the immediacy of individual heroism and the willingness to die for what one believes in became more personally relevant for the average Italian. With the general public attending the opera, the drama on stage was contextualized and, on some levels, made more real by the political drama unfolding outside the opera house. As the political struggle raged for control of Italy's nationhood, the concurrent practices regarding how operatic drama was voiced played out in the multiple soundings encompassing the portrayals of heroism, success, and defeat. In 1849, against the backdrop of many uprisings throughout Europe the previous year, Giuseppe Garibaldi emerged as the central figure promoting Italy's independence and propelled the movement into a new level of self-definition (especially as a separate entity from France) as a nation.

The Romantic heroine in Italian opera from the primo ottocento engages these themes of the Risorgimento.[8] One of the central tenets of feminist criticism in nineteenth-century Italian opera has focused on the death of the heroine. Returning to Catherine Clément's pioneering study *Opera, or the Undoing of Women*, Clément designed a model in which the heroine's death signals a defeat that minimizes her agency and positions her as a victim of an oppressive patriarchal system. Though no one can argue that the Romantic heroine dies, others have noticed that the strength and power of the heroine's voice seem to counter the verdict that her death can only mean weakness and failure. A few of the responses to Clément's work have sought to find strength in operatic women's characters through several thoughtful and compelling theoretical constructions of their voices.[9] I would like to suggest another angle from which to think about different meanings generated by women's voices onstage, an approach prompted by my concept of the period ear.

In the world of the Risorgimento, the climate of dying for what you believe in can be translated into martyrdom. Such a sacrifice may then become a noble death that reveals the steadfastness of holding true to your ideas and principles, despite all the odds. The death of the heroine in opera as a normative situation after 1830 corresponds directly with escalation of Risorgimento fervor after Mazzini's arrest. In the years between 1830 and 1850 operatic practice streamlines the norms for the leading couple. This Romantic soprano and new heroic tenor who struggle mightily, yet end the opera without fulfillment, metaphorically personify the spirit and courage Garibaldi embodied at midcentury when he became a central leader and figurehead. Rather than implying that there is a straightforward cause-and-effect relationship between specific historical political events and changes in operatic casting, I am suggesting, instead, that the general political unrest that led up to 1830 was also articulated artistically inside the opera house. A new voice for heroism and a new outcome for the resolution of the drama onstage reflect the changing social and cultural norms in the daily lives of the members in the audience.[10]

While the nineteenth-century heroine's death is an unambiguous signal of defeat at the local level of the plot—her voice is silenced and her agency is gone—in the context of Italian nation building, her strength is in her presence, the sound of her voice before she dies, and the memory of her desire to remain steadfast in her beliefs. Rather than a sign of abnegation, the character and death of the Romantic heroine may be seen as a conceit for a new type of stylized heroic voice at a specific point in Italian history. As an outgrowth of the older system with the eighteenth-century aestheticized heroic ideal in the castrato, the first decades of the nineteenth century saw a transition in the sound of heroism that had direct repercussions on the types of roles available for men and women on the opera stage. During these early years of the primo ottocento, women's voices sang as female characters with happy endings, heroes who triumphed, and women who were disguised as men only to be unveiled as women at the end.

Around 1830, after the ideals to upset the power of the monarchy in the French Revolution had moved in other directions and the golden dreams of more democratic republics liberated by Napoleon were shattered with his exile and death, heroism was reconfigured. Happiness in the present was deferred for the promise of a reward in the future, and the memory of a benevolent, albeit exploitative, leader who took care of his people no longer guaranteed a peaceful resolution at the end. The balanced phrasing, controlled ornaments, and florid embellishments that were exemplary of the castrato bel canto style gave way to ever-reaching soaring vocal lines that kept striving for more power and increasingly higher notes while also contending with larger and denser orchestral forces.

Shaped by their lives both inside and outside of the theater, composers, singers, and audience members in the early nineteenth century—and I would argue that this is a factor in all opera—experienced Romantic opera as bringing together the legacy of the past with the vision of the future and energy of its time. Women's voices in early-nineteenth-century Italian opera resonated with the sounds of their past, present, and future within a transitional musical and political era. Rather than as linear progressions, the polyphony of sonic meanings coexisted simultaneously for a few decades in the primo ottocento. Such complexity in the relationship between character and voice does not lead to a single interpretation of how nineteenth-century voices were heard, but rather an expanded appreciation for how these voices produced meaning for their contemporary audiences. Such interpretations can, in turn, influence our understanding and hearing of these roles today.

Glossary

The following glossary is a list of terms that are briefly defined as they relate to the content of this book. These definitions are not meant to be comprehensive, but rather a quick general aid to the reader who is interested in opera but might not be familiar with all of the related technical vocabulary. Additionally, I have included new terms that I have introduced and defined in this study.

Adagio: 1. A tempo marking that means slow. 2. The first lyrical portion of an operatic aria or duet that uses the conventions of la solita forma. The Adagio (also called cavatina and cantabile) is usually set in a slow tempo (hence the name) and presents the first principal melody of the number. The technical abilities of the singer(s) are showcased with expressive devices (e.g., trills, portamenti—an expressive carrying of the voice between a small or wide interval—and appoggiaturas). Near the end of the Adagio, usually at the final cadence, the singer has a further opportunity to feature his or her virtuoso singing in a cadenza. The main purpose of the Adagio is to present the first "big tune" of an aria or duet that is memorable, lyrical, and expressive. See also *Solita forma* and *Cadenza*.

Appoggiatura: Derives from the verb *appoggiare*, "to lean." A harmonic and melodic event when a nonharmonic note is given temporary emphasis on a strong beat in the measure. The dissonance is usually resolved by stepwise motion. In opera, this is a frequent melodic device to give a particular word added expressive emphasis.

Aria: A solo number for one singer in an opera. In the early nineteenth century, this usually means a multisectional number that follows the conventions of la solita forma.

Aria di baule: "Suitcase aria," also called "substitution aria." Part of a group of arias that singers would substitute into an opera at his or her will. This practice dates back to the seventeenth and eighteenth centuries and continued through the first half of the nineteenth century. Such an aria was a favorite aria of a singer that highlighted the best capabilities of her or his voice. Singers would insert a substitution aria within an opera when the singer felt that the original aria was not as flattering to his or her voice. Such arias might or might not be written by the composer of the rest of the opera.

Break in the voice: See *Passaggio*.

Cabaletta: The last portion of a vocal number (primarily arias and duets) with multiple sections. The cabaletta is set in a fast rousing tempo and shows off the technical abilities of the singer(s) with vocal leaps, arpeggios, scalar runs, and ornaments (e.g., trills). The text of the cabaletta is generally repeated with even more embellishments added the second time. The main purpose of the cabaletta is to present the last "big tune" of an aria or duet that is flashy, upbeat, and filled with vocal embellishments. See also *Solita forma*.

Cadenza: The term used in instrumental and vocal music for a section that highlights the virtuosic abilities of the performer. In an aria following la solita forma, the cadenza is usually placed near the end of the Adagio slow movement over a V^7 harmony in the accompaniment. The cadenza is an a cappella (unaccompanied) moment that was either improvised on the spot, planned ahead of time, or borrowed from another performer.

Cantabile: 1. An expression marking that means singable, perform in a lyrical singing style. 2. The first, lyrical portion of a vocal number in solita forma. See also *Adagio* and *Solita forma.*

Castrato (pl. castrati): A musician with an uncannily high treble voice, who started life as a young boy and, before the onset of puberty (generally 7–12 years old), underwent an orchiectomy (castration) that did not remove the male genitalia but cut certain blood vessels and altered the circulation of testosterone and growth hormones. The castrati were given a rigorous musical education that included lessons in voice, other instruments, counterpoint, and composition. Most castrati were employed by the Catholic church. Only a few of the best singers (not all castrati had wonderful voices) went on to enjoy fame on the opera stage. Other terms that became synonymous with castrato are *musico* (which can also refer to a cross-dressed hero performed by a woman) and *evirato,* from the verb *evirare* (to emasculate).

Cavatina: 1. A self-contained aria (most often in one tempo and expressing one emotional state, not part of la solita forma) for a solo singer. 2. The first portion of a musical number with multiple sections; see *Adagio* and *Solita forma.* 3. Whether contained within la solita forma or as a freestanding aria, cavatina frequently refers to the first solo aria a character has in an opera—the aria that introduces one of the principal roles. As an entrance aria, the cavatina also may be called an *aria di sortita* (from *sortire,* to go out).

Chest voice: Also called *voce di petto.* A term that is frequently synonymous with the singing style called "Broadway belting." The sound of the singing tone is largely produced and shaped by overtones resonating in the throat and thoracic cavity (primarily the bones in the neck, sternum, and rib cage). Frequently "chest voice" also refers to singing in the lower range of the voice. Like the head voice, the chest voice also can be thought of as a method of vocal placement. An approximation of the sound can be made by singing a note fairly low in one's range then tipping the head forward so as to attempt to cut off the resonance of the upper overtones. The effect is usually a heavy and dark sound with some heft in the voice.

Comprimario/comprimaria: A secondary role that is below a prima donna (or primo uomo) and above the chorus in importance. Generally the comprimario/a role has a few solo lines and could act as the leader of the chorus.

Countertenor: A male singer who has a high voice that is close to the timbre of a female singer. These men are not castrated and achieve their singing timbre and high notes through a development of singing in the head voice falsetto range. In recent years the renaissance of excellent countertenors (such as David Daniels, Brian Asawa, and Bejun Mehta) has produced singers especially successful in repertory originally written for the castrati.

Do di petto: Using the musical solfège system where "do" means the note C, this phrase literally means "C of the chest." In singing terms, this refers to the "chest voice high C," a vocal technique pioneered by the French tenor Gilbert Duprez (1806–96), who was the first to sing the do di petto. This high C (above the treble staff) is supported by the full strength of the chest voice. Formerly this high range was a lighter sound that was produced by the head voice or a "mixed voice" (*voce mista*), the head voice reinforced with a little more power from the chest voice.

First woman: A new term I have developed for the female heroine in opera who loves the hero and is loved by him in return. In the nineteenth century, before the rise of Romantic aesthetics around 1830, this "first woman" survives the end of the drama. In operas written within the new realism of Romanticism (generally after 1830), the "first woman" suffers and dies by the end of the opera.

Head voice: Also called *voce di testa.* In men this sound also can be referred to as "falsetto"; in women's voices, the term falsetto is less commonly used. It is a singing tone whose sound is largely produced and shaped by overtones resonating in the head (primarily in the face, also called the "mask") as opposed to the lower throat and chest. Frequently "head voice" also refers to singing in the upper range of the voice. Like the chest voice, the head voice also can be thought of as a method of vocal placement. An approximation of the sound can be made by singing a note fairly high in one's range and then tipping the head back so as to attempt to cut off the resonance of the lower overtones. The effect is usually a bright and somewhat shallow sound that can have an airy quality to the voice.

Hybrid, hybridity: A term that has meaning in science as well as in cultural studies (especially postcolonialism and feminism) and literary theory. My use of the term relies heavily on Bakhtin's formulation in "Discourse in the Novel" from *The Dialogic Imagination,* where the hybrid presents something new out of the combination of two distinct elements that has specific new aspects and does not reduce to an easy blend of the contributing elements. The hybrid can be thought of as belonging simultaneously to more than one system and can speak with a form of double-voicedness. In my formulation of the Romantic heroine, hybridity works on two interconnected levels: (1) her character is a hybrid of the first woman and the second woman and (2) her voice is a hybrid of what had been the sound of a female character (the first woman and the second woman) plus the sound of a male character (the travesti hero). The period ear of her first audiences could hear the Romantic heroine as double-voiced in character and as an aural phenomenon.

Librettist: Also called the *poeta,* the person who wrote the words of the libretto. In the early nineteenth century, the librettist was usually employed by the theater that commissioned the opera. The librettist was familiar with all of the conventions of versification that were used for recitative and set pieces (arias, ensembles, introductions, and finales).

Libretto (pl. libretti): From the word *libro* (book). The diminutive form, libretto (little book), refers to the full verbal text, all the words, plus occasional stage directions of an opera.

Lieto finale: "Happy ending." Also called *lieto fine.* The convention for happy endings in Italian operas was standard in nineteenth-century operas written up through around 1830. This was true for comic operas, semiserious operas, and opera seria. There were exceptions, but generally an opera's conclusion represented the working out of the conflict in a morally just way so that good triumphed and dishonesty was punished.

Melisma (noun), melismatic (adjective): The musical setting of a vocal text where one syllable of text is given many musical notes. The opposite setting of text is called syllabic or declamatory; this is when each syllable is generally given one musical note. Related terms used to further explain melismatic vocal writing are embellished, ornamented, florid, and coloratura. Generally these terms refer to a heightened style of singing that reflects the nobility of the character and/or social status.

Messa di voce: Literally "placement of the voice." It refers to the ability to start a note very softly, crescendo, and then decrescendo so that the sound is almost imperceptible; an exaggerated and prolonged swell on a note. This vocal practice was associated with the castrati and is mentioned in eighteenth-century singing treatises. This practice was also used by singers in the nineteenth century.

Numbers opera: This term relates to the organization of opera. In Italy, up through the 1870s, most operas were organized into separate numbers (e.g., Verdi's *Rigoletto*). This means that the lyrical sections (arias, ensembles) were closed units that usually had a tonal closure signaling the opportunity to applaud if the performance was especially good. Numbers operas are contrasted with "through-composed" operas, which have less clearly defined breaks in the musical texture and are not organized into such distinct differences between the lyrical sections and the narrative (the recitative) (e.g., Verdi's *Otello*).

Obbligato: Obliged or obligated. In practice this refers to a virtuosic written-out line that the performer is required to play, rather than to freely improvise, as in a cadenza. In opera this frequently refers to a special solo part for an instrument in an aria's accompaniment (e.g., the violin and/or wind instrument—flute, oboe—were often the instruments of choice).

Opera buffa: Comic opera. This is a term that generally refers to operas in the later part of the eighteenth century (e.g., Mozart's *Nozze di Figaro*); however, it also has been used to refer to comic operas into the early nineteenth century (e.g., Rossini's *Barbiere di Siviglia*). In nineteenth-century Italy, comic operas became less popular in favor of operas with tragic elements. The general conventions include a predominance of declamatory (syllabic, parlando) vocal writing instead of the melismatic florid style, characters that come from a wide range of social classes including several stock roles (e.g., the light amorous tenor and a *basso buffo* with "patter"-style writing), and an imbroglio that gets happily resolved, frequently with a wedding.

Opera semiseria: "Half serious" opera, a term that came into use in the beginning of the nineteenth century for operas that combine elements of both comic and serious genres. It frequently includes an eleventh-hour resolution that leads to happy ending. Semiseria operas usually employ pastoral settings (e.g., Bellini's *La sonnambula* and Donizetti's *Linda di Chamounix*).

Opera seria: "Serious opera." This term generally refers to operas in the later part of the eighteenth century, but it also has been used for noncomic operas in the early nineteenth century. Before 1830 operas with "serious," dramatic content had peaceful resolutions. Around 1830 the conflicts in the plot led to tragic conclusions with the death of the leading heroine (and sometimes the hero as well).

Passaggio: "Passage" or "crossing." It refers to the points in the voice when there is a break in the voice and a shift between registers. As the placement of the voice moves, most dramatically between head and chest voices, there is a vulnerable section that is not as secure vocally. One of the principles of the eighteenth-century bel canto tradition is to even out this transition in the voice so that the singer performs a smooth vocal line from the lowest note to the highest note in her or his range.

Period ear: A new term I am presenting that derives from Michael Baxandall's "period eye." As Baxandall has connected cultural experience to how people of a specific time see art, I use the period ear as a similar aural experience for an audience. In opera the period ear takes into account other roles the performer has sung and infuses the action onstage with the added drama of this broader information.

Period eye: Refers to the skills based in cultural experience that a person brings to interpreting visual art of a specific period. The term was developed by Michael Baxandall in his *Painting and Experience in Fifteenth-Century Italy,* first published in 1972, and has been used by scholars such as Clifford Geertz in anthropology and Linda Nochlin for later periods in art history.

Primo ottocento: Literally, "the early 1800s." This term is frequently found in opera scholarship to refer to the first half of the nineteenth century in Italy with an emphasis on the operatic conventions employed and developed by Rossini, Bellini, Donizetti, and their Italian contemporaries. The term is more precise than "bel canto" because bel canto can refer to either the age of the castrato in the seventeenth and eighteenth centuries or the early nineteenth century (which invoked the vocal style of the castrato).

Recitative: A sung style of speaking; the narrative sections of opera that propel the plot forward. In Italian opera, the recitative is usually less densely orchestrated than the arias and ensembles (sometimes still accompanied by only a keyboard instrument as in eighteenth-century opera), and the versification is in *versi sciolti* (broken verse) rather than the more measured poetic *versi lirici* (lyric verse). *Secco recitative* (dry recitative), recitative that is accompanied by very sparse orchestral (or keyboard) chords or figuration, may be contrasted with *recitativo accompagnato* (accompanied recitative), which still has a more syllabic style of voice setting than found in an aria, but the orchestral accompaniment is fuller and more prominent.

Risorgimento: "Revival," from the verb *risorgere,* to rise again. The term refers to a period in the nineteenth century when Italy sought to unite itself as a nation and expel foreign rulers. This unification movement was especially strong in the first half of the nineteenth century when seminal leaders emerged, such a Giuseppe Mazzini and Giuseppe Garibaldi. The first Italian parliament was founded in 1861.

Romantic heroine: A new term I have developed for the singular heroine that became a popular character in Italian opera after 1830 (in operas that did not have two leading roles for women) and the normative heroine in opera after 1850 (when operas with two leading roles for women were rare). The Romantic heroine is a hybrid of the first woman and the second woman in early-nineteenth-century Italian opera; she incorporates the characterizations of both women and the variety of voices who performed these roles.

Second woman: A new term I have developed for a principal female heroine in opera who loves the hero but is not loved, or loved less, by him in return. This second woman is juxtaposed with the "first woman," the woman in opera who loves the hero and is loved in return. In the nineteenth century, before the rise of Romantic aesthetics around 1830, the singer who sang second woman roles frequently also sang heroic travesti roles in other operas. The second woman survives the end of the opera.

Seconda donna: "Second woman," this refers to a designation in opera for a small secondary role for a woman that is contrasted to the "prima donna" (the leading, first, woman). My construction of the "second woman" is quite different from this Italian term (see *Second woman*).

Secondo ottocento: Literally, "the second [part of the] 1800s." This term, less frequently used than primo ottocento, refers to the second half of the nineteenth century in Italy.

Signature role: An opera role that is associated with a specific singer, usually because it fits the voice and temperament of the singer and leads to very compelling performances. Such a role becomes one of the singer's most performed and famous parts (e.g., Leontyne Price as Aida or Denyce Graves as Carmen).

La solita forma (plural: le solite forme): "The usual convention." A set of conventions that helped organize certain standard numbers in opera from the operas of Rossini (generally seen as the first to perfect these forms) through Verdi's early mature works. The most common numbers to use la solita forma are the *introduzione* (the introduction or opening of the opera after an instrumental overture), duets, arias, and a central finale (the end of an act that is not the end of the opera). Though the separate movement titles differ, the basic premise between the multiple sections is one of contrast and alternation between *versi sciolti* (blank verse) and *versi lirici* (lyric verse). Generally, *versi sciolti* is used for the narrative sections that advance the plot and are more sparsely orchestrated. *Versi lirici* is used for the contemplative sections that usually stop the dramatic action. These lyrical sections are the more tuneful and richly orchestrated and present the primary melodic material of the number. See also *Adagio, Cabaletta, Cantabile, Cavatina, Tempo d'attacco, Tempo di mezzo*.

Tempo d'attacco: "Movement of the beginning." The first portion of a vocal number (e.g., duets) that uses the conventions of la solita forma. The tempo d'attacco generally uses *versi sciolti* (broken verse) in a narrative form that propels the dramatic situation into the first lyrical section (Adagio) of the number. Frequently this section is fairly short and generates action in juxtaposition to the following lyrical and contemplative tuneful Adagio section.

Tempo di mezzo: "Movement of the middle." The section between the two big lyrical moments—the "big tunes" (the adagio and the cabaletta)—in a mutisectional vocal number (e.g., arias and duets). Like the tempo d'attacco, this section usually uses *versi sciolti* (broken verse) and is in a narrative form. The main job of the tempo di mezzo is to provide the dramatic impetus to move from the slow Adagio section to the fast and rousing cabaletta. Sometimes this is accomplished through a literal interruption, such as an offstage cannon that is shot or the quick entrance and exit of a messenger; sometimes the shift is more psychological with a change in mood. This section is frequently short (though it is sometimes expanded in secondo ottocento operas) and provides a contrast with its faster dramatic pacing to the more introspective lyrical numbers that surround it.

Tessitura: Not to be confused with the range of a role (the highest and lowest notes written), the tessitura is the general range where the vocal part is sung. As a noted opera scholar once said to me, the tessitura is like the general "cruising altitude" of a role (personal conversation with Roger Parker, fall 1993).

Travesti role, breeches part, musico, pants role, trouser role: Terms used to refer to a cross-dressed role where the gender of the singer is not the same as the gender of the character being portrayed. In the early nineteenth century these terms usually refer to a female singer performing in pants (or trousers) as a male character. The term *musico* was also used to refer to castrato singers.

Notes

Prelude

1.   The scope of this book focuses on Italian opera written in the first half of the nineteenth century. Though I concentrate on Italian opera, these operas were performed across Europe and, as the century progressed, all over the world. This book also discusses Italian operas performed throughout Italy (both in northern and southern houses where local tastes differed in, for example, the preference for heroic travesti roles in the north and for the tenor in Neapolitan theaters in the south), as well as in Paris and London. These cases will be discussed primarily in terms of the repertoire performed by individual singers.

2.   André, "Azucena, Eboli, and Amneris."

3.   In the nineteenth century the divisions between soprano, mezzo-soprano, and contralto were less defined when it came to different roles. For example, Giulia Grisi, the first Adalgisa in Bellini's *Norma,* went on to add the title character to her signature roles. The other woman in each of my chosen operas was Leonora (*Il trovatore*), Elisabetta (*Don Carlos*), and the title character in *Aida.*

4.   Angier, *Woman: An Intimate Geography,* 11.

1. Sounding Voices

1.   I will briefly define Italian terms the first time I use them. For expanded definitions relevant for this study, please see the Glossary I have included at the end. Frequently used Italian terms, such as travesti, will appear in italics the first time and then in Roman text afterwards.

2.   Trouser role and pant role are other terms used for a travesti role, a female singer who dons trousers (or pants) and portrays a male character.

3.   This point is also taken up by Carolyn Abbate and Paul Robinson in reference to the sound of the operatic heroine's voice contradicts her narrative defeat in the plot. (Abbate quotes Robinson in the *New York Times Book Review,* January 1, 1989, 3. Abbate also refers to Robinson's "A Deconstructive Postscript," in Groos and Parker, *Reading Opera,* 328–46, esp. 337.) Ralph Locke also grapples with the assessment of all women in opera as victims in his provocative article "What Are These Women Doing in Opera?"

4   Cone, *Composer's Voice;* Abbate, *Unsung Voices* and "Opera: Or, the Envoicing of Women"; Smart, "Lost Voice of Rosine Stolz" and "Verdi Sings Erminia Frezzolini."

5.   Dunn and Jones, *Embodied Voices;* Abel, *Opera in the Flesh;* Smart, *Siren Songs.* Two pioneering collections in queer theory and music from the 1990s that also address representations of gender and sexuality are Brett and Wood, *Queering the Pitch,* and Blackmer and Smith, *En Travesti.* Koestenbaum's *The Queen's Throat* provides a provocative exploration of the reception of operatic voices in queer culture.

6. Story's *And So I Sing* creates a chronology of African American female singers from the second half of the nineteenth century through the end of the twentieth century. Recovering the voice of the most famous African American singers in the second half of the nineteenth century is Graziano's "The Early Life and Career of the 'Black Patti.'" A few books that examine the diva's voice from historical and other angles include Rupert Christiansen's informative *Prima Donna: A History,* and Ethan Mordden's wonderfully opinionated *Demented: The World of the Opera Diva.* Terry Castle's "In Praise of Brigitte Fassbender: Reflections on Diva-Worship," Wayne Koestenbaum's *The Queen's Throat,* and Leonardi and Pope's *The Diva's Mouth,* are just a few of the most well-known examples of diva worship as it is theorized by self-identified homosexual men and lesbian women.

7. Poizat, *Angel's Cry;* Miller Frank, *Mechanical Song.*

8. Hadlock "Career of Cherubino" and *Mad Loves.* Hadlock discusses primo ottocento female heroic travesti singers in "A Voice for the Hero: The Italian *Musico* Tradition, 1800–1840," presented at the national meeting of the American Musicological Society, Phoenix, Arizona, November 1, 1997.

   In her essay "Women Playing Men," Hadlock's discussion of the move from treble (castrati and women's voices) heroes to the new heroic tenor in the 1830s has much in common with the aural history I lay out in this book. One area Hadlock and I differ is in our interpretations of the careers of Rosamunda Pisaroni, Giuditta Pasta, and Marietta Brambilla. While Hadlock focuses on the progression of the hero from the *musico* female singer to the tenor, my reading complicates the picture by exploring the crossing between genders that these three singers performed in the roles they sang throughout their career. Pisaroni was best known in travesti roles; however, Rossini also wrote female roles for her contemporaneously with Malcolm Graeme, the travesti role he created for her in *La donna del lago* (Teatro San Carlo in Naples, September 1819). The other two roles Rossini wrote for Pisaroni at the San Carlo in 1818 and 1819 were female characters and fit into the second woman category: Zomira in *Ricciardo and Zoraide* (December 1818) and Andromache in *Ermione* (March 1819). Later in her career, in 1827–30 during Pisaroni's first seasons at the Théâtre Italien, she continued to sing travesti roles (Arsace in *Semiramide* and the title role of *Tancredi*) as well as interpret and create new female roles, from the comic heroine Isabella (*L'italiana in Algeri*) to the premiere of Lady Aston in Michele Carafa's *Le nozze di Lammermoor.* Though not as well known for her portrayal of women on the opera stage, Pisaroni sang them all through her career, even after she was popular as a travesti singer.

   Throughout her career Pasta's signature roles included travesti heroes and female leading heroines (Pasta was too famous to sing second woman roles). As late as the 1837 season (near the end of her stage career) Pasta sang Mayr's Medea (*Medea in Corinto*), Rossini's Tancredi, and Zingarelli's Romeo (*Giulietta e Romeo*) at London's King's Theatre (Stern, "Documentary Study of Giuditta Pasta," 244). Even Marietta Brambilla, the best known of the three singers for her travesti roles, would sometimes sing female roles; like Pisaroni, she more commonly sang the second woman roles. For example, a couple of months after its premiere (which she did not sing) Brambilla sang Irene in Donizetti's *Belisario* at La Scala in August 1836 (Weinstock, *Donizetti,* 350).

   As Hadlock points out, Marietta Brambilla's career as a travesti singer was at the end of this tradition's heyday. In premiering Donizetti's Maffio Orsini (*Lucrezia Borgia,* 1833) Romani (the librettist), Donizetti, and Brambilla furthered the evolution of the heroic travesti roles into what Hadlock characterizes as an "elegantly irresponsible hedonist" ("Women Playing Men," 299). To emphasize this progression, Hadlock cites Marco Beghelli's appraisal "if the *musico* had played the protagonist of the drama [in Rossini's operas], the *musichetto* symbolized the social and geographical ambience in which the drama takes; he is the indefatigable protagonist of games, of parties, of jokes. . . . Musically his presence is marginal, almost never essential. . . . His song is not courtly but rather part of everyday life" (298). I present a complementing reading of the heroic travesti's development to these in-between categories of "elegantly irresponsible hedonist" (Hadlock) and *musichetto* (Beghelli). In chapter 4, where I discuss two further Donizetti roles—Smeton in *Anna Bolena* (1830) and Arturo in *Rosmonda d'Inghelterra* (1834)—I examine the move from the heroic travesti to the adolescent court pageboy. My analysis demonstrates that such pageboys were a special type of hybrid role that combine characteristics of both the travesti hero and an adolescent boy's character.

The biggest difference between Hadlock's and my interpretation is my contention that the three women, especially Pasta, went back and forth between male and female characters throughout their careers. Rather than a period when these women specialized in travesti roles and then only sang female roles (or vice versa), my analysis highlights the years of the 1810 through the mid-1830s as a transitional time when the multiplicity of singing practices happened simultaneously.

9. For a brief survey of these developments, see Celletti, *History of Bel Canto,* particularly section 4 on Rossini (pp. 135–87) and Rosselli, "Age of the Tenor," in *Singers of Italian Opera*. Scott (*Record of Singing,* vol. 1) and Steane (*Voices, Singers & Critics*) have also written on this phenomenon.

10. "Primo uomo," the leading man, is an equivalent term to "prima donna" but is not used as frequently. I am using the term to refer to the leading male character, a role that—in the primo ottocento—had the potential to be written for a castrato, female travesti singer, or tenor.

11. A select bibliography on the rise of the tenor in the early nineteenth century includes Rosselli, *Singers of Italian Opera* (especially ch. 8, "The Age of the Tenor") and "Grand Opera"; Celletti, *History of Bel Canto;* and Pleasants, *Great Tenor Tragedy.* In Italian opera the baritone and bass were not real contenders to be the new heroic voice. Given the preference for high timbres it would have been a large leap for the period ears of the time to switch from the castrato/female heroic travesti to the deep tones of the bass and baritone.

12. Clément, "Through Voices, History," 21–22.

13. Ibid., 22.

14. Ibid., 23.

15. Ibid., 25.

16. Ibid., 24.

17. Hadlock, "Career of Cherubino," 68–69.

18. This is not to say that comic opera disappeared altogether, but it held a less important position in mainstream opera in Italy after 1840 than it had when

Rossini and the Ricci brothers (Luigi and Federico) were composing. One probable contributing reason was the serious nature of the Risorgimento in Italy and the tendency for it to permeate the themes in operas written during the time (e.g., the operas of Giuseppe Verdi provide several examples). For more information on comic opera as a genre in nineteenth-century Italy, see Izzo's Ph.D. dissertation and Gossett's introduction to the facsimile score of Luigi Ricci's *Un'avventura di Scaramuccia* (1834).

19.   For more on "semiserious" opera, specifically those of Rossini, see Zedda's "Preface" to the critical edition of Rossini's *La gazza ladra*, xiv.

20.   A notable exception is the title character of Rossini's *Semiramide* (Venice, 1823) where Arsace (the travesti role) is Semiramide's son and fulfills the Oedipal curse of matricide, so that he does not end up marrying her. Instead, the opera ends "happily" as Arsace avenges his father's murder and is proclaimed king.

21.   This situation outlines the norm before 1830, where both women survive the end of the opera. After 1830, the same pairings would take place, but the first woman would die at the end (and the second woman would survive without getting the hero).

22.   Examples will be given of these situations in chapters 4 and 5 that deal with the plots of Donizetti's *Anna Bolena* (1830) and *Rosmonda d'Inghilterra* (1834).

23.   Baxandall, *Painting and Experience,* 40. Section II is entitled "The Period Eye." For more information on Michael Baxandall's contribution as an art historian, including the "period eye," see Rifkin, *About Michael Baxandall.* No one in Rifkin's essay collection discusses the adaptation of the period eye to music or audio culture.

24.   Ibid., 152.

25.   For discussion of the relationship between dancing and arrangement of people, see ibid., 77–81; for discussion of religious meanings, including the content and gesture, see ibid., 40–71; for discussion about mathematical developments and the importance of gauging the size and shape of objects and images, see ibid., 86–108.

26.   Geertz, "Art as a Cultural System," 108–9.

27.   Nochlin, "Camille Pissarro," 61.

28.   Ibid., emphasis in the original.

29.   Laqueur, *Making Sex;* Garber *Vested Interests.*

30.   I discuss all six of Meyerbeer's Italian operas in "Gendered Voicings: Roles for Female Singers in Meyerbeer's Italian Operas," in a collection of writings on French and Italian operas coedited by Victoria Johnson and Jane Fulcher, forthcoming from Cambridge University Press.

31.   Most of the composers whose operas I examine in chapters 4 and 5 (Rossini, Donizetti, and Bellini) were Italians who also had success in Paris.

2. Haunting Legacies

1.   For a partial list of scholarship on the castrato, see Barbier, *World of the Castrati;* Celletti, *History of Bel Canto,* Heriot, *Castrati in Opera;* Rosselli, *Singers of Italian Opera.*

2. This photograph is mentioned in Barbier, *World of the Castrati,* 239.

3. This is not to imply that Velluti was the last castrato ever to sing in opera, just that he was the last of the great to retire. In 1844 the castrato Pergetti is reported to have sung in London (Poizat, *Angel's Cry,* 119).

4. An incomplete list of these castrati, and the years in which they died, includes Giuseppe Aprile (1813), Andrea Martini (1819), Gasparo Pacchierotti (1821), Vincenzo Del Prato (1828), Giovanni Maria Rubinelli (1829), and Luigi Marchesi (1829). Dates are taken from Heriot, *Castrati in Opera,* and singer entries in *The New Grove Dictionary of Opera.*

5. Movie about the life of the famous castrato Farinelli, stage name of Carlo Broschi (1705–82): *Farinelli,* directed by Gérard Corbiau (1994), DVD available from Columbia TriStar Home Entertainment (2000).

6. Movie sound track for *Farinelli.* Music Direction by Christophe Roussett. Auvidis Travelling K 1005. Not everyone has found the digitally combined voice of Eva Mallas-Godlewska and countertenor Derek Lee Ragin to be provocative and compelling as the voice of Farinelli. For another opinion, see that of Handel scholar Ellen T. Harris in her article "Twentieth-Century Farinelli."

7. The CD liner notes refer to this effect as "grace notes" and *acciaccature,* which are assumed to be approached from below the note. For an additional discussion of Moreschi's singing see Joe K. Law, "Alessandro Moreschi Reconsidered: A Castrato on Records," especially 9–12.

8. The opening measures of the vocal melody (as well as points later on in the aria) of Leonora's act 4 aria, "D'amor sull'alli rosee" in Verdi's *Il trovatore* provides one such well-known example.

9. John Wolfson, "Producer's note," *Alessandro Moreschi: The Last Castrato.* Complete Vatican Recordings. London: Opal, CD9823, 1987. Emphasis added.

10. Barbier briefly mentions reactions of Mendelssohn, Liszt, and Marie d'Agoult in *World of the Castrati,* 237.

11. As quoted in ibid.

12. The female companion is identified in Barthes's commentary in *Sarrasine, S/Z,* 211. All further references to Balzac's *Sarrasine* and Barthes's *S/Z* are taken from this edition, where Balzac's novella is reprinted in an appendix at the end, in English translation by Richard Miller. For a discussion of the erotics surrounding the structure of the narrative and how the seductive dynamic between the unidentified male narrator and the Countess reenacts Sarrasine's pursuit of La Zambinella, see Chambers's "Seduction Denied." Barbara Johnson also discusses the sexual tension between the narrator and the Countess and offers a deconstructive analysis of Balzac's novella by examining how Barthes's terms "readerly" and "writerly" are both at work in *Sarrasine;* see her "Critical Difference: BartheS/BalZac." Patrick McCreless discusses narrative structures in *S/Z* as a model for examining tonal procedures in music in "Roland Barthes's *S/Z*." Mary Ann Smart addresses gender binaries and performance in her Introduction to her edited collection *Siren Songs,* 8–9.

13. The exact date of the ball is a little unclear. Barthes claims the date to be 1838 (*S/Z,* 209) and then around 1830 (211). Balzac wrote the novella in 1830, and the references in the text to the singers (Malibran, Sontag, Fodor; 223) and the cava-

tina Marianina sings from *Tancredi* (228) support either date, yet point more strongly to 1830 when Rossini's Italian operas were performed more regularly (than in 1838) and Malibran was still alive (she died in 1836).

14. Ibid., 237.

15. Ibid., 238 and 239.

16. A perfectly logical premise given the Roman setting in 1758 that takes place before the ban had been lifted for women to appear onstage.

17. Ibid., 230.

18. Ibid.

19. Balzac's use of the picture of the "Adonis lying on a lion's skin" in the de Lanty mansion, first mentioned early in the novella (Balzac, *Sarrasine,* 231) references a real picture painted in 1791, Anne-Louis Girodet's *The Sleep of Endymion* (Paris, Musée du Louvre). In *Sarrasine* Balzac mentions Girodet as the artist, but cleverly works this painting into his fictionalized world of his novella. This picture of the "Adonis" returns near the end of the novella when the narrator tells his young companion: "Madame, Cardinal Cicognara took possession of Zambinella's statue and had it executed in marble; today it is in the Albani Museum. There, in 1791, the Lanty family found it and asked Vien to copy it. The portrait in which you saw Zambinella at twenty, a second after having seen him at one hundred, later served for Girodet's *Endymion:* you will have recognized its type in the Adonis" (Balzac, *Sarrasine,* 253). Like the scene with Marianina singing the excerpt from Rossini's *Tancredi,* Balzac's mention of Girodet's *Endymion* (even citing the correct date, 1791, when Girodet completed the picture) references another historical code that gave his story an added connection to his time. Not only was Balzac very interested in Girodet's work (he arranged to see Girodet's *Endymion* himself), but his first readers of *Sarrasine* in 1830 would have had the opportunity to read Girodet's *Oeuvres posthumes,* which were published in Paris in 1829. For more information about Girodet's *Endymion* and its relationship to Balzac and *Sarrasine,* see Crow, *Emulation,* 273–78. Many thanks to Eleanor Lumm, who first brought Girodet's *Endymion* to my attention, and to art historian Susan Siegfried for her expertise in this area.

20. The painting was based on the sculpture Sarrasine made of La Zambinella in 1758 when the latter was twenty (ibid., 207–209). The Countess is twenty-two years old (211, 228).

21. Barthes, *S/Z,* 38. Ross Chambers also comments on the connection between Marianina and her great-uncle as a "symbolic marriage" ("Seduction Denied," 93). My construction of the relationship between Marianina and her great-uncle brings their musical talents together in the form of legacy rather than marriage. Nonetheless, the common thread is the extended meaning embedded within Marianina's voice, approached from different angles.

22. Balzac, *Sarrasine,* 223.

23. Ibid.

24. Ibid.

25. Balzac quotation taken from F. Claudon, "Balzac, Honoré de," *Grove Music Online,* ed. L. Macy, www.grovemusic.com (accessed February 10, 2005).

26. Rossini revised two of his Italian operas for the Paris Opéra: *Maometto II* (1820) became *Le siège de Corinthe* (1826), and *Mosè in Egitto* (1818) became *Moïse et Pharaon* (1827). Rossini wrote three new operas for Paris, one of which was for the Théâtre Italien, *Il viaggio a Reims* (1825)—a one-act *dramma giocoso* (jocular drama—a term generally used for operas with a combination of light and more serious subjects and characters) written for the coronation of Charles X. The other two newly composed operas for the Opéra were *Le Comte Ory* (1828) and *Guillaume Tell* (1829).

27. Rossini also mentions that he himself was almost made a castrato in his youth for his beautiful voice, but was not operated on at his mother's refusal (*Richard Wagner's Visit to Rossini*, 108–109). Edmond Michotte, the scribe for the conversation, was a trusted friend of Rossini's and was allowed to take notes on some of Rossini's conversations.

28. "Di tanti palpiti" is the cabaletta to Tancredi's cavatina. A cavatina is the term frequently given to an entrance aria of a main character; in terms of form, this aria usually has two sections, a slow cantabile and a faster rousing cabaletta. The widespread popularity of "Di tanti palpiti" resonated in nineteenth-century literature and music. Richard Osborne ("*Tancredi*," *The New Grove Dictionary of Opera*, vol. 4, 644) and Charles Osborne (*Bel Canto Operas*, 32–34) have noted such music examples as Wagner's parody in the "Tailor's Song" in act 3 of *Die Meistersinger*. Even within a few years of when the opera was written, Lord Byron refers to "The 'Tanti Palpiti's' on such occasions," and such occasions were the "long evenings of duets and trios," in his epic poem *Don Juan* canto 16, stanza 45, line 4 (Byron worked on *Don Juan* from 1818 until his death in 1824). Thanks to David Anderson for bringing this Byron reference to my attention.

29. Text and translation from liner notes to *Tancredi*, conducted by Roberto Abbado, RCA Victor, 09026-68349-2, 1996. Translation by Lucy E. Cross.

30. Balzac, *Sarrasine*, 228.

31. The two versions of Rossini's *Tancredi* are discussed by Philip Gossett in "Tancredi: From Venice to Ferrara, from Joy to Sorrow," liner notes to *Tancredi*, RCA Victor Red Seal (1996), 13–16, 09026-68349-2. This recording includes both finales.

32. Peschel and Peschel, "Medicine and Music," 27.

33. A few sources for iconography of the castrati can be found in the illustrations of Barbier's *World of the Castrati*, Heriot's *Castrati in Opera*, and Heartz's "Farinelli Revisited."

34. A reproduction of Pierleone Ghezzi's caricature of Farinelli in a woman's costume can be found in Heartz, "Farinelli Revisited," 432 (illustration 3).

35. Peschel and Peschel, "Medicine and Music," 27.

36. Ibid., 29–30. "A number of evirati, however, looked like women" and Lalande, a traveler from the 1760s, discusses the castrati "in disguise who play the women's roles, sometimes in such a way as to create an illusion, as much for their voices as for their figures." Barbier also cites several cases of the castrati "passing" as women (*World of the Castrati*, 153–56).

37. Casanova, *History of My Life*, quoted in Keyser "Cross-sexual Casting," 50. Casanova relates another event in his memoirs about his encounter with "Bellino,"

whose identity is kept secret by his family. Throughout Casanova's acquaintance, Bellino passes as a young boy, a castrato, and a young woman. Casanova, *History of My Life,* vol. 2, 3–51. My thanks to Anthony Cantrell for bringing Bellino to my attention.

38. Quoted in Oberlin, "Castrato," 50.

39. Peschel and Peschel, "Medicine and Music," 26–27. In Table 1 (26) the lengths of the vocal chords are given: boys and girls, 7–8 mm; adult female, 8–11.5 mm; adult male, 12–16 mm.

40. "L'apparato fonatorio dei castrati si rivelava estremamente originale. La taglia della laringe era simile a quella di una donna di piccola statura, la taglia del mantice toracico a quella di un uomo di grande statura, l'altezza e la consistenza laringea erano quelle di un fanciullo." Jean Pierre Sauvage, *Les cahiers d'oto-rhino-laryngologie et de chirurgie cervico-faciale,* Limoges, Chaire de Clinque ORL. Cited in Appolonia, "Il fenomeno della voce castrata," 170, my translation.

41. Barbier, *World of the Castrati,* 17.

42. Koestenbaum, *Queen's Throat,* 167.

43. Mancini, *Practical Reflections,* 59–60.

44. Rosselli, "Castrato," *The New Grove Dictionary of Opera,* vol. 1, 766; Barbier, *World of the Castrati,* 87.

45. Harris, "Baroque Era," 113–14; Heriot, *Castrati in Opera,* 17.

46. Distribution of parts for the Roman 1683 performance was taken from "*Pompeo*" by Malcolm Boyd in *The New Grove Dictionary of Opera,* vol. 3, 1055. Distribution of parts for the Neapolitan 1684 performance was taken from Heriot, *Castrati in Opera,* 33. Heriot lists the names of performers but does not mention the vocal type designation except for the castrato (*musico*) roles.

47. What worked in tandem with the period ear's ability to accept castrato and female voices as interchangeable in roles for male (and sometimes female) characters was the availability of specific singers and who was contracted at a theater for a specific season. If a castrato was not available, a female singer could step into a male role. Additionally, singers could be contracted at a theater and then need a role to be adapted for his or her voice.

48. Harris, "Baroque Era," 113.

49. Celletti, *History of Bel Canto,* 9.

50. Harris, "Baroque Era," 114.

51. Keyser, "Cross-sexual Casting," 47.

52. For more detail on the process of the training, see Barbier, *World of the Castrati,* (ch. 3, "Training the Singers") and Rosselli, *Singers of Italian Opera* (ch. 2, "The Castrati," and ch. 5, "Training").

53. Barbier, *World of the Castrati,* 57–61.

54. Ibid., 84.

55. Celletti, *History of Bel Canto,* 113, n. 4.

56. Ibid.

57. Three fairly well-known castrati were born in Siena and, because of this, were all

known as "Senesino." Francesco Bernardi was the most famous one, and the one most frequently referred to as Senesino (Heriot, *Castrati in Opera,* 91). His exact birth and death dates are not known; 1680–1759 is an approximation made by Heriot (ibid.) and Winton Dean in "Senesino," *The New Grove Dictionary of Opera,* vol. 3, p. 314.

58. Cuzzoni and Senesino sang together in Handel's operas: *Ottone* (1723), *Flavio* (1723), *Giulio Cesare in Egitto* (1724), *Tamerlano* (1724), *Rodelinda* (1725), *Scipione* (1726), *Alessandro* (1726), *Admeto* (1727), *Ricccardo Primo* (1727), *Radamisto* (originally written in 1720 and revised in 1728), *Siroe* (1728), and *Tolomeo* (1728).

59. Bordoni premiered roles with Cuzzoni and Senesino in five Handel operas: *Alessandro* (1726), *Admeto* (1727), *Ricccardo Primo* (1727), *Siroe* (1728), and *Tolomeo* (1728). Though she did not premiere a role, she sang with Cuzzoni and Senesino in the revival of *Radamisto* in 1728.

60. It was in the June 6, 1727, performance of *Astianatte* that the rivalry between Cuzzoni and Bordoni reached climactic heights. Rumors of a fist fight between the two women onstage led to John Gay's 1728 parody of them as Polly Peachum and Lucy Lockhart in his *Beggar's Opera.* (Lowell Lindgren, "*Astianatte,*" *The New Grove Dictionary of Opera,* vol. 1, 232).

61. Tosi's treatise was reprinted in Dutch translation, 1731; English translation as *Observations on the Florid Song* by J. E. Galliard, London, 1742; German translation edited by J. F. Agricola, Berlin, 1757; and French translation in 1874 (John Rosselli, "Tosi," *The New Grove Dictionary of Opera,* vol. 4, 770). Mancini's treatise was revised in 1777 by the author and translated into French as *L'art du chant figure* in 1776 and as *Reflexions pratiques sur le chant figure* in 1796 (trans. Pietro Buzzi as *Practical Reflections on the Figurative Art of Singing,* 1912).

62. A few authors of nineteenth-century singing treatises that claim to come out of bel canto techniques are Manual García, Laure Cinti-Damoreau, Luigi Lablache, and the father and son Francesco and Giovanni Battista Lamperti.

63. García, *Complete Treatise.*

64. Treatises by Pier Francesco Tosi: *Opinioni de' cantori antichi e moderni, o sieno osservazioni sopra il canto figurato* (ed. Michael Pilkington, 1987); Giambattista Mancini, *Practical Reflections on the Figurative Art of Singing by Giambattista Mancini, Singing Master at the Imperial Court of Vienna,* trans. Pietro Buzzi (Boston: Gorham Press, 1912); and Manuel García II: *École de García; Traité complet de l'art du chant* (Mainz: B. Schott's Söhne, 1847, English trans. of part 1, Boston: Oliver Ditson, n.d.; part 2, ed. Donald Paschke, New York: Da Capo Press, 1975) are just a few of the most well known. For a more comprehensive bibliography see Harris. "Baroque Era "; "Singing: A Bibliography," *The New Grove Dictionary of Opera,* vol. 4, 387–92; and Monahan. *Art of Singing*

65. "Nell'istesso solfeggio cerchi il modo di fargli guadagnare a poco a poco gli acuti, acciò mediante l'esercizio acquisti tutta quella dilatazione di corde, che sia possibile. Avverta però, che quanto più le note son'alte, tanto più bisogna toccarle con dolcezza per evitare gli strilli." Mori, *Maestri di bel canto,* 40. The English translation was made by John Ernest Galliard in 1743 (Tosi, *Observations on the Florid Song,* 4).

66. "La voce di testa è facile al moto, possiede le corde superiori più che le inferiori,

ha il trillo pronto, ma è soggetta a perdersi per non aver forza, che la regga." Ibid., 42; trans. Galliard (Pilkington, *Observations on the Florid Song*, 6). The bracketed words were added by Pilkington.

67. Giambattista Mancini's treatise *Practical Reflections on the figurative Art of Singing* (1774, rev. 1777) is the first treatise to talk in some depth about registers in the voice (see Coffin, *Historical Vocal Pedagogy Classics*, 6). Mancini's treatise, based heavily on Tosi's treatise, speaks of two registers where the chest voice is distinguished from the head voice. Mancini uses falsetto synonymously with head voice. See Mancini's treatise, ch. IV, "Concerning the Voice in General—The Chest Register and the Head Register or 'Falsetto'" (Mancini, *Practical Reflections*, pp. 57–60).

68. Mancini, *Practical Reflections*, ch. 9, 116–22.

69. Tosi, *Observations on the Florid Song;* Baird, notes to Agricola, *Art of Singing.*

70. Tosi, *Observations on the Florid Song*, 47.

71. Ibid., 48.

72. Mancini, *Practical Reflections*, 147–48.

73. Ibid., 68.

74. Ibid., 103.

75. Celletti, *History of Bel Canto*, 113.

76. Celletti even calls the tenor do di petto a "mixed note," referring to a similar blending of head and chest voices that was developed by the castrati's voce mista (*History of Bel Canto*, 113).

77. Laqueur, *Making Sex*. Nina Treadwell has very compellingly used Laqueur's construction of the one- and two-sexed model in her examination of cross-dressing as it interacts with sex and gender roles in seventeenth-century comic opera, specifically Neapolitan *commedia per musica*. See Treadwell, "Female Operatic Cross-dressing," 135–40 (especially in footnotes 32 and 44–48) and 152 (footnote 81).

78. Ibid., 124–25.

79. This could be visualized as a vertical continuum where the "perfect" male is at the top. As you move down you find increasing less perfect males; at the bottom is the female (the least "perfect" articulation of male).

80. Laqueur, *Making Sex*, 6. Scare quotes are Laqueur's.

81. Alice Domurat Dreger discusses the gendered and sexed categorization of hermaphrodites (people born with intersexed potential) in the nineteenth and twentieth centuries in her book *Hermaphrodites and the Medical Invention of Sex*. The word "hermaphrodite" is a term that refers back to Greek mythology and denotes the combining of Hermes and Aphrodite into a being with both male and female sexes. Until recently the term hermaphrodite has been used to talk about people born with, and categorized as having, genetic and/or physical attributes of maleness and femaleness together (see Dreger, *Hermaphrodites and the Medical Invention of Sex*, and Laqueur, *Making Sex*). Current movements are suggesting that the term "intersex" be adapted to replace hermaphrodite. The website of the Intersex Society of North America (www.isna.org, accessed February 28, 2005)

states: "In a paper that will be coming out in the *Journal of Pediatric Endocrinology and Metabolism* in 2005, five ISNA-associated experts recommend that all terms based on the root "hermaphrodite" be abandoned because they are scientifically specious and clinically problematic. The terms fail to reflect modern scientific understandings of intersex conditions, confuse clinicians, harm patients, and panic parents." In *Voicing Gender* I am concerned with the eighteenth- and nineteenth-century conceptualization of the castrato and the coming together of male/female and masculine/feminine characteristics. Given the historical focus of my discussion, I have decided to use the older term, hermaphrodite.

82. Laqueur cites Paolo Zacchia's *Questionum medico-legalium* (1653). Zacchia argues "that humans cannot have two valid sexes" (141); quoted in Laqueur, *Making Sex,* 140–42.

83. Garber, *Vested Interests,* 35. Treadwell also uses Garber's idea of category crisis in transvestism both on and offstage; Treadwell, "Female Operatic Cross-dressing," 135.

84. Ibid., 36.

85. Ibid., 17, emphasis in the original.

86. Ibid., 11.

3. Meyerbeer in Italy

1. Of notable exception is the work of Andrew Everett, "Bewitched in a Magic Garden," and Jeremy Commons in his notes to Opera Rara recordings: *Il crociato in Egitto* (1991), *Meyerbeer in Italy* (2002), and *Margherita d'Anjou* (2003). Additionally there are the facsimile editions published by Garland in their Early Romantic Opera: 1810–1840 series edited by Philip Gossett.

2. Meyerbeer's works for Germany are *Der Fischer und das Milchmädchen oder Viel Lärm um einen Kuss* (divertissement, March 26, 1810, Berlin Court Opera); *Jepthas Gelübe* (opera, December 23, 1812, Munich Court Opera); *Wirth und Gast oder Aus Scherz Ernst* (comedy, January 6, 1813, Stuttgart Court Theater). During these years Meyerbeer also wrote *Das Brandenburger Tor,* a lyrical drama, for Berlin in 1814, but there is no documented date for a performance. Many years later Meyerbeer wrote *Ein Feldlager in Schlesien* for Berlin (opera, December 7, 1844).

3. Giacomo Meyerbeer to Jacob Herz Beer in Berlin, Vienna, November 1814; quoted in Becker and Becker, *Giacomo Meyerbeer,* 32.

4. The words in quotation marks were used by Meyerbeer to describe his Italian years to his biographer Dr. Jean F. Schucht in 1856. Everett, "Bewitched in a Magic Garden," 166.

5. Ibid. Schucht's biography of Meyerbeer was published in 1869.

6. Meyerbeer's travel included at least one trip (and in many cases several) to Genoa, Naples, Padua, Venice, Milan, Turin, Bologna, Rome, Florence, and Trieste. In Sicily (July–October 1814) he visited Palermo and Messina. Appendix 1 of Everett's "Bewitched in a Magic Garden," 186–87, lists a "Time and Place Sequence" for Meyerbeer's years between 1814 and 1825.

7. Of Rossini's last nineteen operas for Italy, only four were written for the north

(Milan and Venice), and fifteen were written for southern theaters (Rome and Naples). Rossini's four operas for Milan and Venice after 1815 were *La gazza ladra* (Milan, La Scala, 1817), *Eduardo e Cristina* (Venice, Benedetto, 1819), *Bianca e Falliero* (Milan, La Scala, 1819), and *Semiramide* (Venice, La Fenice, 1823).

8. Wittmann discusses the rising prominence of Mercadante during the time Meyerbeer was in Italy, which is borne out by Mercadante's appointment to succeed Rossini as the composer-in-residence at the Teatro San Carlo (1823–25). The evidence regarding Meyerbeer's increasing success as an opera composer in Italy seems hardly to merit Wittmann's statement that "Meyerbeer was a dilettante who could scarcely be expected to obtain a commission in the face of professional competition" (Wittmann, "Reception of Meyerbeer in Italy," 119). Wittmann's essay focuses on the reception of Meyerbeer's French operas in Italy rather than his six early Italian operas. Brief mention is made of *Il crociato in Egitto.*

9. Rosselli writes about the difficulties of putting on operas in this time period (Rosselli, *Opera Industry in Italy*).

10. In his study of primo ottocento librettist Salvadore Cammarano, John Black describes Romani and Rossi, along with Cammarano, as the leading librettists of their time (Black, *Italian Romantic Libretto,* 292–95).

11. For more information on Romani and his working relationships with Meyerbeer and Bellini, see Roccatagliati, "Felice Romani."

12. Almanzor is the one exception where the voice of the "second woman" is a not a female character, but a travesti singer. However, the sound is the same as the second woman because the singer, Rosamunda Pisaroni, was the same singer who premiered Romilda, the second woman of Meyerbeer's first Italian opera.

13. Treadwell discusses the use of female characters disguised as men who are later revealed to be women near the opera's conclusion in seventeenth-century Neapolitan comic opera; see "Female Operatic Cross-dressing," especially 135, 143–56.

14. I discuss these five Italian operas by Meyerbeer in more depth in "Gendered Voicings: Roles for Female Singers in Meyerbeer's Italian Operas," in a collection of essays on Italian and French opera coedited by Victoria Johnson and Jane Fulcher, forthcoming from Cambridge University Press.

15. Given the different definitions, and problematic nature, of the term, I hesitate in calling these five Meyerbeer operas "rescue operas" (see David Charlton, "Rescue Opera," *The New Grove Dictionary of Opera,* vol. 3, 1293–94; and Charlton, "On Redefinitions of 'Rescue Opera'"). However, there are similar elements with the recurrence of a political imbroglio that leads to certain disaster only to be mitigated at the eleventh hour due to a human heroic deed (and not a deus ex machina). As in Beethoven's *Leonore* (1805, 1806) and *Fidelio* (1814) operas, Meyerbeer also uses the disguised female heroine to be the agent who helps save the day. A few other "rescue" operas that use the element of disguise, though to lesser degrees than Beethoven and Meyerbeer, are Grétry's *Richard Coeur-de-lion* (1784) and Cherubini's *Lodoïska* (1791).

16. Meyerbeer and Rossi completed four operas together: *Romilda e Costanza* (1817),

Semiramide riconosciuta (1819), *Emma di Resburgo* (1819), and *Il crociato di Egitto* (1824). They worked together on other projects that, for various reasons, were never finished, including *Almanzore* (1821) and *Malek Adel* for Naples in 1824 (see Everett, "Bewitched in a Magic Garden," 184).

17. Meyerbeer and Rossi, *Il crociato in Egitto*. *Il crociato* was also the first of Meyerbeer's Italian operas for which a complete commercial recording was made: Opera Rara Limited, ORC 10, Peter Moores Foundation, London, 1991 (B000003LNQ). Conducted by David Parry with the Royal Philharmonic Orchestra. Armando sung by Diana Montague and Felicia sung by Della Jones. Opera Rara released a recording of Meyerbeer's *Margherita d'Anjou* in 2003 (B0000BX5L9).

18. Mark Everist has written compellingly about different configurations of the exotic and Orientalism in "Meyerbeer's *Il crociato in Egitto*."

19. The Knights of Rhodes descend from the twelfth-century Order of the Hospital of St. John in Jerusalem, initially founded to care for sick pilgrims. It soon took on an additional military role and was organized under a Grand Master. Members came from Western European nobility that included Castilian Provence, the Auvergne, France, Italy, Aragon, and England. Evicted from Jerusalem at the end of the thirteenth century, the Knights of St. John moved on to Cyprus before they settled in Rhodes in 1309. For more information on the Order of the Hospital of St. John in Jerusalem and the Knights of Rhodes, see Seward's *The Monks of War,* 43–76 and 223–42. Many thanks to David Anderson for bringing this source to my attention.

20. A compelling discussion of the exoticism in this opera, specifically relating to the character of Armando/Elmireno has been treated by Everist, "Meyerbeer's *Il crociato*."

21. In the list of characters for his essay, Steven Huebner mentions Felicia as being a contralto and "a relative of Adriano in male attire" ("*Il crociato in Egitto*," *The New Grove Dictionary of Opera*, vol. 2, 1015). Don White includes pictures of the costume designs for the Paris 1825 production that identifies Felicia in male garb in a costume resembling a herald or page (Opera Rara ORC 10, p. 48).

22. Combined with the many other performances this hugely popular opera received, it is difficult to speak of one "definitive" version of the opera. In his introduction to the Garland facsimile edition of a manuscript copy (by a copyist, not in Meyerbeer's hand) of the opera from the Venetian first performance, Gossett writes: "It poses more textual problems than practically any other opera of the early nineteenth century, problems which are only partially resolved." Gossett, introduction to Garland edition of Meyerbeer's *Il crociato in Egitto*.

23. The information from table 3.2 comes from Gossett's introduction to the Garland edition of Meyerbeer's *Il crociato;* Everett's "Bewitched in a Magic Garden," 170–92; Don White, "Meyerbeer in Italy," 18–71.

24. Tosi's voice is discussed above, and Méric-Lalande premiered the title roles in Donizetti's *Elvida* (1826) and *Lucrezia Borgia* (1833) as well as four Bellini heroines: Bianca in the first version of *Bianca and Fernando* (1826), Imogene in *Il pirata* (1827), Alaide in *La straniera* (1829), and the title role in *Zaira* (1829).

25. Romani and Bellini collaborated in all of Bellini's subsequent operas with the ex-

ception of his last, *I puritani,* whose librettist was Count Carlo Pepoli. A brief overview of *Bianca e Gernando* and *Bianca e Fernando* can be found in Osborne's *Bel Canto Operas,* 312–15.

26. As quoted in White, "Meyerbeer in Italy, 58.

27. As quoted in ibid.

28. Osborne, *Bel Canto Operas,* 162–63.

29. Felicia says she is Armando's brother twice, both occasions in act 1. The first time is when she first meets Palmide and tries to gain information as to whether or not Armando is alive; she eventually finds out that not only is he alive, but he and Palmide have a child (Mirva). The second time is in the act 1 finale when Felicia jumps in front of Aladino's sword for Armando, and she claims to be Armando's brother.

30. In his essay accompanying the Opera Rara recording of *Il crociato in Egitto,* White identifies the complications surrounding the different vocal makeup of the cast and the role of Felicia: "we should realize that in those early days of the nine-teenth century, any opera containing leading roles for a castrato and a mezzo so-prano posed a major problem when the castrato role was later taken by another mezzo soprano. Understandably in these instances the role of Felicia virtually disappeared" (34).

31. "Caro mano" is not a strict rondò (an aria form that became popular in the late eighteenth century); however, there are similarities: it is a showpiece aria for a lead-ing character and has an alternation between solo verses for Armando/Elmireno and a repeating section for the chorus. Unlike other nineteenth-century rondò us-age, such an aria usually appeared closer to the end of the opera (in the second act of a two-act opera or the second act of a three-act opera). Don Neville, "Rondò," *Grove Music Online,* ed. L. Macy, www.grovemusic.com.proxy.lib .umich.edu (accessed February 12, 2005). The Opera Rara recording of *Il crociato* includes the Florence "Caro mano" scene in its appendix (compact disc 4, track 11, liner notes pp. 173–76). Don White discusses these changes to the Florence version in his liner notes (p. 43).

32. Nicola Tacchinardi (1772–1859). He made his debut at La Scala in Paer's *Griselda* in 1805 and had a successful career until he retired from the stage in 1831. In 1822 he was made principal singer of the grand ducal chapel in Florence but was allowed to continue his operatic career, which led to performances throughout Italy and in Vienna and Barcelona. He was the father of Fanny Tacchinardi-Persiani, Donizetti's first Lucia. Francesco Bussi, "Tacchinardi, Nicola," *The New Grove Dictionary of Opera,* vol. 4, 630.

33. The one exception is in *Margherita d'Anjou,* where the high soprano (Margherita) is in love with the tenor, the Duke of Lavarenne. The travesti role in this opera is a small one, Edoardo, and plays the part of Margherita's son.

34. Though the castrato character was a heroic voice, occasionally this character was also a father, as a few Handel operas illustrate. In Handel's first opera for Italy, *Rodrigo* (Venice, 1707), the title character (soprano castrato) has a son with Florinda. In *Rodelinda* (London, 1725) the title character and Bertarido (written for the alto castrato Senesino) have a young son—Flavio. I thank Ellen T. Harris for bringing these Handel opera plots with castrato father roles to my attention.

35. Indeed, trouble does erupt more than once. From the act 1 finale through the end of the opera, the plot shifts several times so that it seems as though peace between Aladino (the Sultan) and Adriano (Grand Master of the Knights of Rhodes) is achieved, but then keeps getting deferred. Ultimately, the two leaders are united when, in an uprising by Osmino to become the new sultan, Armando and the Knights fight to defend Aladino.

36. In addition to the innovation of having two bandas and the spatial organization Meyerbeer notes for the accompanying drum corps, Philip Gossett has already noted the descriptive orchestration Meyerbeer uses to represent the two different groups. Gossett discusses these two bandas in the introduction to facsimile edition of Meyerbeer's *Il crociato in Egitto*. The first act finale appears as no. 11 (493–608). The full score for the two bandas is given at the end of vol. 1 as "Secondo Supplemento alla stretta del Primo Finale (Banda for #11)" (660–78.) In the score the two bandas are noted as "Banda prima dei Cavalieri" (with 2 C trumpets, 2 F trumpets, 2 B♭ trumpets, 2 horns and trombones) and "Banda seconda degli Egitiani" (with quartino, piccolo clarinetto in C, 5 C clarinets, 2 oboes, 2 bassoons, 2 horns in F, 2 C trumpets, trombone, and a "Serpentone" [Serpent]). Both bandas are accompanied by several drums.

37. In the Garland facsimile score from the premiere of *Il crociato* in Venice, Armando does not sing in the stretta of the finale (574–608). In the Opera Rara recording, Armando sings the last line of the final section with Palmide, Felicia, and Alma (129).

38. At the beginning of the cantabile section of the duet, Armando refers to the spell—"Non sai quale incanto/quest'alma sorprese" (You do not know what a spell was cast over my soul).

39. These conventions were established in the first decades of the nineteenth century and are best exemplified by Rossini and his contemporaries. A short bibliography of these conventional forms are Gossett, "Rossini and the Conventions," and Powers, "La solita forma." Recently, the conventions of la solita forma have been challenged by Roger Parker in "'Insolite forme.'" For working definitions of la solita forma and the four movements (tempo d'attacco, cantabile, tempo di mezzo, and cabaletta) see the Glossary.

40. *A piacere* and *dolce* literally mean "pleasing" and "sweet," which has some relevance here for the manner of performance. However, these directions primarily indicate that the section should be rendered at the pleasure (or discretion) of the singer, for example—out of meter as an expressive opportunity for ornamentation.

41. White, "Meyerbeer in Italy," 60. The text that Rossi describes in the letters from this time and the final version of the trio are somewhat different, yet still support Rossi's general sentiments. By "white" voices, Rossi is referring to the three treble timbres: the two women's voices and Velluti's castrato voice.

42. "Giovinetta, col cuor dell'innocenza, sotto il bel ciel della natià Provenza. / Tenero Trovatore, al raggio amico / D'argentea luna . . . l'ispirava amore . . . / Odi come'ei parlava a questo core." (A young girl with an innocent heart, beneath the beautiful sky of her native Provence. He a tender troubadour, in the friendly rays of a silvery moon . . . he awakened my love. . . . Hear how he spoke to my heart.) This

text is in the recitative immediately preceding the trio stanza (Opera Rara recording libretto, 109).

43. In Greek mythology Chloe is another name for Demeter, the earth goddess, and means "the young green" (Encyclopedia Mythica, www.pantheon.org, accessed April 10, 2004). Chloe has also appeared as a nymph and shepherdess in seventeenth- and eighteenth-century English verse, including Thomas D'Urfey's "Chloe Divine" and Matthew Prior's "The Question to Lisetta" and "Song" (#424) in the *Oxford Book of English Verse,* ed. Arthur Quiller-Couch (1919), Bartleby.com, www.bartleby.com (accessed April 10, 2004).

44. Beethoven's opera *Fidelio* (1814) had seen two earlier versions: the three-act *Leonore* (1805) and and a revised two-act revival (1806). In Beethoven's operas the plot stays basically the same: Florestan (tenor) has been unjustly imprisoned for political reasons. His wife, Leonore (soprano), disguises herself as an adolescent boy (Fidelio) and works for the jailor (Rocco, baritone) as a means for finding her imprisoned husband. Rocco's daughter (Marzelline, soprano) is pursued by Jaquino (tenor), but Marzelline has fallen for Fidelio—who she does not know is really the disguised Lenore.

45. In Beethoven's *Fidelio,* Marzelline thinks she is in love with "Fidelio," who turns out to be the cross-dressed Leonore; Jaquino feels betrayed by Marzelline; and Leonore is aware that she is deceiving Marzelline, Jaquino, and Rocco with her convincing disguise. In a related side note, Meyerbeer's *Il crociato* contains a canon quartet, "O cielo clemente," near the middle of the second act, in which Palmide, Felicia, Armando, and Adriano all sing the same music and the same words. Unlike in Beethoven's canon quartet from *Fidelio,* the characters in *Il crociato* are in agreement as they proclaim their united devotion to the Christian God.

46. In Italian verse forms the type of line is determined by the total number of syllables, and where the accents fall in each line. *Ottonario tronco* means that there are seven syllables with an accent on the final syllable (hence a syllable is "added" in the count to get the correct verse type). *Rima alternata* (abab cdcd) and *rima baciata* (aa bb cc) both refer to the rhyme scheme pattern of the final syllable of the word at the end of the line of a poetic text (e.g., the end of each line of a quatrain). A clear and concise discussion of the metrical structure of nineteenth-century Italian poetry can be found in Parker, "Note on Italian Prosody," ix. Another helpful treatment is Black, "Language and Versification" in his *Italian Romantic Libretto,* 246–71.

47. In the facsimile score from the Venetian premiere of *Il crociato,* Felicia has the stage direction (a few measures after Armando enters the scene onstage) "Felicia si ritira in disparte agitato" (Felicia withdraws aside with agitation) (Garland, *Il crociato,* 455).

48. For more on exoticism in this opera, see Everist, "Meyerbeer's *Il crociato,*"

Interlude

1. Unless the performance was in Rome (where women were not allowed onstage), it was extremely rare to have a castrato play the female soprano heroine; hence, the pairing of two castrati was unlikely.

2. Bonnie G. Smith discusses the importance of expanding the view of history to in-

clude the different contrasting and complementing roles women and men occupied in the nineteenth century. She uses the term "separate spheres" to provide a space for women's activity that largely had been ignored in the narrative of a "normative" history of men's activities. See Smith, *Changing Lives* (especially 222–24) and *Gender of History* (1–13, especially 2–3).

3.   At an earlier point in this study there were eight "Queen" operas; the current four plus Rossini's *Elisabetta d'Inghilterra* (1815), Donizetti's *Maria Stuarda* (1834) and *Roberto Devereux* (1837), and Pacini's *Maria, regina d'Inghilterra* (1843). All eight operas confirm the same trends. I ended up shortening the list to make it easier to follow the overlapping plots (e.g., several operas with Elizabeth I as a character) and to be able to go into more depth with each opera.

4.   At the earlier stage in this study with eight operas, six were based on British subjects (Rossini's *Elisabetta d'Inghilterra*, 1816; Donizetti's *Anna Bolena*, 1830; *Rosmonda d'Inghilterra*, 1834; *Maria Stuarda*, 1834; *Roberto Devereux*, 1837; and Pacini's *Maria, regina d'Inghilterra*, 1843, based on Mary Tudor) and better reflected the large number of primo ottocento operas that were set in England.

5.   Italy's fascination and looking toward England in the beginning of the nineteenth century is not just seen in these few Queen operas I've indicated; there are many other Italian operas from this time based on British sources and history. An extremely short sampling includes seven based on Rosamond Clifford (died c. 1176), the alleged mistress of Henry II: Coccia, *Rosamonda* (1829); Luigi Majocchi, *Rosmonda* (Milan, 1831); Donizetti, *Rosmonda d'Inghilterra* (1834); Antonio Belisario, *Rosmonda* (Rovigo, 1835); Pietro Tonassi and Pietro Collava, *Il castello di Woodstock* (Venice, 1839) Otto Nicolai, *Enrico II* (1839); Giulio Eugenio Abramo Alari, *Rosmonda d'Inghilterra* (1840) (see Jeremy Commons, liner notes to Opera Rara recording of Donizetti's *Rosmonda*, ORC 13, esp. 14 and 42, and Weinstock, *Donizetti*, 343). Several settings of Sir Walter Scott's novels include Donizetti's *Il castello di Kennilworth* (1829); two popular settings of *The Bride of Lammermoor* by Donizetti and Carafa, both called *Lucia di Lammermoor*; and Otto Nicolai's *Il templario* (1840; based on *Ivanhoe*). This rich area deserves further inquiry. I thank Kali Israel and Kathryn Lowerre for their helpful comments on framing this topic.

6.   "Hybrid 1. The offspring of genetically dissimilar parents or stock, especially that of breeding plants or animals of different varieties, species or races. 2a. Something of mixed origin or composition." The first two definitions of "hybrid" in the *American Heritage College Dictionary*, 3rd ed. (Boston: Houghton Mifflin, 1997), 665.

7.   Like Bakhtin, I am not denying the potential for a hierarchical interrelationship between the two concurrent messages. However, for my purposes here, I am not interested in emphasizing the power structure of the relationship. The term and concept of hybridity has been used in postcolonial studies to explore the interaction and confrontation of two cultures where one has a clear political hierarchy. In *The Location of Culture*, Bhabha discusses "cultural hybridity" (2, 5, 15). See also Goldberg, "Heterogeneity and Hybridity."

8.   Bakhtin, *Dialogic Imagination*, 358.

9.   Maria Callas released two recordings of *Norma* with EMI/Angel both conducted by Tullio Serafin. On the first, from 1954, Ebe Stignani sings Adalgisa and Maria

Filippeschi sings Pollione. Callas's second *Norma* (my personal favorite), from 1960, features Christa Ludwig as Adalgisa and Franco Corelli as Pollione. Leontyne Price recorded Aida twice. The first was in 1961 with Decca/London with Georg Solti conducting. The second is from 1970 on the RCA/BMG label with Erich Leinsdorf conducting. One of Renée Fleming's early signature roles was Mozart's Countess (from *Le nozze di Figaro*). She then has added, with much success, Richard Strauss's Marschallin (from *Der Rosenkavalier*).

10. Tatiana Troyanos (1938–1992), American mezzo-soprano who studied at the Juilliard School with Hans J. Heinz.

11. Cecilia Bartoli: *The Vivaldi Album* (with Il Giardino Armonico, Decca 466569, released in October 1999); *Dreams & Fables—Gluck Italian Arias* (with the Akademie für Alte Musik, Berlin; Decca, 467248, released in September 2001); *Rossini Arias* (Decca 425430, released in August 1989); *Il barbiere di Siviglia* (Decca 42520, released in October 1989); *Rossini Recital—Giovanna d'Arco/19 Songs* (Decca 430518, released in December 1990); *Rossini Heroines* (Decca 436075, released in January 1992). Bartoli's full discography—as well as her biography, picture gallery, and tour dates—may be found on her web site, which is maintained by Decca & Philips Worldwide, www.ceciliabartolionline.com (accessed February 15, 2005).

12. More than any other family from the time, the Garcías were responsible for championing the "bel canto" sound favored by Rossini throughout the nineteenth century. A singer, composer, and teacher, Malibran's father, Manuel García, premiered several Rossini roles (notably Almaviva in *Barber,* Norfolk in *Elisabetta,* and the title role of *Otello*). In October 1825 he traveled with his family to New York and sang in the first performances of Italian opera in the United States. Her brother, Manuel García II, did not have much success as a singer; yet he pioneered the study of vocal technique and become one of the leading pedagogues in the nineteenth century. Her younger sister Pauline (whose married name was Viardot) continued the family's singing legacy through the second half of the nineteenth century.

13. Malibran's Rossini repertory is given in Appolonia, *Le voci di Rossini,* 360–65.

14. Donizetti's *Maria Stuarda* was scheduled for its first performance at the Teatro San Carlo in Naples. Due to radical alterations imposed by the censors, it was offered as *Buondelmonte* with a different cast in 1834. *Maria Stuarda* was first performed at La Scala in 1835 with Malibran in the title role. There were still problems with the censors, and it was not performed regularly until the twentieth century. The *Puritani* adapted for Malibran was delayed because of a cholera outbreak in Naples. With Bellini's death in 1835 and Malibran's in 1836, this performance version was not performed until it was reconstructed in the 1990s.

15. Rossini scholar Philip Gossett has written on Rossini's operas and the conventions of the time, notably how they helped define the formal patterns of the time, *le solite forme.* See Gossett's unpublished Ph.D. dissertation, "Rossini and the Conventions of Composition," and "Verdi, Ghislanzoni and *Aida.*"

16. The comparison between Maria Callas and Giuditta Pasta is fitting given the legendary status they both held. It is not inconsequential that Callas became famous for reviving the "bel canto," primo ottocento repertory that Pasta was instrumental in creating, being the first interpreter of several Bellini roles. Additionally, ac-

counts of both Pasta's and Callas's voices comment on their worn-out quality near the ends of their careers. Both singers lived rather reclusive years out of the spotlight after their heydays on the stage.

17. Pasta's Rossini repertory found in Appolonia, *Le voci di Rossini,* 338–41, and in Stern's Ph.D. dissertation on Pasta.

4. Taming Women's Voices

1. Most of Rossini's operas were written for the San Carlo; a couple were also premiered at the Teatro del Fondo and Teatro dei Fiorentini in 1816 when the San Carlo was destroyed by fire. Rossini's operas for the Teatro San Carlo were *Elisabetta* (1815), *Armida* (1817), *Mosè in Egitto* (1818), *Ricciardo e Zoraide* (1818), *Ermione* (1819), *La donna del lago* (1819), *Maometto II* (1820), and *Zelmira* (1822). He wrote one opera each for the Teatro dei Fiorentini (the unsuccessful comic opera *La gazzetta* in September 1816) and Teatro del Fondo (*Otello* in December 1816; it was the temporary home of the San Carlo that season).

2. Osborne, *Bel Canto Operas,* 103.

3. The other Italian opera Rossini reworked for the Paris Opéra was his *Mosè in Egitto* (San Carlo, 1818) which became *Möise et Pharaon* in 1827.

4. *La donna del lago* remained in the San Carlo's repertory for the next twelve years. Within five years of its premiere it was staged in many other Italian cities and throughout Europe: Amsterdam, Barcelona, Budapest, Dresden, Graz, Lisbon, London, Malta, Munich, Paris, St. Petersburg, and Vienna (Osborne, *Bel Canto Operas,* p. 94).

5. Giovanni David (1790–1864) created six roles for Rossini: Narciso (*Il turco in Italia,* 1814); Rodrigo (*Otello,* 1816); Ricciardo (*Ricciardo e Zoraide,* 1818); Oreste (*Ermione,* 1819); Giacomo (*La donna del lago,* 1819); and Ilo (*Zelmira,* 1822). David also sang in *Tancredi, La gazza ladra, Matilde di Shabran, Bianca e Fallier, Mosè in Egitto, Semiramide,* and the title role of *Otello.* Andrea Nozzari (1775–1832) created a total of nine roles for Rossini. Eight roles were at the San Carlo in Naples: Leicester (*Elisabetta,* 1815); Rinaldo (*Armida,* 1817); Osride (*Mosè in Egitto,* 1818); Agorante (*Ricciardo e Zoraide,* 1818); Pyrrhus (*Ermione,* 1819); Roderick of Dhu (*La donna del lago* 1819); Erisso (*Maometto II,* 1820); and Antenore (*Zelmira,* 1823). One role was created at the Teatro del Fondo: the title role in *Otello* (1816).

6. Pisaroni was already known in the north as a travesti singer and would go on to become best remembered for her heroic roles. After premiering King Almanzor in Meyerbeer's *L'esule di Granata* (Milan, 1821), she continued to sing Rossini's Malcolm Graeme and later added his Arsace (*Semiramide* in 1824) and Tancredi (1825) to her signature roles.

7. Adelaide Comelli later married the tenor Giovanni Battista Rubini, hyphenated her name to Comelli-Rubini, and created two roles by Donizetti at the Neapolitan Teatro del Fondo (Matilde in *Gianni di Calais* in 1828 and Nina in *Il giovedì grasso* in 1828 or early 1829). She was not as experienced or well known in 1820 when she sang Calbo.

8. Further contributing reasons are also possible. As Osborne readily admits, "it is

not easy now to understand why Rossini's Neapolitan audience should have acclaimed one opera while rejecting another. . . . It may well be that their response to each new work was dictated largely by the standard of the actual performance they were witnessing" (*Bel Canto Operas,* 103). This speculation is supported by the different performance versions outlined by Gossett in his introduction to the facsimile edition of *Maometto II.* Gossett discusses the innovation in formal conventions regarding the structure of arias and ensemble numbers (especially the *terzettone* in act 1) in the Naples version that were subsequently made more conventional in the Venetian revival and the French revised opera.

9. Cherubino's first entrance in the opera is in the recitative that immediately precedes this aria.

10. I am referring to the physiology of how a sound is produced and where it resonates in the singer's body. The term "mask" is also used to designate the areas in the face; singers are often told to keep the sound forward and resonating in the mask. There are different theories regarding the number of registers in the voice. My discussion here is not concerned with endorsing one over the other.

11. Throughout the rest of the aria, this tug of war continues as his melody continues its helium-like tendency to ascend and his persistent efforts to try and push the melodic contour downwards.

12. "Voi, che sapete"—"Gelo e poi sento / l'alma avvampar / e in un momento / toro na gelar." "Non so più"—"Or di foco, ora sono di ghiaccio."

13. Susanna's accompaniment, however, is played by the strings in the orchestra. To achieve the effect of having Susanna play for him, most productions include Susanna miming an accompaniment on the guitar.

14. Gossett, *Artistic Maturity of Gaetano Donizetti,* 177.

15. As Susanna only mimes playing the guitar for Cherubino in "Voi, che sapete," Smeton also mimes playing the "harp," and the "real" accompaniment is in the orchestra.

16. In the first act during the "Cosa sento" trio (with the Count, Susanna, and Basilio) the Count pantomimes how he found Cherubino hiding in Barbarina's room right as he finds Cherubino hiding in Susanna's room.

17. In the first act, right after Cherubino sings "Non so più," the Count comes to visit Susanna. Not having enough time to escape, and already in trouble with him for having been caught with Barbarina, the gardener's daughter, Cherubino hides behind a chair (or in some productions he crouches in the chair hidden by a cloak or dress). The danger of his being found out is mitigated by the comedic effect when Basilio enters and the Count also has to hide (so Susanna is hiding two men in her room). Cherubino is discovered later in the scene when the Count (who emerges when Basilio starts talking about the Countess and Cherubino) retells how he found the page hidden in Barbarina's room. As he reenacts his search of Barbarina's room, the Count lifts up the covering of the chair, and Cherubino magically appears. Because of the stage business with the Count's pantomime, this moment always causes big laughs when the mischievous page is revealed to the Count for a second time that day. In the second act, the threat to the Countess's reputation becomes a more dangerous possibility when Cherubino is almost caught alone with her by the Count. Though this nearly leads to disaster, Susanna

is able to exchange places with him when the Count goes out to get some tools to break down the door. Again, the comedic effect is present when Susanna lets Cherubino jump out the window and then nonchalantly emerges from the closet, much to the great relief of the Countess and to the Count's consternation. This sets off a chain reaction of entrances where independently Figaro, Antonio (the gardener), Marcellina, Basilio, and Bartolo eventually all come rushing in, creating the climax of the second act finale.

18. In Anna's defense, Smeton says to the King: "Kill me if I am lying: naked, unarmed, I offer you my breast" (Uccidetemi s'io mento: / nudo, inerme io v'offro il petto).

19. In addition to several page travesti roles Donizetti wrote around the time of *Anna Bolena*, he also wrote roles that have characteristics of the heroic travesti: Luigi V, King of France in *Ugo, Conte di Parigi* (1832, Milan, La Scala); Maffio Orsini, a young nobleman in *Lucrezia Borgia* (1833, Milan, La Scala); Aurelio, son to Eustachio, the Mayor of Calais in *L'assedio di Calais* (1836, Naples, San Carlo); and Rodrigo in *Pia de' Tolomei* (1836, Venice, Apollo).

20. Jeremy Commons, "*Rosmonda d'Inghilterra*," liner notes for Opera Rara recording of Donizetti's opera, ORC 13, (see 14). Donizetti was not the last to set this subject. Commons (42) mentions three others: Antonio Belisario, *Rosmonda* (Rovigo, 1835); Pietro Tonassi and Pietro Collava, *Il castello di Woodstock* (Venice, 1839); Otto Nicolai, *Rosmonda* (Trieste, 1839). Weinstock also mentions another opera on the Rosamond legend: Jules Eugène Abraham Alary (also known as Giulio Eugenio Abramo Alari), *Rosmonda d'Inghilterra,* 1840 (*Donizetti,* 343). For a discussion of the changes in the size of Arturo's character from Coccia's *Rosmonda* (1829) and the decreased importance of his role as Donizetti's opera developed, see Common's liner notes, 19–24 and 52–54.

21. Jeremy Commons characterizes Arturo's participation in Rosmonda's "Perchè del vento" as contributing "fairly extensive *pertichini*" (*Rosmonda* liner notes, 52). Pertichini are interjections by other singers into a musical number sung by one or two principal characters. Sometimes the pertichini are substantial enough to temporarily change the nature of the number from an aria to a duet (as is the case here with Rosmonda and Arturo) or a duet into a trio. See "Pertichini," *The New Grove Dictionary of Opera,* vol. 3, 973. Since Arturo not only comments on and repeats Rosmonda's music, but also has his own stanza, I extend Commons's discussion by elevating Arturo's stance in the cantabile section to be almost on par as an equal partner. In the aria as a whole, Arturo plays a less significant role; however, in the cantabile section, the form is very similar to that of a duet.

22. It was common in operas of this time to have improvised cadenzas and not written out by the composer. On the Opera Rara recording, Renee Fleming (Rosmonda) and Diana Montague (Arturo) sing a beautiful cadenza that is motivically related to the last two verses of the first two stanzas and features the intertwining of the voices as well as singing in thirds.

23. For an explanation of the italicized lines in the libretto, please see the discussion of chapters 4 and 5 in the "Overview" section at the end of chapter 1.

24. A provocatively relevant example may be found in Meyerbeer's *Il crociato in Egitto.* Though the situation is a little different, a trio rather than a duet, Armando makes his vocal entrance from offstage when he, Felicia, and Palmide all sing

about love and seduction (act 1, "Giovinetto cavalier"). The voices in the trio reflect the different vocal types of the time: Armando was premiered by the castrato Giambattista Velluti, Palmide is the high soprano, and Felicia is the second woman who is dressed in men's attire—directly invoking the heroic travesti tradition. (A more in-depth discussion of this scene may be found in chapter 3.)

25.   Elisabeth Hudson has written very compellingly about absent tenor-soprano seduction scenes and how they can be reflected in opera in "Gilda Seduced." Hudson's article explores the way Verdi and Piave adapted Hugo's play *Le roi s'amuse* into their opera *Rigoletto* when the bedroom seduction scene between Blanche (Gilda in their opera) and the King (turned into the Duke) could not get past the Italian censors. While Hudson expertly shows how the Duke's tenor voice is made "seductive" despite the absence of the critical seduction scene, my comparison is to evoke the connection between the tenor voice seducing the soprano outside of the opera.

26.   John Warrack and Sandro Corti, "Duprez, Gilbert(-Louis)," *The New Grove Dictionary of Opera,* vol. 1, 1281. Rossini was not a fan of the new singing style and the do di petto. Edmond Michotte relates Rossini's horrified reaction when Gilbert Duprez demonstrated the new technique for which he became so famous. When Duprez asked Rossini if he liked the sound, Rossini replied, "Very sincerely, what pleases me most about your C is that it is over, and that I am no longer in danger of hearing it. I don't like unnatural effects. It strikes my Italian ear as having a strident timbre, like a capon squawking as its throat is slit" (Michotte, "Evening at Rossini's," 98–99).

5. Women's Voices in Motion

1.   Rossini's *Armida* was unusually cast at the San Carlos in Naples for one soprano (Isabella Colbran) and roles for six tenors (two of which were sung by the same singer in the premiere) and two basses (cast list from Osborne's *Bel Canto Operas,* 76). Though Rossini's *Semiramide* has multiple roles for women's voices (Semiramide, Arsace is a travesti role, and Azema), the plot is a little unusual with the death of Semiramide at the opera's conclusion. Nevertheless, the Queen's death allows for an ordered resolution. Since Semiramide and her lover Assur had murdered her husband (King Ninus) in the prehistory to the opera, her death at the end not only prevents a situation of incest (were Semiramide to marry Arsace, her long lost son and current love interest), but also acts as a punishment for her earlier crimes.

2.   The title of Catherine Clément's groundbreaking book on women in opera cites the "undoing" of women: *Opera, or the Undoing of Women.* Michael Scott refers to the "fey" and "hapless" heroines in *Record of Singing,* vol. 1, 16–17. Examples of second women who survive the end of the opera and are without a spouse at the end are Medea; Elizabeth in several operas based on the historical Queen Elizabeth I (Rossini's *Elisabetta, regina d'Inghilterra,* 1816; Donizetti's *Maria Stuarda,* 1834, and *Roberto Devereaux,* 1837); and the title character in Pacini's *Maria, regina d'Inghilterra* (1843), based on the historical Queen Mary I (Mary Tudor).

3.   Others have discussed Lucia's madness as liberation or a sign of her defeat (see

Clément, *Undoing of Women,* 88–91, and Smart, "Silencing of Lucia"). I am not debating whether or not Lucia's madness is liberating. Instead, I note that she does not passively expire for love. Rather, she takes an active stance. Though unfortunate, she takes action by murdering her bridegroom and setting things in motion for her own death.

4. Pasta sang the following roles: Pacini (Adelaide, *Adelaide e Comingio;* Zora, *La schiava in Bagdad;* and she created the title role in *Niobe*), Mercadante (Elisa, *Elisa e Claudio,* the title roles in *Didone* and *Emma d'Antiochia,* which was written for Pasta in 1834 and the last new role she created), Mayr (the travesti roles of Linceo in *Danao* and Enrico in *La rosa bianca e la rosa rossa* and the title role in *Medea in Corinto*), Cimarosa (travesti roles of Telemaco, *Penelope;* Curizaio, *Gli Oriazi e i Curazi*), Nicolini (the travesti roles of Clodomiro, *Giulio Ceasare nelle Gallie;* Gonzalvo, *La conquista di Granata;* and she created the title role in *Malek Adel*), and Giuseppe Farinelli (Diana, *La festa patria* and the travesti role of Clearco, *I riti d'Efeso*). These roles and others are mentioned in Stern's "Documentary Study of Giuditta Pasta."

5. From 1818 through 1820 Pasta sang at the San Benedetto in Venice, the Teatro Nuovo in Padua, the Teatro Grande in Brescia, the Teatro Nuovo in Trieste, and other houses. See Stern, "Documentary Study of Giuditta Pasta," 26–58.

6. Zingarelli's Romeo was created by soprano castrato Girolamo Crescentini (1762–1846) in 1796. Crescentini was particularly well known in this role for "Ombra adorata," an aria Crescentini composed and added to act 3 (Maria Caraci Vela, "*Giulietta e Romeo* (i)," *The New Grove Dictionary of Opera,* vol. 2, 435).

7. Bellini's total operatic output was ten operas. His first (*Adelson e Salvini,* 1825) was a student opera, and *Zaira* (1829) failed to find success. Bellini later reworked ten sections of *Zaira* for *I Capuletti e i Montecchi,* and two sections each for *Norma* and *Beatrice di Tenda.* See Simon Maguire and Elizabeth Forbes, "*Zaira,*" *The New Grove Dictionary of Opera,* vol. 4, 1202–1203.

8. Henriette Méric-Lalande premiered the heroines in Bellini's first four operas (not including his student opera, *Adelson e Salvini*). Her roles were Bianca in *Bianca e Fernando* (1826), Imogene in *Il pirata* (1827), Alaide in *La straniera* (1829), and the title character in *Zaira* (1829).

9. For the history of the compositional genesis of Donizetti's *Anna Bolena* and its place in his career, see Gossett, *Anna Bolena.*

10. John Rosselli discusses the notion of repertory operas catching on in Italy by around 1840. However, Rosselli does mention earlier examples going back to the 1820s, especially with the more prominent singers (Rosselli, *Opera Industry in Italy,* 5, 169–71).

11. In order of performance, Pasta sang all three women in Mozart's *Don Giovanni:* Donna Elvira in 1816 at the Théâtre Italien, Donna Anna in 1821 at the Théâtre Italien, and Zerlina for a benefit performance in Naples in January 1827 (Stern, "Documentary Study of Giuditta Pasta," 13–14, 73, 172).

12. Opera scholar Hilary Poriss has done important work on substitution arias (Poriss "Madwoman's Choice").

13. Meyerbeer wrote the cabaletta for Pasta, "L'aspetto adorabile" when she premiered Armando in Paris. The opening recitative, "Eccomi giunto ormai," was the origi-

nal beginning of the number that was first written for the castrato Giambattista Velluti. The cavatina Pasta preferred, "Oh, come rapida," was originally written for Carolina Bassi (when she sang Armando in Trieste in 1824) and was a re-worked version of an aria for Rosmonda Pisaroni from *L'Esule di Granata* (Stern, "Documentary Study of Giuditta Pasta," 138–39).

14.   Rossini's "Dolci d'amor parole" was written in 1813 at Adelaide Malanotte's (the first Tancredi) request when she felt that the original was not elaborate enough. Ironically, the first version of Tancredi's entrance aria ("Tu che accendi questo core" and especially the more famous cabaletta, "Di tanti palpiti") were later among Rossini's most popular tunes in the nineteenth century. This situation is discussed in Philip Gossett's "Prefazione" to the critical edition of *Tancredi* in the series of Rossini's works by the Rossini Foundation in Pesaro, Italy, and publish-ed by Ricordi, pp. xxi–xxii, xvii–xviii.

15.   Nicolini's aria, "Dolci d'amor parole," and Rossini's added embellishments for Pasta's performances in Brussels and Paris are reproduced in the critical edition of *Tancredi,* Appendix V, No. 17b, 533–49. This case of substitution is also men-tioned in Stern, "Documentary Study of Giuditta Pasta," 143–44.

16.   These twenty roles do not include the few comic roles that Pasta sang but was never well known for. The most complete listing of Pasta's repertory throughout her career is Stern, "Documentary Study of Giuditta Pasta."

17.   The list of these roles is gleaned from ibid.

18.   The list of these roles is gleaned from ibid. and Appolonia's *Le voci di Rossini.*

19.   Edwards, *Prima Donna,* 192.

20.   I am not implying that madness is an invention in nineteenth-century opera; seventeenth- and eighteenth-century opera provide numerous cases of madness and, a related genre, rage arias. In the nineteenth century, madness takes on an added association with feminine hysteria and becomes an even more Romanti-cized theme in opera, literature, dance, and the visual arts.

21.   Bellini's first opera, *Adelson e Salvini,* was first performed at the Real Collegio di Musica di San Sebastiano with an all-male cast. Bellini revised the opera from three acts with spoken dialogue into two acts with recitativo secco, but this ver-sion was not staged until the 1992. The original three-act version was restaged (the first time since its premiere season) in 1985 at a Bellini conference com-memorating the 150th anniversary of his death (see Osborne, *Bel Canto Operas,* 309–310). Bellini's second opera, *Bianca e Gernando,* was revised as *Bianca e Fernando* and performed at the Teatro Carlo Felice in Genoa in April 1828, after the premiere of *Il pirata* at La Scala in of 1827.

22.   Stern, "Documentary Study of Giuditta Pasta," 203.

23.   The terms *prima donna* (first lady) and, less frequently, *prima donna assoluta* (ab-solute first lady) came into use in opera at the end of the eighteenth century and originally referred to the leading female member of the company for that season (there also could be *primo tenore, primo basso,* etc.). In the nineteenth century the terms were used more frequently and could refer to several singers in a company in a given season. Such titles implied that the singer could more easily choose and refuse roles. *Musico assoluta* was less common a term but provided the same rights to singers performing leading travesti roles. Similar to Pasta's request from

John Ebers in London, Giulia Grisi wrote to impresario Alessandro Lanari in July 1830 to say that she wanted *prima donna* and *primo musico soprano* written into her contract (John Rosselli, "Primo musico," *The New Grove Dictionary of Opera*, vol. 3, 1097).

24. Ebers, *Seven Years at the King's Theatre*. Pasta's contract is reprinted as Appendix V, "Madame Pasta's Engagement for 1826," pp. 387–90 (also found in Stern, "Documentary Study of Giuditta Pasta," 156).

25. Stern, "Documentary Study of Giuditta Pasta," 201.

26. Ibid., 203.

27. Ibid., 207–14.

28. Ibid., 234.

29. *New Times,* July 6, 1827. Quoted in Stern, "Documentary Study of Giuditta Pasta," 183, emphasis in the original.

30. The castrati were praised for their ability with the messa di voce. Such a term is common in the two leading eighteenth-century singing treatises, both written by castrati: Pierfrancesco Tosi and Giambattista Mancini. In *Observations on the Florid Song* (1723) Tosi mentions it several times in passing (8, 12–3, 40, 45 in Pilkington's edition), and in *Practical Reflections on the Figurative Art of Singing* (1777), Mancini devotes an entire chapter to it (ch. 9 is entitled "Messa di voce").

31. Stendhal, *Life of Rossini,* 376, emphasis added.

32. Ibid., 377, emphasis added.

33. Chorley, *Thirty Years' Musical Recollections,* 45. Chorley's book was originally published in two volumes in 1862.

34. Ibid., 88.

35. *Morning Herald* (London), May 18, 1837. As quoted in Stern, "Documentary Study of Giuditta Pasta," 246.

36. Bellini's original idea of setting Hugo's *Hernani* (where Pasta would be a heroic travesti role) was most likely abandoned because of the troubles such a political subject would attract, at least according to a letter Bellini wrote to his friend Giovanni Battista Perucchini on 3 January 3, 1831. See Osborne, *Bel Canto Operas,* 333.

37. Ibid.

38. In addition to both Rossini's *Armida* (1817) and Mayr's *Medea in Corinto* (1813) being written for the Teatro San Carlo in Naples, both operas were headed by the same two singers. Isabella Colbran in both title roles and Andrea Nozzari as Rinaldo (in *Armida*) and Giasone (in *Medea*).

39. "Sommi Dei" was most likely not in the first version of the opera but was probably added at Colbran's request. It was not included in the score of the opera that was published by Carli of Paris, which is thought to be the version sung by Pasta. "Sommi Dei" is in the appendix of the Garland score of the opera and included on the Opera Rara recording (1994) as Medea's entrance aria. For further discussion see Gossett's introductory essay to the Garland edition of the opera and Commons's liner notes to the Opera Rara recording (36). Though "Sommi Dei" was not in the first version of Mayr's opera, it was definitely part of the version

that Pasta sang when Medea became one of her signature roles in the 1820s and 1830s.

40. Two of Medea's arias, "Sommi Dei" and "Miseri pergoletti," each survive in two versions. One version has an obbligato solo line for the violin (the more florid version), and the other version is written with a less ornamented solo for the English horn. See Gossett's introductory essay to the Garland edition of the opera and Commons's liner notes to the Opera Rara recording (35–37). The Opera Rara recording includes both arias. The version with the solo violin is included in an appendix at the end of the recording.

41. In this discussion of "Miseri pergoletti" I will refer to the English horn solo, though my general comments about the obbligato solo may also apply to the solo violin in the other, more ornamented, version of this aria.

42. Henry's monologue after the chorus of councilors ends with "Ite; e il consiglio intero / oda, e approvi il grand'atto: al dì novello / fia che rivarchi il mar, non più Regina / l'altera Leonora" (Go; and let the full Council hear and approve the great resolution: tomorrow at dawn let the proud Leonora, no longer Queen, retrace her path across the sea). Opera Rara, *Rosmonda* libretto, trans. Jeremy Commons, 102.

43. In *Medea,* as Giasone and Ismene (Medea's attendant) are talking, Medea enters and orders Giasone to stop ("Femati," using the imperative command). Giasone's response is "Oh Dei!" (Oh gods!). In *Rosmonda,* after Henry's councilors leave, she uses the same word as Medea, "Fermati."

44. Donizetti revised *Rosmunda d'Inghilterra* in 1837 for an intended performance of the opera in Naples. Unfortunately, due to a cholera outbreak in Naples and tragedy in Donizetti's personal life (the death of his newborn child in June and then the death of his wife Virginia at the end of July), this revised score was not performed. Despite Donizetti's attempts to have it performed later that year in Venice (during the time he was mounting the premiere of *Maria di Rudenz*), this never happened. In addition to changing the name of the opera to *Eleonora di Gujenna,* there were a few changes to the score, including the addition of two numbers for Leonora: a cabaletta for her act 1 aria and a cabaletta for her act 2 aria, which ends the opera. Leonora's final cabaletta, "Tu! Spergiuro, disumano," added in 1837 briefly extends the action of the last moments in the opera. The original 1834 ending of the opera (without the cabaletta) is basically the same as the revision, except that after Leonora stabs Rosmonda the action is compressed with short interjections by Leonora, Enrico, Clifford, and the chorus. See Commons, liner notes to *Rosmonda d'Inghilterra,* 33–34.

45. See Kimbell, *Norma,* 16–17; Parmentola's edition of *Norma,* 94–96; and Stern, "Documentary Study of Giuditta Pasta," 224.

46. In *Medea,* the act 1 finale wedding chorus concludes both sections with the same refrain: "Stringe, propizio Imene, le tenere catena, e arrida all'opra Amor" (Propitious Hymen, bind the tender chains and may love smile upon your work) (libretto, 81, 82).

47. *Medea* was written at the beginning of Romani's career and was his second libretto. His first libretto was also for a Mayr opera, *La rosa bianca e la rosa rossa,* written earlier the same year (1813).

48. In the libretto, Norma: "Adalgisa fia punita, / nelle fiamme perirà!"

49. As Anna inquires about the offstage cheering, the chorus informs Anna, "Acclamata dal popolo contento / è regina . . . " (The people happily acclaim the [new] Queen . . .).

50. However, after becoming Queen, Jane and Anne's histories differ: Jane gave Henry a son (Edward VI) and then died days after giving birth.

51. Norma's words to release Adalgisa from her vows: "Ah! Tergi il pianto! / Te non lega eterno nodo, / Eterno nodo all'ara." (Ah! Dry your weeping! An eternal bond does not tie you to the altar.) Norma's next response is "Si, fa core e abbracciami./ Perdono e ti compiango. / Dai voti tuoi ti libero, / i tuoi legami io frango. / Al caro oggetto unita/vivrai felice ancor." (Yes, take heart and embrace me. I forgive you and sympathize with you. I free you from your vows, I break your bonds. United to the object of your love, you shall yet live happily.) *Norma* libretto, trans. William Weaver, 7.

52. Several singers have performed Adalgisa relatively early and have gone on to notable careers (even if Adalgisa did not stay in their repertory). Among others, this has included Christa Ludwig (EMI 1960 with Maria Callas as Norma), Marilyn Horne (Decca/London 1964 with Joan Sutherland as Norma), Fiorenza Cossotto in two recordings (Decca 1967 with Elena Souliotis as Norma and RCA/BMG 1972 with Montserrat Caballé), and Tatiana Troyanos (CBS/Sony 1979 with Renata Scotto).

53. A wonderful exception to the exclusivity of the roles of Norma and Adalgisa is in the career of Shirley Verrett, a singer who defies strict categorization and has performed both leading roles in her career. As far as I can tell, she made only one commercial recording of the opera, and that was as Adalgisa (with Beverly Sills as Norma, 1973 EMI/Angel). Montserrat Caballé has recorded both the title role, her normal performance role (RCA 1972 with Fiorenza Cossotto as Adalgisa), and Adalgisa in a glamorous case of luxury casting with Joan Sutherland as Norma, Luciano Pavarotti as Pollione, and Samuel Ramey as Oroveso (Decca/ London 1984).

54. Bellini and Donizetti's two operas for the 1831–32 season at La Scala share several characteristics in their roles for Pasta and Grisi. In both *Norma* and *Ugo,* the two women love the tenor, and he loves Grisi's character (in *Norma* the tenor returns Norma's love at the very end; in *Ugo* the tenor marries Grisi's character and loves her through the end). In the two operas, Pasta's character has the opportunity and motivation to dictate Grisi's death, but she changes her mind and decides to sacrifice herself.

   An important difference between the two operas is the presence of Luigi V, a heroic travesti role, in Donizetti's opera. Like Bellini, Donizetti was important for pioneering the new Romantic aesthetic of whittling down the number of principal roles and focus of the drama on the tenor and soprano couple. However, Donizetti also continued to write operas in an older style with travesti roles and two female characters. His late use of the travesti can be seen in the heroic roles of Aurelio in *L'assedio di Calais* (1836), Rodrigo in *Pia de' Tolomei* (1837), and the revision of Armando di Gondi for Marietta Brambilla for the performance of *Maria di Rohan* in Paris in November 1843 (the opera had premiered June 5, 1843, in Vienna's Theater am Kärntnertor with Armado's part much smaller and written for a tenor). Additionally there is the page role of Pierotto in *Linda di Chamounix* (1842). Operas with two leading women include *Roberto Devereux* (1837) and *Maria Padilla* (1841).

55. Giulia Grisi did not return to Italy to sing until 1863. She traveled widely and sang in St. Petersburg, New York, and Madrid. See Elizabeth Forbes, "Grisi, Giulia," *The New Grove Dictionary of Opera,* vol. 2, 549–50.

56. Robert D. Hume and Arthur Jacobs, "London, History, 1830–90," *The New Grove Dictionary of Opera,* vol. 3, 12 (caption for the illustration of Giulia Grisi as Norma).

57. As quoted in Kimbell, *Norma,* 112.

58. A striking picture of Giulia Grisi in the title role of *Norma,* holding a knife over a sleeping child (act 2, scene 1), was printed on the cover of a nineteenth-century sheet music excerpt from the opera. The picture caption reads: "Giulia Grisi in the title role of Bellini's *Norma* (Act 2, scene I), which she sang almost every season from 1837 until 1861 at both Her Majesty's Theatre and Covent Garden: lithograph from a contemporary sheet music cover." This picture can be seen in Robert D. Hume and Arthur Jacobs, "London, History, 1830–90," *The New Grove of Dictionary of Opera,* vol. 3, 12.

59. In *Anna Bolena* Percy declares his still ardent love for Anna at the end of the first act. Anna does not allow herself to articulate her love for him until her mad scene at the end of the opera. For Norma, Pollione finally reaffirms his love in the last moments of the opera.

Coda

1. As quoted in Arblaster's *Viva la Libertà!* 65. In the notes to the chapter (321), Arblaster cites his source for this Heine quotation as the Welsh National Opera program book for *The Barber of Seville* (1986).

2. Stendhal, *Life of Rossini,* 457.

3. Ibid., emphasis in the original.

4. Ibid., 458, emphasis in the original.

5. Arblaster, *Viva la Libertà!* 3.

6. See Elvidio Surian's "A Chronology of Verdi's Life and Works" in Weaver and Chusid, *Verdi Companion,* 256–324. He discusses Verdi's name as a political slogan (284) and Verdi's service in the first Italian parliament (286, 291).

7. *The Donizetti Society Journal,* especially the careful scholarship of Jeremy Commons and Don White, has provided critical steps in the examination of primo ottocento opera from a political-historical angle. Also important to this area is the work that Opera Rara, in association with the Peter Moores Foundation, is doing through their recordings of the primo ottocento repertory. Arblaster has written about the political overtones in several operas throughout the nineteenth and twentieth centuries (*Viva la libertà!*). Though he does not spend much time on the operas outlined in my study, he comments that in Rossini's *Tancredi,* the "essential ingredients are love, patriotism and the possible conflict between them" (68) and calls Bellini's *Norma* "a story of national resistance to imperial occupation" (81; more on *Norma* on 82–84). Another study that addresses politi-

cal themes in primo ottocento operas is Ashbrook's *Donizetti and His Operas.*
The situation regarding scholarship on the political and economic operatic enterprise in Paris, notably with French grand opera, has been quite different. In studies that trace the development of French grand opera leading up to its heyday in
the middle of the century, ca. 1830–70, the larger political and cultural context
has been thoughtfully examined (Fulcher, *The Nation's Image;* Pendle, *Eugène
Scribe and French Opera of the Nineteenth Century;* and Gerhard, *The Urbanization of Opera* are a few examples). Stephen C. Meyer's *Carl Maria von Weber and
the Search for a German Opera* has opened up this arena for German opera.

8.   Mary Ann Smart has approached the topic of Verdi's warrior women in five of
his operas, with a focus on two operas in some depth in her "Proud, Indomitable,
Irascible." The five "warrior women" and operas are Abagaille in *Nabucco* (1841),
the title character in *Giovanna d'Arco* (1845), Odabella in *Attila* (1846), Lady
Macbeth in *Macbeth* (1847), and Hélène in *Les vêpres siciliennes* (1855). Her argument provides a beginning context for making a connection between the political
message in the opera and the politics of the time in relation to vocal writing and
aria form. Other studies have treated the topic of the connection between the Risorgimento and opera; however, these studies look more at the political subjects
and references in opera rather than interpreting the way the structure of the plot
and conventions of opera could reflect the political times. A few strong studies
are Arblaster's *Viva la Libertà!* John Bokina's *Opera and Politics,* and Robinson's
Opera and Ideas.

9.   A quick list includes a narrative voice (Abbate, *Unsung Voices*), a triumphant singing voice over the orchestra (Paul Robinson, "It's Not Over until the Soprano
Dies," *New York Times,* January 1, 1989) and a "more rhapsodic approach, an ear
for vocal *jouissance*" (Smart, *Siren Songs,* 4).

10. Bonnie G. Smith provides an entry point for looking at women's activities in
nineteenth-century Italian Risorgimento history. Smith mentions Christina Belgiojoso (who started the newspaper *Gazetta Italiana* in Paris in the early 1840s),
Rosa Donato (who aided a Sicilian uprising in 1847), Anna Mozzoni (who published *Woman and Her Social Relations* in 1864), and Alaide Gaulberta Beccari
(who at eighteen founded the political newspaper *La Donna,* in 1868), among
others who were politically active for women's rights in nineteenth-century Italy
(see Smith, *Changing Lives,* 222–67, esp. 222–23, 236–38, and 256–58). These well-
known offstage Italian heroines of the Risorgimento present another strata of experience for the nineteenth-century Italian audience and provide potential
connections to the characterizations of the Romantic heroines on the opera stage.

Bibliography

Abbate, Carolyn. 1991. *Unsung Voices: Opera and Musical Narrative in the Nineteenth Century*. Princeton Studies in Opera. Princeton, N.J.: Princeton University Press.
———. 1993. "Opera: Or, the Envoicing of Women." In *Musicology and Difference,* edited by Ruth Solie, 225–58. Berkeley: University of California Press.
Abel, Samuel D. 1996. *Opera in the Flesh: Sexuality in Operatic Performances*. Boulder: Westview Press.
Agricola, John Friedrich. 1997. *Introduction to the Art of Singing*. Translated and edited by Julianne C. Baird. Cambridge Musical Texts and Monographs. Cambridge: Cambridge University Press. Original edition, *Anleitung zur Singkunst.* Berlin: G. L. Winter, 1757.
André, Naomi. 1996. "Azucena, Eboli and Amneris: Verdi's Writing for Women's Lower Voices." Ph.D. dissertation, Harvard University.
Angier, Natalie. 1999. *Woman: An Intimate Geography*. Boston: Houghton Mifflin.
Appolonia, Giorgio. 1992. *Le voci di Rossini*. Turin: Edizioni Eda.
———. 1998. "Il fenomeno della voce castrata." *Nuova Rivista Musicale Italiana* 1 (4): 164–77.
Arblaster, Anthony. 1992. *Viva la Libertà! Politics in Opera*. London: Verso.
Ashbrook, William. 1982. *Donizetti and His Operas*. Cambridge: Cambridge University Press.
———. 1998. "The Evolution of the Donizettian Tenor-Persona." *Opera Quarterly* 14 (3): 25–32.
Bakhtin, Mikhail Mikhailovich. 1981. *The Dialogic Imagination: Four Essays*. Edited by Michael Holquist. Translated by Caryl Emerson and Michael Holquist. University of Texas Press Slavic Series, no. 1. Austin: University of Texas Press.
Balthazar, Scott L. 1989. "Music, Poetry, and Action in *Ottocento* Opera: The Principle of Concurrent Articulations." *Opera Journal* 22: 13–34.
———. 1995. "Aspects of Form in the Ottocento Libretto." *Cambridge Opera Journal* 7: 23–35.
———. 1995. "Tectonic and Linear Form in the *Ottocento* Libretto: The Case of the Two *Otellos*." *Opera Journal* 28: 2–14.
Balzac, Honoré de. 1974. *Sarrasine*. In *S/Z*, edited by Roland Barthes, 221–54. New York: Hill and Wang.
Barbier, Patrick. 1995. *Opera in Paris, 1800–1850: A Lively History*. Translated by Robert Luoma. Portland: Amadeus Press. Original edition, *La vie quotidienne à l'Opéra au temps de Rossini et de Balzac: Paris, 1800–1850.* Paris: Hachette, 1987.
———. 1996. *The World of the Castrati: The History of an Extraordinary Operatic Phenomenon*. Translated by Margaret Crosland. London: Souvenir Press. Original edition, *Histoire des castrats*. Paris: Éditions Bernard Grasset & Fasquelle, 1989.
Barthes, Roland. 1974. *S/Z*. Translated by Richard Miller. New York: Hill and Wang.
Baxandall, Michael. 1988. *Painting and Experience in Fifteenth-Century Italy: A Primer in the Social History of Pictorial Style*. 2nd ed. Oxford: Oxford University Press.

Becker, Heinz, and Gudrun Becker. 1989. *Giacomo Meyerbeer: A Life in Letters.* Translated by Mark Violette. Portland: Amadeus Press.

Bellini, Vincenzo. 1974. *Norma: Melodramma in due atti di Felice Romani.* Edited by Carlo Parmentola. Opera collana di guide musicali, vol. 5. Turin: Unione Tippografico Editrice Torinese.

Bergeron, Katherine. 1996. "The Castrato as History." *Cambridge Opera Journal* 8 (2): 167–84.

Bhabha, Homi K. 1994. *The Location of Culture.* New York: Routledge.

Bianconi, Lorenzo, and Giorgio Pestelli, eds. 1998. *Opera Production and Its Resources.* Translated by Lydia G. Cochrane. Volume 4, Part II: *Systems.* The History of Italian Opera. Chicago: University of Chicago Press. Original edition, *Storia dell'opera italiana,* vol. 4: *Il sistema produttivo e le sue competenze.* Turin: Edizioni di Torino, 1987.

Black, John. 1984. *The Italian Romantic Libretto: A Study of Salvadore Cammarano.* Edinburgh: Edinburgh University Press.

Blackmer, Corinne E., and Patricia Juliana Smith, ed. 1995. *En Travesti: Women, Gender, Subversion, Opera.* Between Men—Between Women: Lesbian and Gay Studies. New York: Columbia University Press.

Bokina, John. 1997. *Opera and Politics: From Monteverdi to Henze.* New Haven, Conn.: Yale University Press.

Boyd, Malcolm, ed. 1992. *Music and the French Revolution.* Cambridge: Cambridge University Press.

Brett, Philip, Elizabeth Wood, and Gary C. Thomas, ed. 1994. *Queering the Pitch: The New Gay and Lesbian Musicology.* New York: Routledge.

Bull, Michael, and Les Back, eds. 2003. *The Auditory Culture Reader.* Sensory Formations Series. Oxford: Berg.

Casanova, Giacomo, and Chevalier de Seingalt. 1997. *History of My Life.* Translated by Willard R. Trask. Volumes 1 and 2. Baltimore, Md.: Johns Hopkins University Press. Original edition, *Histoire de ma vie,* édition intégrale. Wiesbaden: F. A. Brockhaus, 1960.

Castanet, Pierre Albert, ed. 2000. *Honoré de Balzac et la musique: Charges, Gambara, Massimilla Doni, Sarrasine.* Paris: Éditions Michel de Maule.

Castle, Terry. 1995. "In Praise of Brigitte Fassbender: Reflections on Diva-Worship." In *En Travesti: Women, Gender, Subversion, Opera,* edited by Corinne E. Blackmer and Patricia Juliana Smith, 20–58. New York: Columbia University Press.

Celletti, Rodolfo. 1969. "Lo stile vocale di Verdi e di Wagner." *Colloquium Verdi-Wagner Rom 1969,* edited by Friedrich Lippmann, 328–41. Vienna: Böhlau, 1972.

———. 1969. *Il vocalismo italiano da Rossini a Donizetti. Parte II: Bellini e Donizetti.* Edited by F. Lippmann. Studien zur italienisch-deutschen Musikgeschichte VI. Vienna: Böhlau Verlag. *Analecta Musicologica* 6(7): 214–47.

———. 1975. "La vocalità di Donizetti." *Atti del Primo Convegno Internatzionale di Studi Donizettiani, Settembre 22–28, Bergamo, 107–47.*

———. 1977. "La vocalità." In *Storia dell' opera,* vol. 3, part 1, edited by Guglielmo Barblan and Alberto Basso, 105–81. Turin: Unione Tipografico-Editrice Torinese.

———. 1996. *A History of Bel Canto.* Translated by F. Fuller. Oxford: Oxford University Press. Original edition, *Storia del belcanto.* Fiesole: Discanto Edizioni, 1983.

Chambers, Ross. 1984. "Seduction Denied: 'Sarrasine' and the Impact of Art." In *Story and Situation: Narrative Seduction and the Power of Fiction.* Minneapolis: University of Minnesota Press.

Charlton, David. 1992. "On Redefinitions of 'Rescue Opera.'" In *Music and the French Revolution,* edited by Malcolm Boyd, 169–90. Cambridge: Cambridge University Press.

Chorley, Henry Fothergill. 1926. *Thirty Years' Musical Recollections.* Edited with an introduction by Ernest Newman. New York: Alfred A. Knopf. Original edition, London, 1862.

Christiansen, Rupert. 1984. *Prima Donna: A History.* New York: Penguin Books.

Clark, Martin. 1998. *The Italian Risorgimento.* Seminar Studies in History. New York: Longman.

Clément, Catherine. 1988. *Opera, or The Undoing of Women.* Translated by Betsy Wing. Minneapolis: University of Minnesota Press. Original edition, *L'opéra ou la défaite des femmes.* Paris: Bernard Grasset, Éditions Grasset & Fasquelle, 1979.

———. 2000. "Through Voices, History." In *Siren Songs: Representations of Gender and Sexuality in Opera,* edited by Mary Ann Smart, 17–28. Princeton, N.J.: Princeton University Press.

Coffin, Berton, ed. 1989. *Historical Vocal Pedagogy Classics.* Metuchen, N.J.: Scarecrow Press.

Collins, Michael. 1982. "The Literary Background of Bellini's *I Capuleti e i Montecchi.*" *Journal of the American Musicological Society* 35 (3): 532–38.

Commons, Jeremy. 1994. "Medea in Corinto." Liner notes to the recording of Mayr's *Medea in Corinto.* Opera Rara 11, 10–51.

Cone, Edward T. 1974. *The Composer's Voice.* Berkeley: University of California Press.

Covell, Roger. 1984. "Voice Register as an Index of Age and Status in Opera Seria." In *Opera and Vivaldi,* edited by Michael Collins and Elise K. Kirk, 193–210. Austin: University of Texas Press.

Crow, Thomas. 1995. *Emulation: Making Artists for Revolutionary France.* New Haven, Conn.: Yale University Press.

Crutchfield, Will. 1989. "Voices, Part Two: The Classical Era." In *Performance Practice,* vol. II: *Music after 1600,* edited by Howard Mayer Brown and Stanley Sadie, 292–319. New York: W. W. Norton.

———. 1989. "Voices, Part Three: The 19th Century." In *Performance Practice,* vol. II: *Music after 1600,* edited by Howard Mayer Brown and Stanley Sadie, 424–58. New York: W. W. Norton.

Dellamora, Richard, and Daniel Fischlin, eds. 1997. *The Work of Opera: Genre, Nationhood and Sexual Difference.* New York: Columbia University Press.

Della Seta, Fabrizio. 1998. "The Librettist: The Nineteenth Century." In *Opera Production and Its Resources,* edited by Lorenzo Bianconi and Giorgio Pestelli, translated by Linda G. Cochrane, 255–72. Chicago: University of Chicago Press. Original edition, *Storia dell' opera italiana,* vol. 4: *Il sistema produttivo e le sue competenze.* Turin: Edizioni di Torino, 1987.

Dreger, Alice Domurat. 1998. *Hermaphrodites and the Medical Invention of Sex.* Cambridge, Mass.: Harvard University Press.

Dunn, Leslie C., and Nancy A. Jones, eds. 1994. *Embodied Voices: Representing Female Vocality in Western Culture.* New Perspectives in Music History and Criticism. Cambridge: Cambridge University Press.

Durante, Sergio. 1998. "The Opera Singer." In *Opera Production and Its Resources,* edited by Lorenzo Bianconi and Giorgi Pestelli, translated by Lydia G. Cochrane, 345–417. Chicago: University of Chicago Press. Original edition, *Storia dell' opera italiana,* vol. 4: *Il sistema produttivo e le sue competenze.* Turin: Edizioni di Torino, 1987.

Ebers, John. 1828. *Seven Years at the King's Theatre.* London: William Harrison Ainsworth.

Edwards, Henry Sutherland. 1888. *The Prima Donna: Her History and Surroundings from the Seventeenth to the Nineteenth Century.* Volume 1. London: Remington.

Everett, Andrew. 1988. "'Bewitched in a Magic Garden': Giacomo Meyerbeer in Italy." *Donizetti Society Journal* 6: 163–92.

Everist, Mark. 1996. "Meyerbeer's *Il crociato in Egitto:* Mélodrame, Opera, Orientalism." *Cambridge Opera Journal* 8 (3): 215–50.

Ferranti-Giulini, Maria. 1935. *Giuditta Pasta e i suoi tempi: Memorie e lettere.* Milan.

Festa-McCormick, Diana. 1979. *Honoré de Balzac.* Twayne's World Author Series, TWAS 54: France. Boston: Twayne.

Fulcher, Jane F. 1987. *The Nation's Image: French Grand Opera as Politics and Politicized Art.* Cambridge: Cambridge University Press.

Garafola, Lynn. 1985–86. "The Travesty Dancer in Nineteenth-Century Ballet." *Dance Research Journal* 17–18 (1–2): 35–40.

Garber, Marjorie. 1992. *Vested Interests: Cross-dressing and Cultural Anxiety.* New York: Routledge.

———. 1995. *Vice Versa: Bisexuality and the Eroticism of Everyday Life.* New York: Simon & Schuster.

García, Manuel, II. 1975. *A Complete Treatise on the Art of Singing: Complete and Un-abridged.* Collated, edited, and translated by Donald V. Paschke. New York: Da Capo.

Geertz, Clifford. 1983. "Art as a Cultural System." In *Local Knowledge: Further Essays in Interpretive Anthropology,* edited by Clifford Geertz, pp. 94–120. New York: Basic Books.

Gerhard, Anselm. 1998. *The Urbanization of Opera: Music Theater in Paris in the Nine-teenth Century.* Translated by Mary Whittall. Chicago: University of Chicago Press. Original edition, *Die Verstädterung der Oper: Paris und das Musiktheater des 19. Jahrhunderts.* Stuttgart: Carl Ernst Poeschel Verlag, 1992.

Gillett, Paula. 2000. "Immortal Tones: Woman as Public Singer." In *Musical Women in England, 1870–1914: "Encroaching on All Man's Privileges."* New York: St. Martin's Press.

Gilman, Sander L., et al. 1993. *Hysteria beyond Freud.* Berkeley: University of California Press.

Gilman, Todd S. 1997. "The Italian (Castrato) in London." In *The Work of Opera: Genre, Nationhood and Sexual Difference,* edited by Richard Dellamora and Daniel Fischlin, 49–70. New York: Columbia University Press.

Goldberg, David Theo. 2005. "Heterogeneity and Hybridity: Colonial Legacy, Postcolonial Theory." In *A Companion to Postcolonial Studies,* edited by Henry Schwarz and Sangeeta Ray, 72–86. Malden, Mass,: Blackwell

Gossett, Phillip. 1970. The Operas of Rossini: Problems of Textual Criticism in Nineteenth-Century Opera." Ph.D. dissertation, Princeton University.

———. 1971. "Gioacchino Rossini and the Conventions of Composition." *Acta Musicologica* 42: 48–58.

———. 1974. "Verdi, Ghislanzoni, and *Aida:* The Uses of Convention." *Critical Inquiry* 1: 291–334.

———, ed. 1981. "Introduction." In Gioacchino Rossini, *Maometto II.* Early Romantic Opera, vol. 11. New York: Garland.

———. 1985. *Anna Bolena and the Artistic Maturity of Gaetano Donizetti.* Studies in Musical Genesis and Structure. Oxford: Oxford University Press.

———, ed. 1985. "Introduction." In Michele Carafa, *Le nozze di Lammermoor.* Italian Opera: 1810–1840, vol. 2. New York: Garland.

———, ed. 1986. *Un'avventura di Scaramuccia.* Libretto by Felice Romani. Music by Luigi Ricci. Italian Opera, 1810–1840, vol. 44. New York: Garland.

———. 1987. "Music at the Théâtre Italien." In *Music in Paris in the Eighteenth-Thirties,* edited by Peter Bloom, 327–63. Stuyvesant, N.Y.: Pendragon Press.

———, ed. 1991. *Gioachino Rossini, Tancredi.* Milan: Ricordi.

———. 1998. "Donizetti: European Composer." *Opera Quarterly* 14 (3): 11–16.

Graziano, Jon. 2000. "The Early Life and Career of the 'Black Patti': The Odyssey of an African American Singer in the Late Nineteenth Century." *Journal of the American Musicological Society* 53 (3): 542–96.

Groos, Arthur, and Roger Parker, eds. 1988. *Reading Opera.* Princeton, N.J.: Princeton University Press.

Hadlock, Heather. 2000. *Mad Loves: Women and Music in Offenbach's* Les Contes d'Hoffmann. Princeton Studies in Opera. Princeton, N.J.: Princeton University Press.

———. 2000. "The Career of Cherubino, or the Trouser Role Grows Up." In *Siren Songs: Representations of Gender and Sexuality in Opera,* edited by Mary Ann Smart, 67–92. Princeton, N.J.: Princeton University Press.

———. 2004. "Women Playing Men in Italian Opera, 1810–1835." In *Women's Voices across Musical Worlds,* edited by Jane A. Bernstein, 285–307. Boston: Northeastern University Press.

Hamm, Charles. 1966. *Opera.* Boston: Allyn and Bacon.

Harris, Ellen T. 1989. "Voices, Part One: The Baroque Era." In *Performance Practice,* vol. II: *Music after 1600,* edited by Howard Mayer Brown and Stanley Sadie, 97–116. New York: W. W. Norton.

———. 1997. "Twentieth-Century Farinelli." *Musical Quarterly* 18 (2): 180–89.

———. 2001. *Handel as Orpheus: Voice and Desire in the Chamber Cantatas.* Cambridge, Mass.: Harvard University Press.

Hearder, Harry. 1983. *Italy in the Age of the Risorgimento, 1790–1870.* Longman History of Italy, vol. 6. New York: Longman.

Heartz, Daniel. 1990. "Farinelli Revisited." *Early Music* 18 (3): 430–43.

Heller, Wendy. 1993. "The Queen as King: Refashioning Semiramide for *Seicento* Venice." *Cambridge Opera Journal* 5 (2): 93–114.

Heriot, Angus. 1975. *The Castrati in Opera.* Opera Library History of Opera Series. London: Calder and Boyars. Original edition, London: Secker and Warburg, 1956.

Hudson, Elizabeth. 1992. "Gilda Seduced: A Tale Untold." *Cambridge Opera Journal* 4 (3): 229–51.

Izzo, Francesco. 2003. "Laughter between Two Revolutions: Opera Buffa in Italy, 1831 1848." Ph.D. dissertation, New York University.

Johnson, Barbara. 1980. "The Critical Difference: Barthes/Balzac. In *The Critical Difference: Essays in the Contemporary Rhetoric of Reading.* Baltimore: Johns Hopkins University Press.

Kaufman, Tom. 1999. "A Performance History of *Aureliano in Palmira.*" *Opera Quarterly* 15 (1): 33–38.

Kerman, Joseph. 1988. *Opera as Drama.* New and revised edition. Berkeley: University of California Press. Original edition, New York: Alfred A. Knopf, 1956.

Keyser, Dorothy. 1987–88. "Cross-sexual Casting in Baroque Opera: Musical and Theatrical Convention." *Opera Quarterly* 5 (4): 46–57.

Kimbell, David R. B. 1981. *Verdi in the Age of Italian Romanticism*. Cambridge: Cambridge University Press.

———. 1998. *Vincenzo Bellini, Norma*. Cambridge Opera Handbooks. Cambridge: Cambridge University Press.

Klein, Hermann. 1978. *Thirty Years of Musical Life in London, 1870–1900*. Da Capo Press Music Reprint Series. New York: Da Capo Press.

Koestenbaum, Wayne. 1993. *The Queen's Throat: Opera, Homosexuality, and the Mystery of Desire*. New York: Vintage. Original edition, New York: Poseidon, 1993.

Langdale, Allan. 1999. "Aspects of the Critical Reception and Intellectual History of Baxandall's Concept of the Period Eye." In *Michael Baxandall*, edited by Adrian Rifkin, 17–35. Malden, Mass.: Blackwell.

Laqueur, Thomas. 1990. *Making Sex: Body and Gender from the Greeks through Freud*. Cambridge, Mass.: Harvard University Press.

Larue, Steven C. 1995. *Handel and His Singers: The Creation of the Royal Academy Operas, 1720–1728*. Oxford: Oxford University Press.

Law, Joe K. 1984. "Alessandro Moreschi Reconsidered: A Castrato on Records." *Opera Quarterly* 2 (2): 1–12.

Leonardi, Susan J., and Rebecca A. Pope. 1999. *The Diva's Mouth: Body, Voice, Prima Donna Politics*. New Brunswick, N.J.: Rutgers University Press.

Levin, David J., ed. 1993. *Opera through Other Eyes*. Stanford, Calif.: Stanford University Press.

Lindgren, Lowell. 1984. "La carriera di Gaetano Berenstadt, contralto evirato (ca. 1690–1735)." *Revista Italiana di Musicologia* 19 (1): 36–112.

Lindner, Thomas. 1999. "Rossini's *Aureliano in Palmira*: A Descriptive Analysis." *Opera Quarterly* 15 (1): 18–32.

Lippmann, Friedrich. 1966. "Die Melodien Donizettis." In *Studien zur Italienisch-Deutschen Musikgeschichte III,* edited by F. Lippmann. Graz: Böhlau Verlag. *Analecta Musicologica* 3: 80–113.

Locke, Ralph. 1995. "What Are These Women Doing in Opera?" In *En Travesti: Women, Gender, Subversion, Opera,* edited by Corinne E. Blackmer and Patricia Juliana Smith, 59–98. New York: Columbia University Press.

Mack Smith, Denis. 1997. *Modern Italy: A Political History*. Ann Arbor: University of Michigan Press. Original edition, *Italy: A Modern History*. Ann Arbor: University of Michigan Press, 1959.

Maguire, Simon. 1989. *Vincenzo Bellini and the Aesthetics of Early Nineteenth-Century Italian Opera*. Outstanding Dissertations in Music from British Universities. New York: Garland.

Mancini, Giambattista. 1912. *Practical Reflections on the Figurative Art of Singing by Giambattista Mancini, Singing Master at the Imperial Court of Vienna.* Translated by R Buell. Boston: Gorham Press.

Marchesi, Gustavo. 1977. "I cantanti." In *Storia dell' opera,* vol. 3, part 1, edited by Guglielmo Barblan and Alberto Basso, 357–71. Turin: Unione Tipografico-Editrice Torinese.

Mayr, Giovanni Simone. 1986. *Medea in Corinto*. Facsimile edition of the printed piano-vocal score with an introduction by Philip Gossett. Italian Opera, 1810–1840, vol. 12. New York: Garland.

McClary, Susan. 1991. *Feminine Endings: Music, Gender, and Sexuality.* Minneapolis: University of Minnesota Press.

McCreless, Patrick. 1988. "Roland Barthes's S/Z from a Musical Point of View." *In Theory Only* 10 (7): 1–29.

McGeary, Thomas. 1998. "Farinelli in Madrid: Opera, Politics, and the War of Jenkins' Ear." *Musical Quarterly* 82 (2): 383–421.

Meyer, Stephen C. 2003. *Carl Maria von Weber and the Search for a German Opera.* Bloomington: Indiana University Press.

Meyerbeer, Giacomo, and Gaetano Rossi. 1979. *Il crociato in Egitto: Melodramma eroico in Two Acts.* A facsimile edition of a manuscript of the original version. Edited by Philip Gossett. Early Romantic Opera, vol. 18. New York: Garland.

Michotte, Edmond. 1968. *Richard Wagner's Visit to Rossini (Paris 1860) and An Evening at Rossini's in Beau-Sejour (Passy) 1858.* Translated from the French and annotated, with an introduction and appendix, by Herbert Weinstock. Chicago: University of Chicago Press.

Miller, Felicia. 1999. "*Farinelli's* Electronic Hermaphrodite and the Contralto Tradition." In *The Work of Opera: Genre, Nationhood and Sexual Difference,* edited by Richard Dellamora and Daniel Fischlin, 73–92. New York: Columbia University Press.

Miller Frank, Felicia. 1995. *The Mechanical Song: Women, Voice, and the Artificial in Nineteenth-Century French Narrative.* Stanford, Calif.: Stanford University Press.

Monahan, Brent Jeffrey. 1978. *The Art of Singing: A Compendium of Thoughts on Singing Published between 1777 and 1927.* Metuchen, N.J.: Scarecrow Press.

Mordden, Ethan. 1984. *Demented: The World of the Opera Diva.* New York: Simon & Schuster.

Moreen, Robert Anthony. 1975. "Integration of Text Forms and Musical Forms in Verdi's Early Operas." Ph.D. dissertation, Princeton University.

Mori, Rachele Maragliano, ed. 1953. *I maestri del bel canto.* Rome: Edizioni de Santis.

Nochlin, Linda. 1988. "Women, Art and Power (1988)." In *Women, Art, and Power: And Other Essays,* 1–36. Boulder: Westview Press.

———. 1989. "Camille Pissarro: The Unassuming Eye." In *The Politics of Vision: Essays on Nineteenth-Century Art and Society,* 60–74. Boulder: Westview Press.

Oberlin, Russell. 1990. "The Castrato: A Lost Vocal Phenomenon." *American Music Teacher* 40 (2): 18–21, 49–51.

Osborne, Charles. 1994. *The Bel Canto Operas of Rossini, Donizetti, and Bellini.* Portland: Amadeus Press.

Parker, Roger. 1994. "A Note on Italian Prosody." In Pierluigi Petrobelli, *Music in the Theater: Essays on Verdi and Other Composers,* ix. Princeton, N.J.: Princeton University Press.

———. 1997. "'Insolite forme,' or Basevi's Garden Path." In *Leonora's Last Act: Essays in Verdian Discourse,* 42–60. Princeton, N.J.: Princeton University Press.

Parlodari, Gonnolio. 1932. "Giambattista Velluti ultimo dei sopranisti sulle liriche scene." *Revista Musicale Italiana* 39: 263–98.

Pendle, Karin. 1979. *Eugène Scribe and French Opera of the Nineteenth Century.* Ann Arbor, Mich.: UMI Research Press.

Peschel, Enid, and Richard Peschel. 1986–87. "Medicine and Music: The Castrati in Opera." *Opera Quarterly* 4 (4): 21–38.

Pistone, Danièle. 1995. *Nineteenth-Century Italian Opera from Rossini to Puccini.* Translated by E. Thomas Glasow. Portland: Amadeus Press. Original edition, *L'Opéra italien au XIXe siècle de Rossini à Puccini.* Paris: Editions Champion, 1986.

Pleasants, Henry, ed. 1995. *The Great Tenor Tragedy: The Last Days of Adolphe Nourrit—As Told (Mostly) by Himself.* Translated by Henry and Richard R. Pleasants. Portland: Amadeus Press.

Poizat, Michel. 1992. *The Angel's Cry: Beyond the Pleasure Principle in Opera.* Translated by A. Denner. Ithaca, N.Y.: Cornell University Press. Original edition, *L'Opéra, ou le cri de l'ange: Essai sur la jouissance de l'amateur d'opéra.* Paris: Éditions A. M. Métailié, 1986.

Poriss, Hilary. 2001. "A Madwoman's Choice: Aria Substitution in *Lucia di Lammermoor.*" *Cambridge Opera Journal* 13 (1): 1–28.

Powers, Harold. 1987. "'La solita forma' and "The Uses of Convention." *Acta Musicologica* 59: 65–90.

Rifkin, Adrian, ed. 1999. *About Michael Baxandall.* Malden, Mass.: Blackwell.

Ringer, Alexander L. 1984. "Some Socio-economic Aspects of Italian Opera at the Time of Donizetti." *Analecta Musicologica* 22: 229–47.

Robinson, Paul. 1985. *Opera and Ideas: From Mozart to Strauss.* Ithaca, N.Y.: Cornell University Press.

Roccatagliati, Alessandro. 1996. "Felice Romani, Librettist by Trade." *Cambridge Opera Journal* 8 (2): 113–46.

Rogers, Francis. 1919. "The Male Soprano." *Musical Quarterly* 5 (3): 413–25.

Rosand, Ellen. 1978. "Barbara Strozzi, *virtuosissima cantatrice*: The Composer's Voice." *Journal of the American Musicological Society* 31 (2): 241–81.

Rosselli, John. 1984. *The Opera Industry in Italy from Cimarosa to Verdi: The Role of the Impresario.* Cambridge: Cambridge University Press.

———. 1992. *Singers of Italian Opera: The History of a Profession.* Cambridge: Cambridge University Press.

———. 2000. "Grand Opera: Nineteenth-Century Revolution and Twentieth-Century Tradition." In *The Cambridge Companion to Singing,* edited by John Potter, 96–108. Cambridge: Cambridge University Press.

———. 2000. "Song into Theatre: The Beginnings of Opera." In *The Cambridge Companion to Singing,* edited by John Potter, 83–95. Cambridge: Cambridge University Press.

Rutherford, Susan. 1992. "The Voice of Freedom: Images of the Prima Donna." In *The New Woman and Her Sisters: Feminism and Theatre, 1850–1900,* edited by Vivien Gardner and Susan Rutherford. Ann Arbor: University of Michigan Press.

Scott, Joan Wallach, ed. 1996. *Feminism and History.* Oxford Readings in History. Oxford: Oxford University Press.

Scott, Michael. 1993. *The Record of Singing.* 2 vols. Vol. I: *To 1914.* Boston: Northeastern University Press. Original edition, London: Gerald Duckworth, 1977.

Senici, Emanuele. 1998. "Verdi's Luisa, a Semiserious Alpine Virgin." *Nineteenth-Century Music* 22 (2): 144–68.

Seward, Desmond. 1995. *The Monks of War: The Military Religious Orders.* New York: Penguin Books.

Smart, Mary Ann. 1992. "The Silencing of Lucia." *Cambridge Opera Journal* 4 (2): 119–41.

———. 1994. "The Lost Voice of Rosine Stoltz." *Cambridge Opera Journal* 6 (1): 31–50.

———. 1997. "'Proud, Indomitable, Irascible': Allegories of Nation in *Attila* and *Les vêpres siciliennes.*" In *Verdi's Middle Period, 1849–1859: Source Studies, Analysis, and Performance Practice,* edited by Martin Chusid, 227–56. Chicago: University of Chicago Press.

———. 1997. "Verdi Sings Erminia Frezzolini." *Verdi Newsletter* 24: 13–22.

———. 2000. "Introduction." In *Siren Songs: Representations of Gender and Sexuality in Opera,* edited by Mary Ann Smart, 3–16. Princeton, N.J.: Princeton University Press.

———, ed. 2000. *Siren Songs: Representations of Gender and Sexuality in Opera.* Princeton Studies in Opera. Princeton, N.J.: Princeton University Press.

Smiles, Joan E. 1978. "Directions for Improvised Ornamentation in Italian Method Books of the Late Eighteenth Century." *Journal of the American Musicological Society* 31 (3): 495–509.

Smith, Bonnie G. 1989. *Changing Lives: Women in European History since 1700.* Lexington, Mass.: D. C. Heath.

———. 1998. *The Gender of History: Men, Women, and Historical Practice.* Cambridge, Mass.: Harvard University Press.

Solie, Ruth, ed. 1993. *Musicology and Difference: Gender and Sexuality in Music Scholarship.* Berkeley: University of California Press.

Somerset-Ward, Richard. 2004. *Angels and Monsters: Male and Female Sopranos in the Story of Opera.* New Haven, Conn.: Yale University Press.

Steane, J. B. 1995. *Voices, Singers & Critics.* Portland: Amadeus Press. Original edition, London: Gerard Duckworth, 1992.

Stendhal. 1985. *The Life of Rossini.* Translated by R. N. Coe. London: John Calder.

Stern, Kenneth A. 1983. "A Documentary Study of Giuditta Pasta on the Opera Stage." Ph.D. dissertation, City University of New York.

Story, Rosalyn M. 1990. *And So I Sing: African-American Divas of Opera and Concert.* New York: Amistad.

Surian, Elvidio. 1979. "A Chronology of Verdi's Life and Works." In *The Verdi Companion,* edited by William Weaver and Martin Chusid, 256–324. New York: W. W. Norton.

Taplin, Oliver, Fiona Macintosh, and Edith Hall, eds. 2000. *Medea in Performance: 1500–2000.* Oxford: Legenda.

Tortora, Daniela. 1996. *Drammaturgia del Rossini serio: Le opere della maturità da Tancredi a Semiramide.* Biblioteca Musicologica Collana di studi e richerche. Rome: Torre d'Orfeo Editrice.

Tosi, Pier Francesco. 1987. *Observations on the Florid Song.* Edited with additional notes by Michael Pilkington. London: Stainer & Bell.

Treadwell, Nina. 1998. "Female Operatic Cross-dressing: Bernardo Saddumene's Libretto for Leonardo Vinci's *Li zite 'n galera* (1722)." *Cambridge Opera Journal* 10 (2): 131–56.

Vitali, Carlo, ed. 2000. *Carlo Broschi Farinelli: La solitudine amica, lettere al conte Sicinio Pepoli.* Palermo: Sellerio Editore.

Walsh, Basil F. 1998. "Catherine Hayes: An Early Donizetti Prima Donna." *Opera Quarterly* 14 (3): 45–54.

Weaver, William, and Martin Chusid, eds. 1979. *The Verdi Companion.* New York: W. W. Norton.

Weinstock, Herbert. 1963. *Donizetti and the World of Opera in Italy, Paris, and Vienna in the First Half of the Nineteenth Century.* New York: Pantheon Books.

Wettlaufer, Alexandra. 2001. *Pen vs. Paintbrush: Girodet, Balzac, and the Myth of Pygmalion in Post-Revolutionary France.* New York: Palgrave.

Willier, Stephen A. 1995. "A Celebrated Eighteenth-Century Castrato: Gasparo Pacchierotti's Life and Career." *Opera Quarterly* 11 (3): 96–121.

Wittmann, Michael. 1993. "Meyerbeer and Mercadante? The Reception of Meyerbeer in Italy." *Cambridge Opera Journal* 5 (2): 115–32.

Zedda, Alberto, ed. 1989. "Preface." In *Gioachino Rossini, La gazza ladra*. Translated by Tom Hammond, edited and revised by Tom Hawkes and Philip Gossett. Piano-vocal score reduction based on the critical edition of the orchestral score published by the Fondazione Rossini of Pesaro. Milan: Ricordi.

Index

Abbate, Carolyn, 2, 183n3
Acquini, Giuseppe, 33
Adelson e Salvini (Bellini), 206n21
African American female singers, 184n6
Agoult, Marie d', 20
Agricola, John Friedrich, 40
"Ah! parea che per incanto," *Anna Bolena*
(Donizetti), 115
Alary, Jules Eugène Abraham, 203n20
Alboni, Marietta, 96
Anatomy: castrati, 29, 30; orchiectomies' effects on castrati, 28; vocal chords, 190n39;
voice resonance, 202n10
Anderson, David, 189n28, 195n19
Angier, Natalie, xii
Anna Bolena (Donizetti), 5, 91, 210n59; chorus in, 209n49; libretto for, 139; Milan premiere of, 143; *Norma* (Bellini) compared to,
164–170; Giuditta Pasta premiering, 132,
133, *134;* Smeton character compared to
Mozart's Cherubino, 107–118; Smeton character in, 92, 128, 203n18
Aprile, Giuseppe, 187n4
Arblaster, Anthony, 173, 210n7
Arie di baule (suitcase arias), 134–135
Armida (Rossini), 129, 204n1, 207n38
Asawa, Brian, 1
L'assedio di Calais (Donizetti), 203n19, 209n54
Attila (Verdi), 211n8
Aureliano in Palmira (Rossini), 16, 25

"Un bacio, un bacio ancora," *Anna Bolena*
(Donizetti), 114–115
Bakhtin, Mikhail Mikhailovich, 92–93
Balfe, Michael William, 99
Balzac, Honoré de. Anne Louis Girodet and
188n19; Rossini's *Tancredi* in novel of, 26–
27; *Sarrasine,* 13 (*see also Sarrasine* [Balzac])
Barbaja, Domenico, 100, 104
Barbier, Patrick, 16, 31
Baritone voices, 185n11
Barthes, Roland, 187n12
Bartoli, Cecilia, 1, 95–96, 200n11
Bartoluzzi, Gerolamo, 33
Bass voices, 185n11

Bassi, Carolina: in *Bianca e Falliero* (Rossini),
106; in *Il crociato in Egitto* (Meyerbeer),
59, 63, 72, 206n13; heroic travesti roles, 96;
Meyerbeer working with, 53, 54
Baxandall, Michael, 9–10, 186n23
Beatrice di Tenda (Bellini), 132, 133, 139
Beccari, Alaide Gaulberta, 211n10
Beethoven, Ludwig van, 79, 97, 194n15,
198n44
Beggar's Opera (Gay), 191n60
Beghelli, Marco, 185n8
Bel canto singing, 17, 32, 39–44
Belgiojoso, Christina, 211n10
Belisario, Antonio, 203n20
Bellini, Vincenzo, 51; *Adelson e Salvini,*
206n21; *Bianca e Gernando,* 59, 206n21;
early operas by, 205n7; Henriette Méric-
Lalande premiering roles for, 195n24;
Norma, 5, 91 (*see also Norma* [Bellini]);
Giuditta Pasta premiering roles by, 132, 133,
140; *I puritani,* 167–168, 200n14; Felice Romani as librettist for operas, 195n25; setting Hugo's *Hernani,* 207n36
Berenstadt, Gaetano, in Hogarth engraving, *28*
Bernacchi, Antonio, 37
Bernardi, Francesco (Senesino), 38. *See also*
Senesino (Francesco Bernardi)
Beyle, Henri (Stendhal), 141, 142, 172–173
Bianca e Falliero (Rossini), 106, 194n7
Bianca e Gernando (Bellini), 59, 206n21
Black, John, 194n10
Bonaparte, Joseph, 104
Bordoni, Faustina, 38, 191nn59,60
Brambilla, Marietta, 3, 184–185n8
Bravura style of singing, 41
Broschi, Carlo (Farinelli), *19. See also* Farinelli
(Carlo Broschi)
Byron, Lord, 189n28

Cabalettas, 72; in Adriano-Armando duet in
Il crociato in Egitto (Meyerbeer), 75–77,
197n39; "Di tanti palpiti," *Tancredi*
(Rossini), 189n28
Caballé, Montserrat, 209n53
Cadenzas in opera arias, 203n22

Heine, Heinrich, 172
Heriot, Angus, 33
Hermaphrodites, 46–47, 192–193n81
Heroism/Heroic: in Meyerbeer's Italian operas, 55–56; romantic heroines, 129–170 (*see also* Romantic heroines); tenor voices in Romantic era, 89 (*see also* Tenor voices); vocal sound changing, 103; voice timbres and, 21
Hiller, Ferdinand, 20
Hogarth, William, engraving by, *28*
Horne, Marilyn, 1, 95, 209n52
Hubert, Antonio, 37
Hudson, Elisabeth, 204n25
Huebner, Steven, 195n21
Hybrid roles/Hybridity, 14, 92–94, 199n6; cultural, 199n7; Giuditta Pasta and, 132, 142–143; Romantic heroine as hybrid, 130; Smeton (*Anna Bolena*) and Arturo (*Rosmonda d'Inghilterra*) as, 128

Insanity in opera, 206n20
Intersexes, 192–193n81
Israel, Kali, 199n5
Italy, 172–173; enthusiasm for British subjects in nineteenth century, 91–92, 199n5; Meyerbeer in, 13, 51–56 (*see also* Meyerbeer, Giacomo); regional differences for operas, 183n1; Risorgimento in, 92, 172, 186n19, 211n10; Rossini in, 103–107 (*see also* Rossini, Gioachino)

Jepthas Gelübe (Meyerbeer), 193n2
Johnson, Barbara, 187n12

Kasarova, Vesselina, 1
Kerman, Joseph, 173
Keyser, Dorothy, 35
King's Theatre (London, England), 139–140
Knights of Rhodes, 195n19
Koestenbaum, Wayne, 31, 183n5

Lablache, Luigi, 168, 191n62
Lamperti, Francesco and Giovanni Battista, 191n62
Lanari, Alessandro, 207n23
Laqueur, Thomas, 13, 45–46
Larmore, Jennifer, 1
Leonore (Beethoven), 194n15, 198n44
Life of Rossini (Stendhal), 141, 172–173
Lind, Jenny, 96
Linda di Chamounix (Donizetti), 209n54
Locke, Ralph, 183n3
Lodoïska (Cherubini), 194n15
Lorenzani, Brigida, 60–61, 96

Lowerre, Kathryn, 199n5
Lucia di Lammermoor (Donizetti), 130–131, 171, 204–205n3
Lucrezia Borgia (Donizetti), 203n19
Ludwig, Christa, 200n9, 209n52
Lumm, Eleanor, 188n19

Macbeth (Verdi), 211n8
Madness in opera, 206n20
The Maid of Artois (Balfe), 99
Majorano, Gaetano (Caffarelli), 37
Malanotte, Adelaide, 206n14
Malibran, Maria, 96–99; combining characteristics of first and second woman, 130; family of, 200n12; in *Maria Stuarda* (Donizetti), 200n14; mentioned in Balzac's *Sarrasine*, 24, 187–188n13; Meyerbeer working with, 54
Mallas-Godlewska, Ewa, 18, 187n6
Mancini, Giambattista, 207n30; on even sound between registers, 32; *Pensieri e riflessioni pratiche sopra il canto figurato*, 38, 40, 41–42; references to Tosi, 43
Manzuoli, Giovanni, 37
Maometto II (Rossini), 104–105, 189n26, 201–202n8
Marchesi, Luigi, 187n4
Margherita d'Anjou (Meyerbeer), 55, 196n33
Maria, regina d'Inghilterra (Pacini), 199n3
Maria di Rohan (Donizetti), 209n54
Maria di Rudenz (Donizetti), 208n44
Maria Padilla (Donizetti), 209n54
Maria Stuarda (Donizetti), 199n3, 200n14
Mariani, Rosa, 107
Marlacchi, Francesco, 51
Martini, Andrea, 33, 187n4
Mask, voice resonating in the, 202n10
Matilde di Shabran (Rossini), 106
Mayr, Giovanni Simone, 51; as Donizetti's teacher, 158; *Medea in Corinto*, 91, 143–164 (*see also Medea in Corinto* [Mayr]); Giuditta Pasta as Enrico in *La rosa bianca e la rosa rossa, 135;* Giuditta Pasta singing in operas by, 132, 205n4
Mazzini, Giuseppe, 174
McClary, Susan, 1
Medea in Corinto (Mayr), 91, 143–164; Creusa character in, 130; "Miseri pergoletti," 208n40, 208n41; musical characteristics of vocal lines, 143–153; *Norma* (Bellini) compared to, 158–164; Giuditta Pasta, signature role of, 132, 143, *151;* recording of, 208n40; Felice Romani as librettist, 208n47; *Rosmonda d'Inghilterra*

(Donizetti) compared to, 153–158; singers premiering in at Teatro San Carlo, 207n38; "Somme Dei," 207–208n39, 208n40; wedding chorus in, 208n46

Mehta, Bejun, 1

Mercadante, Saverio, 51; Giuditta Pasta singing in operas by, 132, 140, 205n4; rise of, 194n8

Méric-Lalande, Henriette, 195n24; Bellini working with, 133, 205n8; in *Il crociato in Egitto* (Meyerbeer), 59; in *Elvida* (Donizetti), 61; Meyerbeer working with, 54

Meyerbeer, Giacomo, 51–88; *Il crociato in Egitto*, 13, 16, 56–89 (*see also Il crociato in Egitto* Meyerbeer]); early career in Italy, 51–56; Germany, operas in, 193n2; Italian operas, 186n30; rescue operas, 194n15; Rossi as librettist for, 194–195n16; travel within Italy, 193n6

Mezzo-soprano voices, 4, 183n3

Michotte, Edmond, 189n27, 204n26

Miller, Richard, 187n12

Miller Frank, Felicia, 2

Minato, Nicolò, 33

"Miseri pergoletti," *Medea in Corinto* (Mayr), 208nn40,41

Mixed voice of castrati (*voce mista*), 43–44, 192n76, 207n30

Moïse et Pharaon (Rossini), 189n26, 201n3

Mombelli, Ester, 54

Monanni, Angelo, 37

Montague, Diana, 203n22

Morandi, Rosa, 96

Moreschi, Alessandro, 18–19, 21, 48

Morning Herald (newspaper), 142

Mosè in Egitto (Rossini), 189n26, 201n3

Mozart, Wolfgang Amadeus: *Le nozze di Figaro*, 103, 107–118; Giuditta Pasta in *Don Giovanni*, 136, 205n11; performance of his operas after his death, 133–134

Mozzoni, Anna, 211n10

Murat, Joachim, 104

Musico assoluta, 206n23

Nabucco (Verdi), 211n8

Naples, Italy, 104; Teatro dei Fiorentini and Teatro del Fondo, 201n1; Teatro San Carlo, 99, 100 (*see also* Teatro San Carlo [Naples, Italy]); tenor voices, popularity in, 104

Negrini, Vincenzo, 133

Nicolai, Otto, 51, 203n20

Nicolini, Giuseppe, 132, 135–136; Giuditta Pasta singing in operas by, 205n4; substitution aria by, 206n15

Nochlin, Linda, 11–12

"Non so più," *Le nozze di Figaro* (Mozart), 108–109, 112, 202n17

Norma (Bellini), 5, 91, 210n59; Adalgisa role in, 209; *Anna Bolena* (Donizetti) compared to, 164–170; Giulia Grisi as, *169*; *Medea in Corinto* (Mayr) compared to, 158–164; Milan premiere of, 143; Giuditta Pasta premiering, 132, 133, 139, 140, 143; *Ugo, conte di Parigi* (Donizetti) compared to, 209–210n54

Nourrit, Adolphe, 105

Nozzari, Andrea, 207n38

Le nozze di Figaro (Mozart), 103; Cherubino character in, 107–118, 127–128; "Non so più," 108–109, 112, 202n17; "Voi che sapete," 109–110, 202

Observations on the Florid Song (Tosi), 40

"O cielo clemente," *Il crociato in Egitto* (Meyerbeer), 198n45

Opera, or the Undoing of Women (Clément), 1–2, 174, 204n2

Opera as Drama (Kerman), 173

Opera Rara recordings, 210n7

Opera seria tradition, 8

Opinioni de' cantori antichi e moderni, o sieno osservazioni sopra il canto figurato (Tosi), 38, 39–41

Orchiectomies, 28

Order of the Hospital of St. John, 195n19

Osborne, Charles, 105, 189n28

Osborne, Richard, 189n28

Otello (Rossini), 129; Maria Malibran in, *98*; Giuditta Pasta in, *101*, 132, 135, 136

Ottonario tronco, 81, 198n46

Pacchierotti, Gasparo, 187n4

Pacini, Giovanni, 51, 132; *Maria, regina d'Inghilterra*, 199n3; Giuditta Pasta singing in operas by, 205n4

Pageboy roles, 92, 107–128. *See also* Travesti roles

Painting and Experience in Fifteenth-Century Italy (Baxandall), 9–10

Pants roles, 183n2. *See also* Travesti roles

Parlamagni, Annetta, 106

Passi, Antonio, 37

Pasta, Giuditta, 3, 15; as Bellini's *Norma*, with Giulia Grisi, 167; Maria Callas compared to, 200–201n16; career of, 131–140, 169–170; in *Il crociato in Egitto* (Meyerbeer), 59, *65*, 205–206n13; as Donizetti's *Anna Bolena*, *134;* as Enrico in *La rosa bianca e la rosa rossa*, *135;* as Mayr's *Medea in Corinto*, *151;*

NAOMI ANDRÉ is Associate Professor in Women's Studies at the University of Michigan. She received her Ph.D. in musicology from Harvard University. Her research focuses on nineteenth-century opera and issues surrounding women, gender, and voice. Working within feminist theory, she has examined voice as a sounding phenomenon and as a conceptual construct. Her publications include topics on Italian opera, Schoenberg, and women composers. Her current research interests extend to constructions of race, ethnicity, and identity in opera.

Lightning Source UK Ltd.
Milton Keynes UK
UKOW05f1001141016

285193UK00015B/179/P